The Laws of Physics

THE LAWS

OF PHYSICS

Milton A. Rothman

BASIC BOOKS, INC. Publishers
New York   London

~~~~ **FOR DORI**

CONTENTS

Introduction			1
CHAPTER	1	What Is a Law of Nature?	5
	2	Things We Take for Granted	13
	3	Conservation of Momentum	21
	4	Conservation of Energy	36
	5	Conservation of Angular Momentum	52
	6	The Laws of Motion	68
	7	Forces and Fields	95
	8	The Laws of Relativity	122
	9	The Laws of Probability and Entropy	147
	10	The Laws of Quantum Physics	165
	11	Elementary Particles	189
	12	Where Do We Stand Now?	223
Appendix 1			227
Appendix 2			231
Appendix 3			239
References			241
Index			243

The Laws of Physics

INTRODUCTION

During the nineteenth century, perpetual-motion machines were a common source of amazement and amusement. In almost every issue of *Scientific American,* and in newspaper Sunday supplements, there were descriptions of these devices. The inventor was invariably a strong-minded individual, convinced that where others had failed he could build a machine which would give forth more energy than was put into it.

The urge to build such a device is natural. If you could get energy for nothing, obviously you could make a fortune building fuelless power plants.

Occasionally one of these "perpetual-motion" machines would make money for its inventor, but not in the honorable uses of science. One Charles Redheffer swindled his way through Philadelphia and New York in 1812, charging the public a dollar admission to observe a complex contraption of wheels, pulleys, and gears which kept moving round and round with no obvious source of energy. (Until someone discovered the little man sitting in the back room turning a crank.) In 1898, J. M. Aldrich managed to con a number of citizens of Pennsylvania into investing in a machine consisting of a single wheel with "overbalanced weights" which kept going around, again with no visible driving force. When it was discovered that a clockwork mechanism was hidden in the wooden base, the irate investors had Mr. Aldrich sent to jail.

Gadgets like these could become a sensation only because people did not understand why the devices could not possibly work. But as time went on, even gullible investors resigned themselves to the idea that, as far as energy is concerned, you can't get something for nothing. Anybody who has gone through any sort of science course has at least heard of the law of *Conservation of Energy*. Atomic energy seems to have been the clincher. We no longer hear much about perpetual-motion machines.

However, the law of *Conservation of Momentum* is still undergoing the throes of misunderstanding.

During the 1920s and '30s, when men like Robert Goddard and Hermann Oberth began to talk about using rockets to drive a ship to the moon, the indignation and ridicule aroused by the idea were overwhelming. People who should have known better would say: "A rocket can't work in space—there is no air to push against."

The spread of this superstition was probably enhanced by an editorial in the *New York Times* (January 13, 1920) which read in part as follows:

A Severe Strain on the Credulity

As a method of sending a missile to the higher, and even to the highest parts of the earth's atmospheric envelope, Professor Goddard's rocket is a practicable and therefore promising device. . . . It is when one considers the multiple-charge rocket as a traveler to the moon that one begins to doubt . . . for after the rocket quits our air and really starts on its longer journey, its flight would be neither accelerated nor maintained by the explosion of the charges it then might have left. That Professor Goddard, with his "chair" in Clark College and the countenancing of the Smithsonian Institution, does not know the relation of action to reaction, and of the need to have something better than a vacuum against which to react—to say that would be absurd. Of course he only seems to lack the knowledge ladled out daily in high schools. . . .

This was the *New York Times,* a leader of American opinion, giving a display of opaque incomprehension.

We might speculate on how different history might have been if the public had possessed a proper understanding of the conservation of momentum. Goddard was right: a rocket does indeed work in a vacuum; in fact, it is the only kind of engine that can propel a vehicle in that medium. Had it not been for his neighbors' objections and the newspaper ridicule, Goddard would not have retired into his shell and carried on his rocket work in secret. If he had published papers on his theories and experiments at the time, the subject might well have attracted the interest of other American scientists, and the United States might have made great progress in rocketry, so that we would not have been as stunned and chagrined as we were by the sudden appearance of the German V-2 rocket in World War II and of the Russian sputnik in 1957.

An understanding of a few basic laws of nature can go a long way toward guiding us through the mysteries of modern science and technology. We don't need to look into all the details of the machinery to decide whether an idea is sound or silly. Unfortunately, the laws of nature are still not commonly understood. Everyone knows now that a rocket can fly in space, but many are hazy about the principles that make this possible. Within the past year I have read of three ideas for propulsion of space vehicles *without pushing against anything*. Of course, a rocket does have to push against something—it pushes against its own exhaust gases. You cannot gain momentum without application of a force. A proper understanding of the law of conservation of momentum would have saved a lot of talk about these pushless space drives.

The purpose of this book is to explain in some detail a few of the very basic laws of nature. These are laws on which the whole structure of science is built. If you understand them, you understand a great deal about space flight, atomic energy, and many other complexities of the age in which we live.

It is possible to understand the laws without going into complicated mathematics, because basically they are very simple statements. To appreciate just how powerful these laws are, however, we must look at some of the evidence for believing in them. The evidence, and the constant examination and re-examination of the laws and their consequences, are what make science. Scientists never stop testing the basic principles on which their understanding of the universe is founded. In physics, investigators are still working to learn whether the accepted rules hold true for the smallest particles and for the most distant galaxies in the immensity of the cosmos.

CHAPTER I

~~~~~~~~~~~~~~~~~~~~~~

What Is a Law of Nature?

~~~~~~~~

There was once a government whose leaders decided that it would be nice to relieve the people of the effort of carrying their weight around. They reasoned that life would be much easier without the stresses and strains caused by the force of gravity. Therefore they convened their legislature and repealed the law of gravity. As soon as their president signed the bill, everything became weightless. Immediately all the air whizzed off into space. Likewise, all objects not tied down to the ground were flung away from the spinning earth—for, unfortunately, the legislature had forgotten to repeal the law of Inertia.

This, of course, is a fairy tale. The law of gravity is not the kind of law that can be repealed or passed by a congress. It is not a creature of popular vote or even of scientists. Nor does it respect national boundaries: there is no such thing as an American law of gravity or a Russian law of gravity.

The planets move in their orbits; rockets rise and fall; a cat jumping from one fence to another travels along a certain kind of path; a projectile shot from a cannon travels along the same kind of path—all this is governed by the law of gravity.

A scientist investigates the nature of the law by studying motions. He measures the speed of the moon and the shape of its orbit. He measures the acceleration of balls rolling down an inclined plane. He measures the time it takes for a pendulum to swing back and forth and for various weights to drop from a height.

Having collected all these measurements—how fast each object moves, how fast its speed changes, in what direction it moves, how the direction changes, and so on—he tries to find a principle or common property that will account for them. Is there one simple rule that will describe how *every* object will move under the influence of gravity?

If the scientist can find such a rule, he calls it a law of nature.

Not every description of motion can be glorified as a law of nature. We can say that a certain rocket accelerates at the rate of 100 feet per second per second until it reaches a velocity of five miles per second at an altitude of 200 miles, whereupon it proceeds to circle the earth in 88 minutes. But this is only a description of the motion of one particular rocket. We would not call it a law of nature.

We can generalize the description somewhat by saying that every object traveling at a velocity of five miles per second and starting out in the proper direction will travel around the earth in a circular orbit. This is getting closer, and we might call it a useful rule, but it is still not what we would like to call a law of nature. It says nothing, for example, about objects traveling four miles per second, or seven miles per second. It is not very general.

A really good law of nature is a grand statement that encompasses the entire universe. Yet it may be very simple. Like this: *Every object in the universe attracts every other object.*

This, however, is only part of the description of gravity. How *strongly* does one object attract another? The law is not complete until it is stated in quantitative terms.

Sir Isaac Newton's contribution to the law of gravity was not simply to say that an apple falls from a tree. Everybody knew that. Newton did not "discover" gravity. Furthermore, Galileo had already measured how fast an object fell and how its speed increased while it was falling. What Newton did was to show that the earth's force of gravity extended out to the moon; that the earth, the planets, the sun, and the stars all moved according to the same rule; and that the amount of gravitational attraction between two bodies depended on the distance between them and their masses, according to a definite formula. This was his tremendous idea.

The act of falling to the earth is not a law of nature. The planets moving in their orbits are not a law. The attraction that draws you to the earth and the earth toward the sun is not the law of gravity. These are merely phenomena of nature. The law itself is the *generalized* description of these events.

The words and ideas and mathematical symbols we use to describe what happens—these make up the laws of nature.

The attraction between two bodies is called the "force of gravity." What the law does is to give a precise description of this force—how strong it is, what its direction is, how it changes from one place to another.

ᨑᨑ SHOULD WE ASK "WHY?"

It makes many people unhappy and frustrated to be told that a law of nature merely describes what happens in nature. They want to know "why"—why things fall to the ground, for instance.

The trouble is, when you start asking "Why?" you may get involved in a dialogue something like this:

Why does a stone fall to the ground? Well, gravity pulls it to the ground. But what is gravity? Gravity is a force which attracts all objects to the earth. But what causes this attraction? Well, there is a gravitational field that surrounds the earth, and any object in this field is attracted to the earth. But what does the field consist of?

Now the question begins to get sticky. Suppose we answered that the gravitational field was composed of a fluid named "gravitol" which tended to contract and pull all objects together.

This would satisfy some people. It is a curious fact that, if you give something a name, many will feel satisfied that you have explained it.

But a little thought shows that the name itself doesn't tell you anything you didn't know before: replacing the word "field" with the word "gravitol" adds no new information.

The ancients tried to account for phenomena like gravitation by supernatural explanations, endowing all objects with a sort of life of their own. The moon and the planets were propelled through the sky by gods, and a stone fell to the earth because it wanted to fall.

By the eighteenth century, scientists had abandoned such beliefs; they began to offer mechanical explanations which appear very strange today.

One theory said that space was filled with whirlpools, or vortices, in a fluid called the *ether,* and it was these whirlpools that carried the planets in their paths around the sun.

Another theory asserted that space was filled with tiny particles moving very fast, which pushed the planets toward the sun, pushed the moon toward the earth, and, in general pushed everything together.

These ideas did not, however, produce useful results, and scientists, being practical people in many ways, decided that there was no point in pursuing theories that did not lead anywhere in improving understanding. Toward the end of the nineteenth century, they came to the conclusion that the most they could accomplish was to give an accurate description of *how* the universe operates and let philosophers worry about the *why.* They concentrated on studying "what happens."

With this approach, scientists found that their ability to find answers increased by leaps and bounds. By directing their efforts to questions that could be answered by observation, they were able to ignore questions which previously had used up much time and energy but had yielded no meaningful answers.

Consider the question: "What is electricity?" If we say that electricity is a property that belongs to electrically charged particles, we have only pushed the question back a notch; now we have to ask what an electric charge is.

It is much more useful to ask: "What does electricity do?" With this question we can get enough answers to fill a library, merely by making observations.

We can note that an electron is a particle which carries a unit of negative electrical charge, and a proton is a particle which carries a unit of positive electrical charge. We know the charges are different because two negative particles repel each other, and a positive and a negative particle attract each other. We can measure the amount of the charges with great accuracy. We can describe how these particles behave in all kinds of circumstances, and we can show how all the effects of electricity—the heating of wires, the rotation of a motor, the production of a magnetic field—are produced by the motion of electrons and protons.

We can describe these motions in great detail. We can even go farther and say that the motions can be explained by means of the electric and magnetic "fields" that surround the electrons and protons.

If we try to dig deeper than this and explain what causes the fields in terms of something else, then we have to invent a new word. We now run the risk of thinking that we have explained something, when we have done nothing more than invent a new name.

Despite the risk, physicists are trying to describe the behavior of electric, magnetic, and gravitational fields in terms of deeper ideas. If we can learn how the various kinds of fields of force are *related* to one another, we will have a better understanding of fields, not just a new name for them.

When we say that a law of nature describes what things do, we imply that the "things" are in some way observable. In addition, when we invent a theory to explain how something happens, the theory must predict some result that can be tested by observation.

For example, take the idea that a gravitational field consists of a fluid called gravitol. All we have said is that gravitol produces the effects of a gravitational field. We cannot detect or describe it by any other effects: it has no mass, no temperature, no thickness, no friction, no electric charge, nothing that can be measured or observed. We can do just as well by ignoring the gravitol and simply describing the gravitational field itself. What is this field? Well, it is simply a place—a region of space. If we put an object in this region, it will start to move in a certain direction. That is, it will experience a force. The only way we can tell where a field of force is located is to put an object there and see if it starts to move.

We have defined the field of force by describing how we would observe it. (This is called an operational definition.) We have boiled away all the metaphysical explanations and are left with nothing more than the description of how a test object moves.

Much of our progress during the twentieth century is due to our better understanding of the basic laws of nature. These laws are often very simple statements about very simple things. Why, then, did it take so many thousands of years to discover them?

The reason is that nature rarely shows itself in its simple aspects. For instance, the planets are attracted by the sun, but their motion is also affected by other planets, complicating the situation. On the earth, a falling body is affected not only by gravitation but also by air resistance, working against the effect of gravity.

The problem of science is to find basic causes in a universe in which many influences are operating simultaneously.

～～～ ELEMENTARY PARTICLES

At the beginning of the twentieth century it had become clear that all matter was made up of atoms and that the atoms contained elementary particles labeled electrons and protons. It was not yet clear just how these particles were arranged within the atom. Within a few decades atomic physicists learned a great deal about the atom as a whole, but the electrons and protons became more of a mystery than ever. The physicists had learned to ask harder questions for which they had no easy answers. (Questions such as: What produces the magnetic field that electrons and protons carry with them?)

In the second half of the twentieth century we know more about electrons and protons (certainly not all there is to know), and we also know that there are multitudes of other elementary particles to be found within an atom: neutrons, positrons, neutrinos, mesons of many different types, and photons (the units of light).

Since all matter is made up of these elementary particles, an understanding of how they behave is necessary in order to understand how matter as a whole behaves. Therefore the laws of nature governing elementary particles must be considered the most basic of laws.

This is the field of physics that is the most puzzling at the present time. To explore it, we build huge and powerful atom-smashing machines. The machines split up not only atoms but also the particles making up atoms. They have shown that protons and neutrons are not necessarily "elementary" particles; they seem to be built up of smaller particles—the mesons.

What do elementary particles do? Most importantly, they *interact* with one another. Usually this means that two particles attract or repel each other. Or, the two particles may join together to form one or more other particles. Or one particle may be transformed into two or more other particles.

All of nature, it now seems, must eventually be described in terms of interactions between elementary particles, for it is these interactions that produce all the changes in the universe—the motions, the causes and effects.

The interaction is the important thing. A physicist uses an interaction to describe what happens to two particles when they are near each other. We do not say that particle *A* attracts particle *B*, because we could just as well say that *B* attracts *A*. Better to say that they interact with each other. This covers attractions and repulsions, as well as other types of activities such as emission and absorption.

We describe the way particles interact by picturing a field of force surrounding each particle, just as we picture the earth surrounded by a gravitational field. Each elementary particle is surrounded by its own little gravitational field. When very large numbers of particles are lumped together to form a large body, such as a planet, the little individual fields add up to form the field of the planet as a whole.

Four different types of field are known at the present time. They are the gravitational, electromagnetic, "strong nuclear," and "weak nuclear" fields. As always, the word "field" is simply a picture-word to describe the fact that, when two particles interact with each other, some change in their motion or condition results. The space surrounding each particle is labeled a "field of force." To obtain a more complete picture of the ways in which elementary particles interact with each other is the most fundamental study in physics today.

CHAPTER 2

~~~~~~~~~~~~~~~~~~~

Things We Take for Granted

~~~~~~

Many of the "facts" of nature are assumed to be true because they seem so obvious that it is silly to question them. However, occasionally one of these "obvious" facts turns out to be not completely true, and this sometimes leads to the discovery of a new law of nature.

To avoid going astray in our logic, we need to be aware of all the assumptions that go into our theories. We must take nothing for granted without knowing what we are doing. Let us examine some of our assumptions.

~~~~ **REALITY**

First of all, *I believe that I exist.* Most people assume that this is a fairly safe statement, although Tweedledee, in *Through the Looking Glass,* claimed that Alice was only a fiction of the Red King's dream. However, this was a bit of a philosophical joke on the part of Lewis Carroll, the professional logician and mathematician who wrote these grown-up children's stories.

Secondly, *I believe that all of you out there also exist.* (Otherwise I would not be writing this book.) There have been philosophers who have argued: "I exist, but everything else in the universe is only a creation of my mind." Not many of us are so conceited; most people agree on the observation that we actually live on a planet populated by great numbers of other human beings and that this planet is a small item in a vast universe filled with stars and galaxies as far as our largest telescopes can see.

I next assume that *I can learn something about the universe* by looking with my eyes, feeling with my hands, listening with my ears.

Light rays from the sun reach the earth. Some of the rays are reflected from a tree. They then travel through the lens of my eye, strike the retina, and set up a signal which travels to my brain. By a method as yet unknown, I now become aware of the image of a tree.

All this is automatic. I am not conscious of the process—the signals, the image in my brain—nor am I aware that the camera-like image on my retina is actually upside down. I merely perceive that there is a tree "out there."

I further assume that the *only* way I can learn anything about the universe is by means of the information I receive through my senses. This includes pictures, words spoken to me by other people, and words and mathematical symbols which I read. This philosophy of knowledge is a recent one, historically speaking. It represents a great split between modern science and ancient and medieval philosophers, who contended that we could learn all the important truths about the universe solely by logical thinking. Scientists have come to believe that you can invent all the theories you like by pure reason, but you cannot decide whether your theories say anything about the real world until you test them by observation with your senses of perception to find out whether nature behaves as your theories predict.

Your contact with the universe, like everything else, is the result of interactions between elementary particles. The atoms of the sun emit photons which interact with electrons in the surface of the tree. Some of the photons are reflected and interact with electrons in the retina of your eye. These electrons send a chain of interactions through the optic nerve into your brain, and the brain, in turn, produces the sensation of seeing a tree. We have reason to believe that even the intricate operation of the nervous system—the processes of learning and interpretation that result in the recognition of a tree—must be explainable ultimately in terms of elementary particle interactions acting in an organized way.

⋙ REGULARITY

If the purpose of science is to find out the laws of nature, one of our chief assumptions must be that everything in the universe obeys natural laws and that there are no exceptions to these laws. That is, we take for granted that there is regularity in the universe.

The path the earth follows around the sun is not random. It is dictated by the operation of gravitational forces, and we believe that, if we know all the facts, we should be able to predict what this path will be for the next million years.

All massive bodies attract one another by gravitation. All positive electric charges repel one another. All positive electric charges attract all negative electric charges. We have found no exceptions to these rules so far.

When you hit a baseball with a bat, the path followed by the baseball is no accident: the ball goes where it must go. Where it must go is decided by its speed at impact, the speed of the bat, the elasticity of the ball, the angle at which the bat hits the ball, the temperature of the air, the speed and direction of the wind, the attraction of gravity, the rotation of the earth, and no doubt other factors we are not aware of.

In a large room with a thousand tennis balls bouncing around in all directions, there would be quite a scramble of balls hitting the walls and colliding with one another. To anyone looking at this confusion it might appear that the balls were flying around in a thoroughly random and chaotic way. Actually, of course, each ball would strictly obey natural laws. If we had precise measurements of all the factors at play and a computing machine adequate to handle all the information, we could calculate where every ball was going, how it would bounce whenever it made a collision, when it would have its next collision, and where it would be ten minutes from now. In practice, this sort of calculation is much too complicated to do, and so we cannot see the regularity in the seeming chaos.

～～ UNIFORMITY

Before the time of Isaac Newton (1642–1727) it was taken for granted that one set of rules applied to things happening on the earth and an entirely different set of rules regulated events in the heavens.

Newton destroyed this assumption by finding a connection between the apple falling from a tree and the planets revolving around the sun. He began by wondering whether the gravitational attraction observed on the surface of the earth reached out as far as the moon. Eventually Newton was able to show by mathematical proof that the moon's travel around the earth must indeed be ruled by the force of gravity. Furthermore, the same law also explained the captive movement of all the planets in elliptical orbits around the sun.

It was just one more step to say that every two bodies in the entire universe attracted each other, no matter how far apart they were—although, the farther apart they were, the weaker was the force of attraction. In this way the motions of all the planets, stars, and galaxies could be explained in terms of a universal force of gravity.

Another step in logic, together with many years of observing thousands of stars in the sky, leads to the all-encompassing conclusion: *All the laws of nature are the same in all regions of the universe.*

This is a grand conception. We can now see the universe as one unified whole, and it is immensely helpful to science to be able to feel confident that gravity, electricity, light, chemical reactions, atomic reactions—every sort of physical behavior—follow exactly the same rules everywhere in the universe as they do right here on the earth.

But a little warning bell rings in the mind of the skeptical scientist. What are we taking for granted now? How sure can we be that the gravitational force, for instance, has exactly the same strength and obeys the same rules in the distant regions of the universe beyond our observation?

It turns out, indeed, that there *are* exceptions to our elegantly simple assumption. Gravitation is *not* precisely the same everywhere. The astronomers have discovered that in the neighborhood of a very heavy star the strength of the gravitational force differs slightly from what we should expect on the basis of Newton's law of gravity. So we find that, while his law holds true in our region of space, it has to be modified to cover the situation in a very different region.

At the other extreme, physicists also encountered many surprises when they came to investigate the microcosmic world of the atom and elementary particles.

Early in this century physicists began to discover some very peculiar things about the behavior of atoms. For example, when electricity was passed through hydrogen gas in a glass tube, the gas gave off light—but the light consisted only of certain special wavelengths. Why did the hydrogen emit those particular wavelengths and no others?

Even more mysterious was the existence of the hydrogen atom itself, as its structure was analyzed. It had a negatively charged electron circling around a positively charged proton. According to the known laws of electricity, the electron should be drawn to the proton and unite with it, yet it never did. What kept the electron and the proton apart?

The more the atom was studied, the more obvious it became that the particles in this realm simply did not obey the rules that applied to large bodies such as baseballs and planets.

To describe what happened in the world of the atom, physicists had to free themselves of traditional and cherished assumptions and invent an entirely new science—the science of *quantum mechanics.* The theories and laws of this new science were very strange and difficult to understand, even for physicists. But they proved so successful in answering puzzling questions that quantum mechanics has become the foundation of modern physics. It explains the sunshine and uranium fission and the functioning of everyday implements of our technology such as fluorescent lights, photoelectric cells, transistors, photographic film, and X-rays.

Quantum mechanics is based on the idea that an elementary particle such as an electron or proton is not a hard, solid ball of electricity but must be thought of as a *wave packet* moving through space. Thus, an electron is not concentrated at one point but is spread out like a puff of smoke. When tied up inside an atom, it behaves as if it is a cloud around the nucleus, instead of a pellet traveling in an orbit the way the earth travels around the sun. Accordingly, it is impossible to say exactly where an electron is at any given moment. This thought was hard to accept at first, for it contradicted the very concept of a particle.

If such a basic idea must be changed when we talk about elementary particles, perhaps *all* our laws of nature break down within the atom! Fortunately for us, this is not so. It turns out that the grand, basic laws—laws such as the conservation of energy —apply just as well to elementary particles as they do to larger objects. We must, however, interpret the operation of these laws in the light of the special properties of particles in the microscopic world. We shall look into that world and the laws of quantum mechanics in more detail in later chapters.

ᘌᘍᘍ THE PAST AND THE FUTURE

A new-born baby swims in a sea of timelessness. Vague sensations filter through an undeveloped consciousness. As he grows older, the child learns that there is a difference between things that happened yesterday and things happening right now. It takes longer for him to get the idea that there are things which will happen tomorrow.

Gradually he develops a feeling for the direction in which time advances. He learns from experience that certain happenings of the past are very closely connected with things that are going to happen in the future. He learns to say that the first event *caused* the second event. The idea of cause and effect is built up in his mind.

The growing child also observes that certain things always happen in the same way, day after day. He sees the sun rise every day. He sees that every time he drops a stone it falls down. It never falls up. As a result, he gets the feeling that things like this will always happen the same way in the future.

Thus we obtain the principle of regularity in time. In the last section we spoke of the idea that the laws of nature, broadly and carefully interpreted, are the same in all regions of space. We can now go further and say that the laws of nature are the same at all times.

This assumption is so basic and so ingrained in our habits that it controls most of our daily activities. When we put a roast in the oven, we feel confident that it will come out right if we follow the cookbook instruction to let it cook for two hours at an oven setting of 350° Fahrenheit. This formula will be good not just once but every time (if the meat is standard). The laws of heat and the chemistry of cooking are not going to vary from one day to the next.

We know that every time we flip the switch on the wall, the electric light will go on, barring an accident. We are so certain of this that, if the light happened to stay off the next time we flipped the switch, we would not for a moment think that the laws of electricity had broken down but would simply look to see whether the bulb was burned out, or the switch broken, or a fuse blown, or some other mishap interfering with the processes of nature.

This concept that the laws of nature which have worked in the past will continue to work in the future cannot be proved by logic or pure reason. It is merely taken for granted on the basis of experience. But a skeptic may still ask: "Are you absolutely sure that the laws of electricity will be the same tomorrow as they were yesterday?"

The scientist cannot give you a completely unqualified answer to this question. But he can say: "The laws have been tested many times and found to be unchanging within the limits of experimental accuracy; therefore I am willing to bet at odds of billions to one that they will not change significantly in the near future."

This kind of answer may not satisfy people who want to be absolutely certain about everything, but if we relax and allow ourselves to be satisfied with just a little bit less than perfect certainty, we find that we can get along quite well. As far as science is concerned, we are perfectly right.

Yet, just as we must be careful about extending the laws of nature into all the regions of space, we need to be cautious about extending them indefinitely in time. Civilized man's observations have covered only a few thousand years. They do not rule out the possibility that very slow changes in natural laws may take place over periods of millions of years.

Perhaps the strength of gravity, for instance, has slowly changed over the history of the universe. Experiments have been proposed to test this speculation, but so far nobody has been able to do such experiments accurately enough to detect the slight change expected. What we can say is that any change, if present, is so tiny that for all practical purposes we can take the force of gravity to be constant.

CHAPTER 3

Conservation of Momentum

Most basic of all the laws of nature, from the point of view of modern science, are the conservation laws. I should like to begin with the law of conservation of momentum—a subject often overlooked entirely in elementary textbooks of physics.

We shall introduce the subject by considering a seesaw and the problem of two friends, named Walter and William, who mount it for a ride. If both weighed the same, they would balance each other by sitting on the ends of the board—that is, at equal distances from the center. But it happens that Walter weighs twice as much as William; it turns out that their weights will balance only if Walter sits halfway up the board—half as far from the center as William.

Now suppose that the two boys, wearing ice skates, stand on an ice pond and push against each other. They fly apart in opposite directions, sliding backward across the ice. If you timed their speed, you would find that William, weighing half as much as Walter, rebounds from the push at twice the velocity. Thus, if Walter, say, weighs 100 pounds and moves away from the pushing point at ten feet per second, 50-pound Willie will move at 20 feet per second.

Looking at these numbers, we notice an interesting fact: If we multiply Walter's speed by his weight, we get $100 \times 10 = 1,000$.

If we do the same for William, we obtain $50 \times 20 = 1,000$. Both boys, after they are pushed apart, possess a property identical in amount.

We might do other experiments which illustrate the same principle: the recoil in opposite directions of a gun and the bullet, of a rocket and its exhaust gases, of a radioactive nucleus and the particle it ejects. All of these reactions demonstrate the rule that when two bodies push each other apart, the weight times the final velocity of one always equals the weight times the final velocity of the other.

We can put this in a short, general equation:

$$w_1 v_1 = w_2 v_2$$

with w_1 and w_2 standing for the weights of the two bodies and v_1 and v_2 for their velocities.

There is something about this rule, however, that worries us when we think about it. The weight of a body varies from place to place: it decreases with altitude on the earth, and in interstellar space where gravities balance, a body may have no appreciable weight at all. What happens to the equation then?

We might try an experiment. Take two objects that weigh the same at a given altitude and place them at different altitudes— one at sea level and the other atop a mountain three miles up. Now Object 1 (at sea level) weighs more than Object 2. Give both objects equal pushes by means of identical springs. (This means that the same force is applied for the same length of time to both objects.) What do we find? The velocity of Object 1 turns out to be the *same* as the velocity of Object 2, in spite of the fact that w_1 differs from w_2!

In other words, we find that $w_1 v_1$ is *not* always equal to $w_2 v_2$.

Our trouble is that we have chosen the wrong property for the description of the bodies. We should identify them not by w (weight) but by a property which is independent of the position in space where they happen to be placed. The property that answers to this description is *mass*. Two bodies which are identical in weight under a given gravitational force are also identical in mass. Another term equivalent to mass is the *inertia* of a body, which is a measure of the resistance of the body to any change in its motion.

We can now state our rule about the balance of motion as follows: When two bodies of mass m_1 and m_2 are pushed apart by some force, then their final velocities are related by the equation

$$m_1v_1 = m_2v_2$$

This equation gives us a method of measuring mass. It tells us that, if we know one mass and we measure the velocities of the two objects after they are pushed apart, then by using this equation we can calculate the other mass. We must always start out with one mass that we take to be a standard. From this we can determine all other masses.

⁓⁓⁓ MASS

It is easy to become confused about the meaning of "mass." Sir Isaac Newton defined it as "the amount of matter in a body," and his definition has been handed down through generations of textbooks and dictionaries. Unfortunately, it was never a good definition, and in modern physics it has lost all meaning. What do we mean by "amount?" How do we measure it? A single electron is a definite amount of matter, but we find that its mass increases with velocity. When it is traveling at a very high speed, this gain in mass becomes considerable. Furthermore, a beam of light has mass, but we don't usually classify it as "matter."

We used to call a beam of light a "form of energy," but now the distinction between matter and energy has disappeared. We see them as two aspects of the same thing. When a body gets more energy, it gets more mass, so we see that the mass of a body is not an eternal, unchanging attribute. This point is one of the key differences between the "classical" physics developed by Newton and the "modern" physics we have learned in the twentieth century.

The unvarying mass of classical physics we now call the *rest-mass* of a body—the mass it has when it is not moving. When we use the word "mass" alone, we mean the variable mass of the body, the mass that increases when the body is in motion.

Of course, when we talk about the ordinary motion of ordinary objects, such as baseballs, airplanes, rockets, and planets, the increase of mass with velocity is so insignificant that mass can be treated as a constant quantity. The variability of mass is important only when we talk about elementary particles, at least until the day comes when rockets travel at velocities greater than several thousand miles per second.

To formulate a sensible definition of mass we must resort to the operational method: we describe how we measure a mass. This can be done in various ways.

The simplest way is to compare the weight of the unknown object with the weight of a standard mass in the same location, using a balance. To do this we must decide on one lump of material which we define to be a standard kilogram (or whatever unit we happen to be using). The standard kilogram actually exists; it is a piece of platinum stored in a vault in Sèvres, France.

This procedure works well enough for objects large enough to be weighed, but it does not tell us what to do with elementary particles, which cannot conveniently be put on a balance. Nor does it give us a clear method of dealing with objects moving at high speeds or with a beam of light, which will not stand still to be weighed.

In situations like these, often encountered in atomic physics, our procedure is to compare the masses of two particles by using the principle of recoil: we measure their velocities after they collide with each other and push each other apart, just as we did with the boys on skates.

〰〰 MOMENTUM

We have seen that whenever bodies are pushed apart by some force acting between them, the mass times the velocity of one body always equals the mass times the velocity of the other. This product of mass and velocity is an important property of an object and is called the *momentum*. The symbol for momentum is usually the letter p, which stands for $m \times v$. Thus, the balance of momentum between two bodies can be written simply as:

$$p_1 = p_2$$

Or, taking p_2 to the other side of the equation, we write:

$$p_1 - p_2 = 0$$

This simply tells us that the *total momentum* of the two bodies is zero. (Recall that the two bodies are moving in opposite directions, so that we have to put a minus sign in front of p_2 in order to add it to p_1. Momentum has direction, just like velocity.)

What we have discovered from this discussion is that if two bodies start out with zero momentum, when they are pushed apart by some force the total momentum of the two bodies is still zero.

The same idea can be applied to any number of particles. When a bomb explodes, the total momentum of all the fragments (again taking direction into account) adds up to zero.

What happens if the bomb is moving before the explosion? It has some momentum to begin with. After the explosion, the momentum of all the fragments will add up to the same value as the original momentum. The momentum of the bomb is not changed at all by the explosion! Although the fragments are flying in different directions, the group as a whole carries the original momentum of the missile.

From this we can make an extension of our original rule. No changes that take place as a result of forces operating *within* a group of objects can alter the total momentum of the system. This is the law of conservation of momentum.

〰〰 CONSERVATION LAWS

Many of the most fundamental laws of nature can be stated as conservation laws. Such a law simply says that there is some property of matter or energy which never changes, no matter what happens.

These are very powerful laws, for they apply to all objects, large and small, everywhere in the universe. They are the simplest of laws, for it takes very little mathematics to say that something remains constant, or unchanged.

Conservation laws are considered very elegant by scientists because they appeal to a sense of simplicity, as well as to a sense of symmetry. We find that whenever we can do an experiment whose result does not depend upon the direction in which we are facing or the way in which we are moving, a conservation law is involved.

Momentum is conserved in India as in New York, on Mars as on the earth, in the galaxies as in the stars. It is conserved when we are inside a fast-moving jet plane and also when we are standing still on the ground. It does not depend on how fast or which way we are moving.

Although the conservation concept sounds like a very trivial idea, it has taken scientists hundreds of years to become quite clear in their minds about the conservation laws. It is far from obvious what properties of matter or energy will remain forever unchangeable no matter what you do to it. These properties had to be discovered by experiment.

The law of conservation of momentum is usually stated as follows: *The total momentum of an isolated system (i.e., a system unaffected by any outside force) is always constant.*

Ever since this theory was proposed three centuries ago, it has been tested in every conceivable way, and nobody has found a single exception to it. Experiments have been performed in every field of physics—in mechanics, atomic physics, nuclear physics—and in every case it has been found that momentum is always conserved. The definition of momentum has had to be enlarged to take into account discoveries such as the effects of electromagnetic fields and of very rapid motion, but the law has readily accommodated these new facts. Conservation of momentum is now considered to be one of the most fundamental and best established laws we have.

⌁⌁⌁ CENTER OF MASS

A few extremely important consequences of the law of conservation of momentum can be seen right away. Suppose we go back to the experiment in which we pushed two masses apart by a spring and see how far they have traveled after a certain length of time. If we multiply both sides of the equation by the elapsed time, t, we find that

$$m_1 v_1 t = m_2 v_2 t$$

Since vt is the distance traveled in the specified time, we can substitute d, for distance, in the equation and it becomes:

$$m_1 d_1 = m_2 d_2$$

Now this is also the equation of a seesaw, or of two balancing masses on a beam balance.

What does it mean to be in balance? It means that while gravity tends to pull Mass 1 down, which would rotate the beam counter-clockwise, at the same time it also tends to pull Mass 2 down, in the clockwise direction, so that the two rotations cancel out and the beam remains level on its pivot.

Suppose we take the pivot away. The two masses then will fall with equal accelerations; that is, they will fall together so that there still will be no rotation of the beam. If the whole system were enclosed in an opaque box (meaning an "isolated sys-

tem"), we would see only the box falling. To all intents and purposes, the box would act as if there was a single mass located
at the pivot point. This single mass would have the value
$m_1 + m_2$.

The pivot point is often called the center of gravity of the two
bodies. A better term is *center of mass*, because this property of
bodies is not exclusively related to the force of gravity. It applies also to the effects of electrical forces, magnetic forces, or
any other forces.

In general, whenever we have a group of objects which are
acted upon by some force from outside the system, there is a
simple way to predict how the group of objects will move as a
whole. Instead of worrying about a cluster of things milling
around, we think of a single object located at the center of mass
and containing the entire mass of the group. This single object
will travel in the same path as the center of mass of all the
actual objects.

Let us put it another way. Having located the center of mass
of the group, we now imagine the whole conglomeration surrounded by our opaque box. The center of mass of the box is the
same as the center of mass of the cluster, because we assume that
the box itself has no mass. The box, with all the things moving
around inside it, will travel through space under the influence of
outside forces just as if the box were a single object.

Perhaps the most important result of this idea is the following:
If there is no force acting upon a group of objects, then there is
no change in the velocity of the center of mass of the group. If
the center of mass is motionless to begin with, it remains motionless. If it is moving with a certain velocity, the center of mass
will continue to move with the same velocity as long as no outside force acts on the system. (This you may recognize as Newton's First Law of Motion.)

For example, if a projectile is moving with a certain velocity
and then explodes, all the fragments must move in such a way
that the center of mass continues to follow the path of the
original projectile.

Another example: If we imagine a box filled with machinery which is not connected in any way with the outside world, and if the box is at rest, then no matter what the machinery inside the box does, no matter how the wheels spin, gears turn, and motors whirl, the center of mass of the box must always remain in the same position. The box may vibrate back and forth if weights are thrown about inside it, but there is no way in the universe for this box to take off and go in one direction.

We sometimes hear the suggestion that if we have a box filled with molecules of gas moving about at random, there is a small but not zero probability that at some instant of time most of the molecules may happen to move simultaneously in the same direction—purely by chance. At that instant, the box will take off in flight.

We now see that this cannot be so. Although the molecules' motions are so complicated that we have to treat them as if they were random in order to calculate the average motion of the group, the molecules' behavior is not really random. They must strictly obey the law of conservation of momentum. This law is built into the calculations we make to describe the average behavior. An inescapable restriction on that behavior is that the center of mass of the container must always stay in the same place.

⁓⁓⁓ METHODS OF SPACE PROPULSION

We can use what we have learned about momentum to analyze what methods of propulsion might be useful for space travel.

In ground, water, and air transportation, a means of propulsion is nothing more than a device to set the vehicle in motion. Steering—changing of direction—is accomplished by pushing against the roadway, the rails, the water, the atmosphere, etc. In space there is nothing substantial to push against. Steering in space must be accomplished by the spaceship's own propulsive means.

To get a vehicle off the ground requires a large force acting for a relatively short time—the time being determined by the amount of fuel you can carry and the rate at which you burn the fuel, as well as by the final velocity you wish to attain. On the other hand, maneuvering in space can be done with a smaller force acting over a longer time, because you need to overcome only the inertia of the ship, not its gravitational weight on the ground.

This suggests that it is most efficient to use two types of engines: large-thrust motors to get into space and low-thrust motors to steer out there.

In any discussion of methods of propulsion there is one basic rule of the game: conservation of momentum. Any proposal for a propulsion device that promises to operate without obeying this law had better come equipped with a working model to demonstrate that it will work.

When we start thinking about possible means of propulsion for a spaceship, we immediately find certain very serious limitations. First of all, an escape velocity of seven miles per second must be attained. Yet it must not be attained too abruptly, for we do not want the occupants of the ship to be mashed into jelly. This rules out firing from a gun (as in Jules Verne's fantasy). The acceleration must be gradual enough to spare the passengers and to avoid burning up the ship by air friction while it is still in the lower atmosphere. This means that the take-off must be straight up (to get out of the air as quickly as possible), and it rules out acceleration by long magnetic catapults. (This last idea is not implausible for take-offs from the moon, where there is no atmosphere and where the escape velocity is only about 1.4 miles per second.) Futhermore, since most of the velocity must be attained after the ship has left the atmosphere, the motive power must be of a kind that will work in a vacuum.

Immediately we have eliminated almost all the means of propulsion we can think of—except the rocket. The rocket idea answers all the requirements. It provides an acceleration of almost any amount desired, a gradually increasing velocity straight up, and it keeps on exerting thrust after the vehicle has left the atmosphere. These basic principles were recognized as far back as 1895 by a Russian, Constantin Ziolkowsky, who wrote theoretical papers on the subject but was unable to put his ideas into practice. The first man to make a serious experimental start in the direction of a space rocket was the American physicist Robert Goddard (1882–1945), who conceived most of the basic ideas in 1914.

While rockets had been known for hundreds of years, it was not obvious to everybody that this type of device could be used for propulsion in space, and many people protested that a rocket could not work in space because "there is nothing to push against." Today such objections seem inconceivable to us.

Basically, a rocket is a mechanism which pushes two masses apart in order to give one of them a desired velocity. If you fired a machine-gun in space, the repeated recoil of the gun would carry you away from the direction of fire. It used to be thought that only the reaction from solid projectiles could yield enough recoil to drive a heavy vehicle, but as we now know, the exhaust gases of a rocket motor are quite enough to give all the needed thrust.

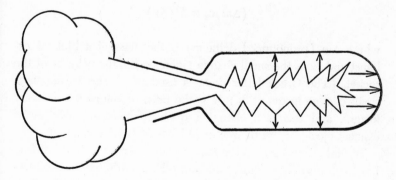

FIGURE 1. The thrust that drives a rocket.

One way of thinking about the operation of a rocket is shown in Figure 1. Fuel burns in the combustion chamber, and the expanding gases push against the closed end but have nothing to push against at the open end. This unbalanced force thrusts the motor forward. To calculate how a rocket moves we do not have to worry about the details of what goes on inside the combustion chamber. Conservation of momentum gives us all the information we need.

We can think of the exhaust as little blobs of mass being ejected from the rocket with a velocity v_e (the exhaust velocity) which is measured relative to the rocket itself (Figure 2). The

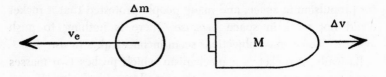

FIGURE 2. Conservation of momentum in a rocket. Each blob of exhaust going to the left gives the rocket a push to the right.

momentum gained by the exhaust to the left is equal to the momentum gained by the rocket to the right, so that every instant we can say:

$$(\Delta m)v_e = M(\Delta v)$$

where Δm (pronounced delta m) is the mass of a blob of exhaust and Δv is the small change (increase) in the velocity of the rocket. (The Greek letter delta is used in physics to denote a small change in quantity.) M is the mass of the rocket at every instant, and this is a changing quantity because each bit of exhaust ejected from the motor reduces M by that amount.

To find the velocity of the rocket after a certain amount of fuel has been burned, we must add up all the little increases in velocity, taking into account the way M changes continually. This sort of calculation is easily performed by the method of the calculus. The result of such a calculation is best visualized by drawing a curve (see Figure 3). The final velocity (v) of the

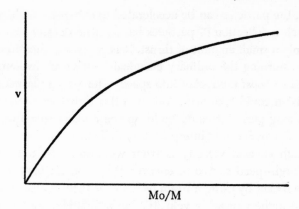

FIGURE 3. A rocket's final velocity (v) depends on the ratio of its mass at the beginning to its mass at the end (Mo/M).

rocket is found to depend directly on the exhaust velocity and also on the ratio of the mass of the rocket at the beginning (including the fuel) to its mass at the end, after the fuel has been burned. The final velocity does not depend on the time it takes to burn the fuel, so that it makes no difference how fast you burn it. (This is strictly true only out in free space. When you start out from the surface of the earth, the situation is complicated by the force of gravity, so that for best efficiency the rocket must reach the top velocity quickly.)

We can see from the curve that doubling the mass ratio does not double the final speed. In order to double the final velocity you must *square* the mass ratio. In other words, you get only a comparatively small increase in speed by increasing the amount of fuel. However, if you can step up the velocity of the exhaust gases, you will get a directly proportional increase in rocket speed. The trick, then, is to find a kind of fuel that will produce a very-high-speed exhaust.

This is the motivation behind the search for devices such as plasma rockets and ion rockets. In a plasma (a very hot gas of electrified particles) or a stream of ions (also electrified particles), the particles can be accelerated to extremely high speeds. But such a collection of particles has so little density that it can give only a small amount of thrust. It is proposed, therefore, that engines burning the ordinary chemical fuels (such as kerosene) be used to boost the rocket into space, after which plasma or ion propulsion could take over. Although this thrust would be small, over a long period it could build up the rocket's speed to velocities sufficient for long interplanetary flights.

If high exhaust velocity is what we want, why not go to a really high-speed source of energy? Why not, for instance, propel the rocket by using a beam of light for the exhaust, since this has the highest possible velocity? Unfortunately, energy in this tenuous form cannot give enough thrust to do us any good. If we used a million watts of power to generate a strong beam of light to drive a rocket, it would produce a thrust of only about one-third of a gram!

Are there other possible methods of propulsion besides the rocket principle? The suggestion has been made that the pressure of the light from the sun might be caught on large sails and thus propel a ship in space. Let us say that the light from the sun would provide about one watt of power per square centimeter of sail surface. Then a sail one kilometer (six-tenths of a mile) square would receive a push amounting to between three and six kilograms (depending on how much of the light the material reflected). In unresisting space, this would be enough to accelerate a ship slowly. But what about that huge sail? It would have to be made of extremely thin material to avoid adding immensely to the mass of the vehicle. So thin a sail might soon disintegrate under the bombardment of the meteorites and radiations in space—fast protons, gamma rays, ultraviolet light, and so on.

Could the magnetic fields in space be used for propulsion in some manner? Though they are rather weak, perhaps some small thrust might be obtained from them. We know that the strength of the fields in space varies from region to region, and this change of field strength might provide a force to propel a ship, as a magnetic field on earth drives an electric motor. The fact is, however, that the magnetic fields in space, besides being extremely weak, change only very gradually, and so the propulsive force obtainable from them is bound to be exceedingly small.

Thus the law of conservation of momentum leads us sternly to the conclusion that, for journeys into space, rockets seem to be the only practicable means of propulsion.

CHAPTER 4

Conservation of Energy

The phenomenon of energy is hard to describe precisely in a simple way, because it exists in so many forms and has so many aspects. When we first encounter the idea in the study of science, our minds have rattling around inside them many loose and vague ideas about the meaning of energy, acquired through common speech. We speak of an energetic person, of mental energy, of psychic energy, of an energetic style of writing, and so on. True, all these uses of the word have a common meaning in that they imply a capability of doing something.

But in physics we must define this capability in a precise way—a way that allows us to measure it.

Let us begin with the form of physical energy known as kinetic energy. We consider our now-familiar situation of two bodies being pushed apart by a spring. The bodies start at rest, and after the spring acts on them for a certain time, each body has a certain momentum. We have found, by experiment, that the momentum of the first body is equal to the momentum of the second body.

We can also find, by experiment, that the final momentum of each body depends upon the length of time that the force of the spring is applied. If it pushes for one second, we get a certain momentum; if it pushes two seconds, the final momentum is twice as great. So the momentum acquired by a body (that is, mass times velocity) equals the force exerted by the spring multiplied by the time during which the force acts:

$$mv = ft$$

Here f is the force, representing the strength of the spring, and t is the time. (This equation is strictly true only when the force is constant. If the force varies from time to time, a somewhat more complicated expression must be used.)

The quantity ft is called the *impulse,* and so we can say that the change of momentum of a body equals the impulse acting on it.

If the body has some momentum to begin with (which we denote as m_0v_0, the subscript zero representing the initial state), then the *change* of momentum produced by the impulse is expressed as

$$mv - m_0v_0 = ft$$

Thus we can say (for the case of a constant force) that

$$f = \frac{mv - m_0v_0}{t}$$

In other words, if we know the change of momentum of a body and the time over which this change has taken place, then the above expression tells us the force. This, in fact, is the way we *define* the concept of force.

In most ordinary cases we can consider that the *mass* of the body does not change enough to count, so the equation can be written:

$$f = \frac{m(v - v_0)}{t}$$

Now the change of velocity divided by the time is the *accelera-tion* of the body. Therefore we customarily find the definition of force given as

$$f = ma$$

a standing for the acceleration. Or, turning the equation around, it is said that the acceleration of a body equals the force acting on it divided by its mass.

While this is quite true for most elementary problems in mechanics, we must be careful when we get into situations where the mass changes while the velocity is changing. These situations are not rare in modern physics and technology. They are common in high-energy nuclear reactions (where the mass of a particle increases significantly when its velocity becomes very great), in rocket mechanics (where the mass of the rocket decreases as it uses up fuel), and in hydrodynamics (where we often speak of the motion of a small volume of material while some of the fluid is leaving or entering it).

Therefore, it is actually more useful (and perhaps more fundamental) to define force in terms of momentum rather than of mass and acceleration. Force is then defined as the *rate of change of momentum* of the body on which the force acts.

What we have just demonstrated, in the foregoing, are Newton's three laws of motion. His First Law says that, to change a body's momentum or direction of motion, an outside force must be applied. The Second Law states that the change is directly proportional to the force and the time over which it is applied. And Newton's Third Law says that every force involves an action and an equal and opposite reaction—that is, the situation illustrated by our two bodies recoiling from each other and thereby acquiring equal and opposite momentum.

So we see that, from our point of view, Newton's First and Third Laws of Motion are included in the law of conservation of momentum, while his Second Law is equivalent to the definition of what we mean by force.

So far we have discussed a force acting upon a body for a given length of time. It is also fruitful to consider a force acting on a body as it moves through a given *distance*.

Again, to avoid complications, we consider the usual situation of a body whose mass does not change appreciably during the motion; this allows us to assume that a constant force acting upon the body increases its velocity at a steady rate.

Now if we multiply the force by the distance over which it acts, we have an equation which defines the work done by the force in moving the body this distance:

$$W = fd$$

For the distance, let us now substitute its equivalent—the velocity produced, v, multiplied by the time the force has acted, t. If the velocity to start with was zero, we must divide the final velocity by two to get the *average* velocity produced over the distance. This quantity, then, is $vt/2$. Substituting it for d, we get

$$W = f\frac{vt}{2}$$

The time, we have already seen in an earlier equation, is equal to the mass times the final velocity divided by the force, or mv/f. Substituting this for t, we get

$$W = f\frac{v}{2} \cdot \frac{mv}{f}$$

which simplifies to

$$W = \frac{mv^2}{2}$$

This last quantity, $mv^2/2$, looks familiar; you may well have seen it before. It is none other than the formula for the *kinetic energy* of a moving body, as it has been known for more than a hundred years.

We have thus shown that the kinetic energy of the body is equal to the work done to set it in motion. As the end product, however, the kinetic energy is measured solely in terms of the mass and velocity of the body itself. It says nothing about the kind or intensity of the force that produced it; it might have been produced in a host of different ways, but it is now simply a property belonging to the moving body.

One reason for considering the kinetic energy of a body to be such an important quantity can be discovered if we look at the problem of two spheres colliding with each other. These could be billiard balls, a neutron striking a proton, two gas molecules in collision—examples of such events abound in physics.

Let the two spheres have masses m_1 and m_2. Their velocities before the collision are v_1 and v_2. After the collision their velocities are v_3 and v_4. We assume, for simplicity, that the collision is head-on. We also assume that the spheres are perfectly elastic. (By elastic, we mean that they rebound from collisions without any loss of velocity, as billiard balls come close to doing.)

We know from the conservation of momentum that the total momentum of the two spheres after the collision will be the same as before the collision. If we wish to write this in the form of an equation, we can say:

$$m_1v_1 - m_2v_2 = m_2v_4 - m_1v_3$$

(The minus signs mean that the velocities v_2 and v_3 represent motion to the left, while v_1 and v_4 are toward the right.)

Starting from this equation, we can show by a mathematical argument (given in Appendix 1) that the following equation also is true:

$$\frac{m_1v_1^2}{2} + \frac{m_2v_2^2}{2} = \frac{m_1v_3^2}{2} + \frac{m_2v_4^2}{2}$$

Here again we have the formula for kinetic energy. The left side of this equation represents the total kinetic energy of the two balls before the collision, and the right side, after the collision. Thus we have proved that in an elastic collision kinetic energy, like momentum, is conserved. It, too, obeys a conservation law.

~~~~ CONSERVATION OF ENERGY

The law of conservation of energy says simply that in any isolated system the total amount of energy remains unchanged.

Is this true in the examples we have examined so far? Take the case of the two balls recoiling elastically from a collision (which we can consider an isolated system if we disregard the friction of the table, air pressure, and all other outside influences). We saw that the balls' total kinetic energy was the same after the collision as before. But what about the situation at the instant of collision? At that instant both balls are stopped dead. In other words, they have no kinetic energy. Where has that energy gone?

Obviously, kinetic energy itself has not been conserved at the instant of collision. But we can salvage our conservation law by noticing that at the moment of collision the two balls become compressed like springs. Their kinetic energy has been converted into the energy of compression. Then, when they decompress, they are shoved apart. (This, in fact, is what we mean by elasticity.) Since the spring is a perfect one, the force and distance of the balls' expansion are exactly the same as the force and distance of the compression. Thus, when the balls are pushed apart, they are given the same kinetic energy that went into the compression.

From this kind of experience we are led to say that the spring stores energy in it while it is compressed. This stored energy we call *potential energy*. While the spring is compressed, there is only potential energy in the system. After the spring expands, there is only the kinetic energy of the masses in motion. While the spring is in the process of expanding, there is a combination of kinetic and potential energy. And if we examine the situation closely, we find that the sum of the potential and kinetic energies is always a constant quantity.

We are now in a position to say that the potential plus the kinetic energy is the *total energy* of the system. What is conserved is not a particular form of energy but the *total* energy.

This is the law of conservation of energy as we know it today. Through all the discoveries and transformations of modern science, this law has stood unaltered. Only our ideas as to what we mean by *total energy* have been modified.

Energy appears in many guises. Besides kinetic energy and the potential energy of a spring, we can talk about electrical energy, heat energy, chemical energy, and the energy in a beam of light. As we shall see later in more detail, all these forms of energy turn out to be versions of either the kinetic energy of molecular motion or the energy of electromagnetic fields. All potential energy may be thought of as the energy stored in a field of force. When you lift a weight, for example, you store energy in the earth's gravitational field.

Around the turn of the century physicists began to run into new phenomena which seemed to threaten the conservation of energy. One was the mysterious behavior of the radioactive elements. Radium, for instance, gave off a little heat. There seemed to be some sort of spontaneous energy within the atom. This potential energy was converted into kinetic energy of the particles shot out during the radioactive breakdown of the atom. Not only was energy apparently coming into existence out of nowhere, but the mass of the atoms was diminished.

The classical physicists were greatly perturbed by this situation, because it appeared that mass was not conserved—and conservation of mass had long been considered one of the foundation-stones of science.

The day was saved by Albert Einstein, who deduced from his principle of relativity that energy possesses mass. This idea could now be applied to the problem of the radioactive nucleus. If you measured the mass of the nucleus before it disintegrated and then measured the mass of all the particles that came out of the disintegration—including the kinetic energy of the particles and the energy of all the other forms of radiation that appeared—these would all add up to equal the original mass.

When uranium fissions, it is often said, some of its "matter is converted into energy." This is not quite the right way to put it, because the energy that appears was present in the nucleus in the form of potential energy.

When we compress a spring, the mass of the spring actually increases, because the potential energy we store in the spring has mass. This is energy residing in the electric fields of the atoms repelling one another within the spring. When the spring expands, this energy goes into kinetic energy of the masses set in motion, and thus the spring loses mass (by a very tiny amount, in any practical case).

The fission of a uranium atom is very similar to the release of a compressed spring: potential energy is converted to kinetic energy. "Matter" is not really destroyed or changed into energy. What we have is simply a release of some of the nuclear force that holds the nucleus together.

When we lift a weight off the ground, we "give it potential energy," the textbooks say. This energy has mass. We might ask: Does the mass of an object change when we lift it off the ground?

The answer is *no*—we could not measure any increase in the object's mass. This seems a paradoxical answer, since we have been emphasizing that all forms of energy have mass. Why not this particular potential energy?

The answer is that the question arises out of a misuse of language. The common statement given in most elementary physics books (and many advanced ones) is that "we give a body potential energy" when we raise it off the ground. This is a bit inaccurate. Actually the energy belongs not to the body but to the gravitational field, just as the potential energy in a compressed spring belongs to the spring, not to the objects compressing it. Therefore, when the body is lifted there is no increase of mass, for the potential energy is not part of the body itself.

We have seen, then, that in most kinds of physical change there is simply a conversion of energy from one form to another. Every elementary particle has a rest-mass which is a definite quantity, and any changes of mass that take place are the result of adding or subtracting energy.

To complete the picture, however, we must remember that there are cases where elementary particles actually change from one form to another. An electron and a positron may combine to form two photons (units of radiation), for example. According to traditional ways of thinking, this represents a case of "matter" changing to "energy." After all, electrons are considered "matter," and photons are considered "energy." But the fact that one can change into the other now leads us to think that matter and energy are two aspects of the same thing. Distinctions between matter and energy become artificial when we observe how readily elementary particles switch from one to the other.

Ignoring these artificial distinctions, we can simply say that every mass has a certain amount of energy connected with it, and every energy has a certain amount of mass. The connection between the two is given by Einstein's famous formula: $E = mc^2$. (In the metric system, m is the mass in grams, c is the speed of light in centimeters per second, and E is the energy of the mass in ergs.)

It follows from all this that the law of conservation of energy is equivalent to the law of conservation of mass—if we make sure that we count up all the contributions of kinetic and potential energy as well as the rest-masses of the bodies within the system.

With this understanding, we can still say: *In an isolated system, the total mass is constant.*

～～ A PARADOX

We may note here, in connection with the question of what belongs to what, the puzzling fact that an object may have different amounts of kinetic energy, depending on who is looking at it.

Suppose we have a spaceship *A*, traveling at a speed of one mile per second relative to an observer *S*, located in an observatory in space. Observer *S* says that spaceship *A* has one unit of kinetic energy. Another observer *G*, located on the ground, measures the speed of spaceship *A* and finds it to be two miles per second, relative to the ground. Therefore, *G* says that *A* has four units of kinetic energy (remember that kinetic energy is proportional to the square of the velocity). So *S* says that *A* has one unit, and, at the same time, *G* says it has four units of energy. Who is right?

Both are right. The paradox arises only because somewhere in our education we got the impression that energy is a kind of substance that permeates a body in a certain definite amount, so that it seems silly to speak of a body containing two different amounts of energy at the same time.

Energy is not a substance. It is merely a concept—an abstraction invented to make easier our interpretation of the things we see happening. By defining kinetic energy in mathematical terms, we can work out meaningful solutions of many problems concerning motion.

In this case, since the amount of kinetic energy depends upon the velocity of the moving body, and the velocity of the body depends upon the motion of the observer, the amount of kinetic energy connected with the body turns out to be a property of the observer as well as of the body itself!

～～ CONCERNING UNITS

It is an interesting historical accident that a physical quantity as basically important as momentum has no unit commonly used for its measurement. All the other concepts we deal with, such as mass, energy, force, length, etc., have an embarrassing variety of units with which the student must struggle.

Another difficulty that makes for unlimited confusion is the fact that the common meanings of certain words have very little to do with their technical meaning in physics. Words such as "work," "force," "power," and "energy" are used almost interchangeably in everyday speech. In technical thought, on the other hand, each one of these words has a precise meaning of its own, with a very specific definition.

This, as a matter of fact, is a fairly recent development. Even among scientists there was often confusion and vagueness about the meaning of these words, so that reading literature more than 200 years old requires a good deal of interpretation.

In present-day physics the word "force" means something that causes a body to change its velocity. Intuitively, we look upon it as a push or a pull. Technically, we become abstract and leave out words such as "push" or "pull." We say instead that when a force acts on a body for a certain time, the force is measured by the change in momentum of the body. Ultimately, all forces boil down to interactions—attractions or repulsions—between elementary particles.

The word "work" really represents an abstraction. In common language, when we say we have done some work we generally mean that we have exerted our muscles in such a way that we feel fatigue. If you held a piano over your head for five minutes, you would say that you had done work, for you feel tired.

However, a physicist would be forced to say that you did work only when you lifted the piano; while you were holding it motionless you did no work at all, no matter how tired your muscles became. In physics, work is done when a force moves a body through a certain distance. The amount of work is always calculated by multiplying the force by the distance traversed.

Power, in common language, often implies some sort of potential for doing things. A king has power over his subjects. A person has a powerful physique. In semi-scientific language, power and energy are very often confused. Nuclear power and nuclear energy are used interchangeably.

In technical language, however, power has one precise meaning: the rate at which work is done. One machine may be able to do the same amount of work as another machine. If it does this work twice as fast as the second machine, it has twice the power. Thus the units for power are always in the form of work (or energy) divided by time.

When work is done, energy is generally changed from one form to another. A spring, an explosive, gravity working on a falling body—these transform potential energy into kinetic energy. A bullet, plowing through a target, transforms its kinetic energy into the heat energy of the target. This heat energy itself is the kinetic energy of the individual molecules of the target.

Thus in physics energy always refers to those properties of matter and space that can be transformed from one form into another by the process of "doing work." The units of energy are always based upon force times distance.

⌇⌇ VICISSITUDES OF CONSERVATION

The complete meaning of the conservation of energy was not recognized until the middle of the nineteenth century. This is rather strange, considering that Newton had recognized the conservation of momentum two centuries earlier. But in the early days of the modern era of science there was great confusion over many matters which every beginning physics student is expected to understand clearly these days. Gottfried Wilhelm von Leibniz and René Descartes (together with their followers) fought for many years over the question of "conservation of force." Descartes chose to measure force by the product mv, which he called the quantity of motion, and he asserted that the total quantity of motion in the universe must remain constant. Leibniz countered this view (in 1686) by saying that a force must be measured by the *vis viva* (energy in motion) produced in a body when the force acted upon it through a certain distance.

It was not until 1743 that Jean d'Alembert pointed out that everybody was just arguing about words—a force could be measured either by the momentum it gave a body or by the energy. In other words, there were actually *two* conservation laws involved during all the quarreling, and both sides were right.

Actually, the general idea that the universe contains a constant amount of motion, or force, or some other dimly understood form of energy goes back a long way. This undoubtedly is connected with the hundreds of years of futile attempts to create a perpetual-motion machine—a machine that would keep running and do work without the benefit of some means of propulsion. The idea of the overbalancing wheel goes back to the thirteenth century and was foisted on gullible believers as late as the nineteenth. (If it has succeeded in fooling anybody in the twentieth century, it has not come to my attention.)

The failure of all attempts to make a successful perpetual-motion machine must have convinced many that it was impossible to get mechanical energy for nothing. Newton, Leibniz, and some of their contemporaries based their work on this conviction. However, it was not so clear to those early thinkers that *all kinds* of energy were conserved. It was possible for a person to think that a mechanical perpetual-motion machine (like the overbalanced wheel) would not work, while at the same time believing that an electric, chemical, or heat device might somehow create energy.

We must remember that it was not then realized that energy could be changed from one form to another and that the concept of interactions among elementary particles as the basis of all energy was completely unknown.

Heat was considered a mysterious fluid; electricity was a mysterious fluid; friction, cohesion, and surface tension were mysterious forces that seemed to have no connection with kinetic or potential energy. Johann and Daniel Bernoulli of Switzerland were able to develop many uses for the idea of conservation of energy during the eighteenth century, especially in the study of fluid motion, but they were unable to make the jump required to apply this idea to other forms of energy.

As a result, the idea of conservation of energy was almost forgotten for many years, except that, as a practical matter, the French Academy formally resolved in 1775 to consider no more designs for perpetual-motion machines, because so much time had been wasted in discovering, over and over again, that these machines did not work.

At the end of the eighteenth century new ideas about energy began to emerge. Alessandro Volta's invention of the battery in 1800 showed that electric current could come from chemical reactions. The electric current could produce heat and light, and through magnetism it could produce motion. Motion, in turn, could produce electricity through friction. A closed cycle of energy conversion had thus been demonstrated: electricity, magnetism, mechanical motion, friction, electricity.

In 1822 the German physicist Thomas Johann Seebeck showed that heat applied to the junction between two different metals could produce an electric current directly. Twelve years later Jean Peltier of France reversed this, showing that a current applied to such a junction could produce heat or cold, depending on the direction of the current. For a time it was fashionable to write papers in the learned journals describing chains of transformations from one kind of energy to another, and people gradually began to speak of a single "force" which could appear in electrical, thermal, dynamical, and other forms.

Earlier, in 1798, the American scientist Benjamin Thompson (who pursued a notorious career in Europe as Count Rumford) had shown that when cannons were bored out with a drill, the mechanical energy of the drill was converted into heat through friction. This discovery made little impact on the world of science until, in the years between 1840 and 1850, James Prescott Joule of England actually measured the amount of heat obtained from a given amount of mechanical energy. When it was demonstrated that mechanical work could be converted into heat without loss, the mental dam seemed to break, and all at once everybody was writing about conservation of energy. The brilliant French engineer Sadi Carnot had actually worked out the theory of the interchangeability of heat and mechanical work in the 1830s, but it took Joule's measurements of heat yields to attract wide attention and acceptance.

Between 1842 and 1847, the theory of conservation of energy was publicly announced by several scientists separately—by Joule, by Hermann von Helmholtz and Robert Mayer of Germany, and by others. It seemed that the idea was "in the air" and just ripe for acceptance by the world of science. There has never been another such example of a theory appearing simultaneously in so many different minds.

There is good reason to believe this was no accident. In the first place, the beginning of the nineteenth century marked a great rise in engineering. People were becoming interested in water, wind, and steam power. The measurement of work and power became important. Use of the word "work" became widespread in physics, and the equivalence of work (force times distance) and kinetic energy became well-known. Between 1819 and 1839 several writers on engineering mechanics derived the expression $fd = \frac{1}{2}mv^2$.

Moreover, some of the German scientists—Helmholtz, Mayer, the chemist Justus von Liebig—had a concept of the indestructibility of energy even before they found evidence for it. When the evidence began to accumulate, they were prepared. They made the mental jump from the various discoveries to the general law of conservation of energy because they were looking for just such a principle.

The original influence behind all these simultaneous discoveries may have been a philosophical movement known in Germany as *Naturphilosophie*. Its adherents sought a single, unifying principle for all natural phenomena. The philosophy professor Friedrich Wilhelm Joseph von Schelling predicted in 1799 ". . . that magnetic, electrical, chemical, and finally even organic phenomena would be interwoven into one great association . . . (which) extends over the whole of nature." This is precisely the point of view that prevails today, many scientists believing that the universe will ultimately be explainable in terms of a few fields and elementary particles.

Schelling's followers dominated the teaching in German universities at the beginning of the nineteenth century, and the influence of this philosophy undoubtedly contributed to the recognition of conservation of energy when the facts were assembled.

Conservation of energy remains one of the cornerstones of modern science. About the only scientists who seriously challenge it at present are a small group of cosmologists who believe that new matter is continuously being created (and, some say, old matter continuously being extinguished) in the expanding universe. Their "steady-state" universe requires the creation of only one atom of hydrogen per liter of space in about a trillion years, according to some calculations. Such a tiny violation of the law of conservation of matter-energy is too small to be detected in any conceivable way, so from a strictly experimental point of view it is difficult to disprove the argument of Fred Hoyle and his fellow "steady-staters." However, certain astronomical observations should enable us to decide for or against the continuous-creation theory when all the facts are in. So far the evidence seems to be against—to the comfort of most physicists, who would be distressed to discover exceptions to the powerful law of conservation of energy.

CHAPTER 5

~~~~~~~~~~~~~~~~~~~~~~~

Conservation of Angular Momentum

~~~~~~~~~

We are all familiar with the trick of the ice skater who starts a spin with outstretched arms and then proceeds to whirl himself into a frenzy by pulling his arms in close to his sides. You can feel the same effect by seating yourself in a freely turning swivel chair and holding out a weight in each hand. If you start rotating and then pull your arms in, you will find that your speed of rotation increases dramatically.

We can examine this situation in a simplified way by picturing a mass being swung around a circle at the end of a rope. We arrange matters so that we can reel in the rope and shorten it while the mass is whirling around.

What do we observe?

We see, first of all, that as the rope shortens, the velocity of the object increases. The increase of velocity, of course, means that both the momentum and the kinetic energy of the object increase. Does this behavior violate conservation of momentum and energy? No, it does not—when we pull in the rope we do work on the object, thus increasing its kinetic energy.

We notice, if we make careful measurements, that when we shorten the rope to one-half the original length, the velocity of the body doubles; when we reduce it to one-third, the velocity is multiplied by three, and so on. It would appear at first thought that we have discovered a constant quantity which describes the rotation of bodies—namely, radius times velocity.

This is not the entire story, however. What would happen if we changed the mass of the object while it was revolving? Instead of whirling a solid mass at the end of a rope, we substitute a hollow glass globe for the solid and whirl it at the end of a hose through which we can pump water into the globe. Keeping the length of the hose constant, we inject water into the globe as it revolves. We find now that, as the mass of the water-loaded globe increases, its velocity *decreases*.

If we make careful measurements of the mass and velocity of the globe, we find that the mass times the velocity times the radius is a constant quantity. This quantity is called the *angular momentum*. We can express it in this simple case in terms of ordinary momentum, *mv*, multiplied by the radius of rotation:

$$L \; (angular \; momentum) = mvr$$

If a number of objects are revolving around the same center, then the total angular momentum is obtained simply by calculating *mvr* for each mass and adding up these numbers, taking the direction of rotation into account.

The reason this is called angular momentum is that as the body revolves in a circle we can measure its position by an angle. The rate at which this angle, called θ (theta), changes as the body moves is called the *angular velocity*. It is useful to measure the angle in *radians* rather than degrees. The radian, as shown in Figure 4, is simply that angle which makes the distance subtended around the circumference equal to the radius of the circle. One radian is approximately 57 degrees. For any angle θ, measured in radians, the distance around the circumference subtended by this angle is simply given by the radius times the angle: $r\theta$. Then, if v is the velocity of the body around the circle, the angular velocity ω (omega) is simply $\omega = rv$. (We should not be alarmed by the use of Greek letters; it is useful to know them, because θ and ω are used by scientists all over the world

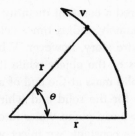

FIGURE 4. Measurement of angular velocity.

for angle and angular velocity. It would be more confusing in the long run if, trying to be simple, we started using English letters for these things.)

The expression mvr represents another great conservation law —the law of conservation of angular momentum. Innumerable observations and experiments have built up our belief in this law. It states that *in a closed system, the total amount of angular momentum is constant.*

The simplicity of this statement is deceptive; actually it contains many hidden pitfalls and problems. In fact, these few words raise some of the deepest problems in physics. We shall try to bring forth, and perhaps clarify, some of these problems here and in later chapters.

The meaning of angular momentum itself requires clarification. Suppose that an object traveling in a straight line collides with a mass attached by a rigid rod to an axle so that it can move only in a circle around this axis (see Figure 5). Upon being struck by the first mass (m), the second mass (M) begins to circle the axis, while m recoils.

At first glance we seem to have something that violates conservation of angular momentum. How can an object traveling in a straight line produce angular momentum where none existed before?

The fact of the matter is that a body moving in a straight line does have angular momentum. Strictly speaking, it is a property belonging to all moving bodies, regardless of the kind of path

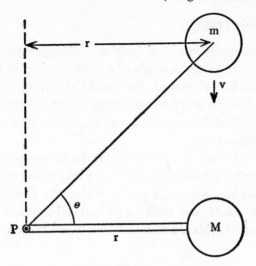

FIGURE 5. Translation of ordinary momentum
into angular momentum.

they travel. The angular momentum of mass m relative to the axis P in our example is mvr, with r equal to the perpendicular, or shortest distance, from P to the straight path traversed by m.

This definition allows conservation of angular momentum to be satisfied. We can prove this by starting with the general law of conservation of momentum. It tells us that the momentum of a moving body before collision with a stationary body equals the momentum of both bodies after the collision:

$$mv = mv_1 + MV_1$$

If we multiply both sides of this equation by r, we obtain:

$$mvr = mv_1r + MV_1r$$

By this operation, translating ordinary momentum into angular momentum, we have proved that the angular momentum before the collision equals the angular momentum after collision.

∿∿∿ TORQUE

Some properties of a body may change while others remain constant. In the example of a mass whirling at the end of a rope which is shortened, the kinetic energy of the mass increases, while the angular momentum remains constant. A force is being applied, but in such a way that it does not change the angular momentum.

What must we do to change the angular momentum of a body? Well, everybody knows that to turn a wheel you should apply force at the rim, not at the center of the axle. Clearly, to make something rotate we must apply an off-center force to it (see Figure 6). This is a *torque*, which we all know as a twisting

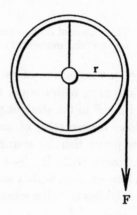

FIGURE 6. Application of a twisting force, or torque.

force. The magnitude of the torque is defined as the applied force multiplied by the distance from the center of rotation:

$$T = Fr$$

If, for simplicity, we consider a wheel which has all its mass located around the rim, experiment shows that the acceleration of any point on the rim is proportional to the applied force according to the equation

$$F = Ma$$

where M is the mass of the wheel.

Angular acceleration is designated by α (alpha). The acceleration of a point at the distance r from the axis (*i.e.*, a point on the rim) is $r\alpha$.

Now let us substitute in the equation $T = Fr$ the equivalents of F (Ma) and of a ($r\alpha$). We get

$$T = Mar$$
$$= M(r\alpha)r$$
$$= Mr^2\alpha$$
$$= I\alpha$$

The quantity I is called the *moment of inertia* of the wheel. In this particular example (a wheel with all the mass at the rim) $I = Mr^2$. For objects of other shapes (a solid wheel, a sphere, a square, etc.) the moment of inertia must be calculated in a more complicated manner. The moment of inertia always takes the part of the mass in problems involving rotation.

This is clearly seen when we calculate the kinetic energy of the wheel after it has been set into rotation, substituting $r\omega$ for v:

$$K.E. = \tfrac{1}{2}Mv^2$$
$$= \tfrac{1}{2}M(r\omega)^2$$
$$= \tfrac{1}{2}Mr^2\omega^2$$
$$= \tfrac{1}{2}I\omega^2$$

(We must emphasize that the final equation can be obtained in this simple way only because we have chosen a wheel which has all the mass located at the same radius, so that all parts of the wheel have the same velocity.)

Now the rotational kinetic energy looks just like ordinary kinetic energy—except that instead of the word "mass" we use "moment of inertia," and instead of "velocity" we use "angular velocity." All the laws and equations that apply to straight-line motion also apply to rotational motion if we make the proper substitutions of words. The table below shows these parallels.

STRAIGHT-LINE MOTION		ROTATIONAL MOTION	
Distance	s	Angle	θ
Velocity	v	Angular velocity	ω
Acceleration	a	Angular acceleration	α
Mass	m	Moment of inertia	I
Momentum	p	Angular momentum	L
Force	F	Torque	T
Impulse:		Angular impulse:	
Ft = change of momentum		Tt = change of angular momentum	
$F = ma$		$T = I\alpha$	
$K.E. = \frac{1}{2}mv^2$		$K.E. = \frac{1}{2}I\omega^2$	
$p = mv$		$L = I\omega$	

~~~ THE ROTATING EARTH

Conservation of angular momentum provides a most useful and simple tool for solving all kinds of problems involving rotation. Consider the problem that started this chapter: a mass is swung around at the end of a rope, and the rope is shortened (or lengthened). If you know the angular momentum at the beginning, before the rope has been pulled in, then you also know the angular momentum after the rope has been pulled in, for they are the same. Indeed you know the angular momentum at any instant of time during this motion, for it does not change as long as no torque is applied. Thus we can immediately write down:

angular momentum (after) = angular momentum (before)

$$Mv_2r_2 = Mv_1r_1$$

so that

$$v_2 = v_1 \frac{r_1}{r_2}$$

Thus, if we know the velocity at the beginning and the length of the rope before and after the length is changed, we can easily calculate the final velocity of the object. We do not have to consider knotty problems such as what forces are acting on the mass at every instant, what its acceleration is at any moment, what its exact path is while all this is going on, etc. We don't care about all that if we just want to know what the object is doing after all the changes of motion have taken place.

An interesting hypothetical problem that can be treated in this manner is the following: We know that the earth is a rotating sphere. Imagine that a long, rigid rod sticks straight out into space from the equator and turns with the earth like a spoke on a wheel. The longer we make the rod, the faster its end will move as it whips around far out in space. The question is: If we made the rod long enough, would the end of it eventually be traveling faster than light? If so, what happens to our belief that no material object can travel faster than light?

The question we have asked turns out to be meaningless, because we have set up an impossible situation. How will we erect such a rod? If we get one somewhere else and attach it to the surface of the earth, it will not start moving with the same angular velocity as the earth unless we apply enough force to give the rod itself (*i.e.*, the extra mass) the required kinetic energy. And there is not enough energy in the universe to make any part of the rod go faster than light! If, on the other hand, we push out material from the earth to form the rod, the law of conservation of angular momentum tells us that, as the rod is extended, the angular velocity of the earth-rod mass must decrease, just as the rotation of a whirling skater slows down when he extends his arms. Calculation shows that the velocity of the end of the rod will become smaller and smaller as it grows longer. If the entire mass of the earth is converted into rod, it will swing around very slowly indeed.

It is a rather fascinating thought that every time we build a skyscraper we slow down the rotation of the earth by a tiny amount. On the other hand, the washing down of material from the tops of mountains into the ocean tends to speed up the earth's rotation rate. Contrariwise, the building up of glaciers on the mountain tops by snow formed from water evaporated from the oceans tends to work in the opposite direction. All effects of this type produce slight changes in the rate of the earth's rotation on its axis.

～～～ TOPS AND GYROSCOPES

The tenacious disposition of a rotating object to preserve its angular momentum provides us with many useful devices. One of them is the device of imparting spin to a bullet by means of rifling in the gun's barrel. The spin, contrary to some beliefs, does not make the bullet travel in a straight line. It merely stabilizes the bullet so that its nose remains pointed in the forward direction. That defends it from deflection by the air. If the bullet nose wobbled, erratically changing air resistance would push it off course.

The fact is that the motion of a bullet in its trajectory cannot be affected by anything going on within the bullet itself. If it were traveling through a vacuum, the path of the bullet's center of mass would not be changed at all by its spin, by machinery moving around inside it, or by anything else you can imagine. The spin only affects the orientation of the bullet—that is, the direction in which its nose points. If the axis of the bullet is oriented in a certain direction when it starts spinning, then it will remain oriented in that direction during its travels.

What causes the spinning bullet to keep its axis pointing in the same direction? This question plunges us into one of the most advanced problems of modern physics.

Let us see what happens when a force acts on a spinning body. We recall that angular momentum has *direction* connected with it, as well as magnitude. This means that it must be represented by a *vector*—an arrow. In the case of ordinary momentum, the vector points in the direction of the body's motion. To indicate the direction of angular momentum, physicists find it most useful to point the vector along the axis around which the body rotates.

The convention accepted by all scientists is that when you see a body spin clockwise, you draw an arrow along the axis facing away from you; when the body spins counterclockwise, the vector points in the opposite direction (toward you). This is illustrated by a screw. In the case of a right-handed screw (turning clockwise as you drive it into the wood) the vector points in the direction of the screw's forward motion.

We now apply this convention to the angular momentum of any rotating body. If the body is rotating clockwise as you look at it, the angular momentum vector points away from you. If you apply a clockwise torque to this body (with a screwdriver, or by any other means), you tend to increase the angular momentum. The change in the angular momentum must be in the same direction as the torque vector. Thus, when you twist a screwdriver in a clockwise direction, the arrow that represents this torque is aimed from the handle to the point of the screwdriver.

Now as long as you apply the twisting force in the direction of the axis of spin, all that happens is that the body spins faster. But if you apply the torque in some other direction, the situation becomes more complicated.

Consider a spinning top. As long as the top stands upright, with its center of mass directly over the point, gravity does not exert any off-center force on it. But if you tilt the top so that its axis of spin is horizontal (you can do this with a gyroscope), the gravitational force produces a torque which is directed at right angles to the axis of spin (see Figure 7). This causes the angular momentum of the spinning gyroscope to swing around in the same direction as the torque. The angular momentum does not

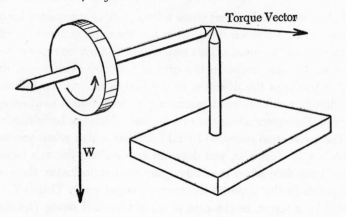

FIGURE 7. Action of gravity (*W*) on a spinning gyroscope.

change in amount, but the direction of the vector (or axis) does change. Since the torque exerted by gravity goes on acting at right angles to the angular momentum, the axis of spin continues to shift around in the horizontal plane, so that the gyroscope slowly swings in a circle around the pivot. In other words, instead of toppling over, as an ordinary weight would if supported only at one end, the axis of the gyroscope moves around in a horizontal plane.

This motion is called *precession*. The angular velocity of the precession motion, *P*—that is, the rate at which the axis of the top turns in a horizontal plane—is given by the formula:

$$P = \frac{T}{I\omega}$$

where *T* is the torque resulting from the weight of the gyroscope, *I* is the gyroscope's moment of inertia, and ω is the angular velocity of the top around its own axis—its rate of spin.

This formula shows us that if the gyroscope has a large moment of inertia, and if it is spinning very rapidly, then the precession is slow. For a given amount of torque, the faster the spin, the slower the precession.

The gyroscope, in fact, behaves as if it does not want to change the position of its axis. Its slow and reluctant response to the right-angle torque suggests that the spinning top has an extremely large amount of inertia.

When a horizontal gyroscope is supported at both ends, there is no unbalanced torque and therefore no tendency to precess. However, if you try to lift one end of the axis, you are in for a surprise. The gyroscope will refuse to obey; it will not tilt but instead will start swinging around in a horizontal direction.

Another most important ability of the gyroscope is this: If it is supported inside a box on gimbals, which allow the axis of spin to hold its position or to move freely, then no matter how the box is turned, the gyroscope will always keep its axis pointed in the same direction. This is the property that makes the gyroscope so useful as an instrument for navigation. It is the heart of the inertial guidance systems in ships and rocket missiles.

When we say that the gyroscope always keeps its axis pointed in the same direction, we mean exactly that: its direction remains constant in space—not with reference to the changing earth. Suppose, for instance, that we start flying around the earth from the Equator toward the North Pole, and at the Equator the axis of the gimballed gyroscope in our airplane is parallel to the earth's surface, pointing north (see Figure 8). As we fly north, the gyroscope will seem to tilt its axis upward, until, at the North Pole, it will point straight up to the sky!

From our point of view, it will appear that the gyroscope has changed its direction. But from the point of view of somebody located outside the earth, the gyroscope has at all times kept its axis pointing toward the North Star (see Figure 8).

Similarly, a gyroscope resting on the surface of the earth seems to turn its direction completely around in 24 hours; actually it is the earth that is turning around under the gyroscope. Over the period of a year, a gyroscope also shows the change of direction of the earth as it swings around the sun in its orbit.

Here we are penetrating to the heart of the mystery of the constancy of angular momentum. The box is turning around the

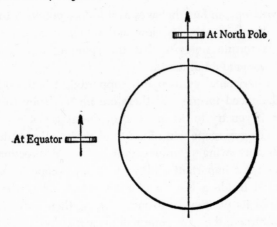

FIGURE 8. A gyroscope maintains its direction in space.

gyroscope, the earth is turning under the box, the solar system is turning, the galaxy is turning—everything is turning except the axis of this gyroscope. Do we really mean that the gyroscope is going to keep pointing in the same direction of space regardless of all these motions going on around it?

When we say that the gyroscope "points in the same direction," we must relate this direction to something. What is the basic framework of the universe that allows us to determine the direction of the gyroscope and say that it does not change? This question brings us to one of the fundamental differences between classical physics and modern physics.

Newton believed that there was an "absolute frame of reference" in the universe and that the rotation of a body could always be measured with reference to this frame. Newton's concept of "absolute" space seemed, indeed, the only way to find any order in the universe, for without the idea of a fixed frame of reference it was hard to understand the behavior of a gyroscope or many other phenomena.

We can illustrate the problem with the following hypothetical experiment. Imagine yourself floating alone out in space (appropriately dressed in a space suit). It appears to you that the distant stars are slowly revolving around you. You stretch out your arms, and the stars seem to slow down. You pull in your arms again, and now the revolution of the stars speeds up. Apparently you have induced the entire universe to move faster.

A nearby observer might say that this is nonsense: nothing so dramatic has taken place. He would say that you yourself were rotating on your own axis to begin with, and when you pulled your arms in you merely speeded up your own rotation.

You might argue in reply: "If that is the case, who applied the force that made me rotate?"

The observer could answer: "That's a ridiculous argument. If you are worried about the force that made you rotate, why don't you worry about the force that made the whole universe rotate, according to your story?"

Newton felt that there was no real paradox here. He thought we should consider the universe as a whole to be absolutely at rest, so that the only proper way of looking at it was to say that the man in the space suit was turning around relative to the universe.

For good and sufficient reasons, a number of physicists decided at the beginning of this century that Newton was wrong. Albert Einstein's principle of relativity became the guiding principle of science, in place of Newton's absolutism. From the relativistic point of view, it makes no difference whether you say the man in the space suit is rotating or the universe is rotating! There is no "absolute frame of reference," no imaginary set of axes in space to which you can point and say: *This is at rest.* But that is no longer of crucial importance, for we can describe the behavior of the physical universe relative to the observer.

It is still proper to say that a gyroscope keeps its axis fixed with respect to the distant stars. The motions of the earth, of the sun, of the solar system, and of our galaxy as a whole all take place in a framework connected with the galaxies far distant from our own. We shall consider this whole subject in more detail in the chapter on relativity.

～～ CAN THE EARTH'S AXIS BE TILTED?

In recent years there has been much playful speculation about the possibility of changing the earth's motion by means of tremendous nuclear explosions. For instance, a science-fiction movie depicted two atomic bomb blasts, set off on opposite sides of the earth, which turned the earth over so that its north-south axis was shifted and also threw the planet off its orbit so that it started falling into the sun.

Looking at these ideas with a critical eye, we must first recognize that, whatever happens, the conservation laws must be satisfied. In order to change the orbit of the earth around the sun, we would have to change its angular momentum. This cannot be done by means of anything happening within the earth itself. Even if we blew up the planet, its fragments as a group would retain the same angular momentum and continue to circle the sun in the same orbit. Only an outside force, such as the gravitational effect of the approach of another planet, could change the earth's orbit.

Likewise, to change the tilt of the earth's axis would require a change in the angular momentum belonging to its spin. The earth is a pretty good gyroscope, and it would take a lot of torque to alter this spin. Moreover, the torque would have to be applied off-center—that is, not through the center of the earth. This means that the attraction of another planet could not do anything to the earth's daily rotation, for the gravitational force between two planets passes through their centers and supplies no torque. That disposes of the theory presented by the much-discussed book, *Worlds in Collision,* which would have had us believe that another planet passing close by caused the earth to stop its rotation for a few days, resulting in all sorts of Biblical catastrophes.

Atomic explosions on the surface of the earth would, under ordinary conditions, press straight down toward the center of the earth and again would produce no torque. If you could arrange things so that a large amount of the earth's material was ejected tangentially from the surface of the earth (as in a fire-works pinwheel), then you could change the angular momentum of the earth. For example, if you scooped out a ball of earth two miles in diameter at the North Pole and shot it away at right angles to the axis of spin at a velocity of ten miles per second, this would tilt the earth's axis by about one ten-millionth of a degree!

In actuality, the crust of the earth is not fastened rigidly to the core, so that such an experiment would probably tear a section of the crust loose, rather than move the earth as a whole. Geologists conjecture that at some time in the past the continents have moved around on the surface of the earth, so that the North Pole was not always where it is now. This kind of motion is allowed by conservation of angular momentum.

CHAPTER 6

The Laws of Motion

Philosophical ponderings on the nature of motion can be traced back to before the time of ancient Greece. The movements of the sun, the moon, and the stars across the sky excited speculations which are recorded in the earliest writings of man. In Greek mythology, Phoebus drove the chariot of the sun through the heavens, spreading light over the world. The coming of the dawn was heralded by Phosphoros (whom we know as the planet Venus), driving white horses through the sky.

Plato (428–348 B.C.) considered the stars to be floating free in space, moved by their own divine souls. Aristotle (384–322 B.C.) believed that continued motion required a continued moving force. He therefore postulated an Unmoved Mover, which provided the motive power for the universe. Aristotle's influence was so great that for the next thousand years his ideas dominated the thoughts of scientists and philosophers. As a result, astronomical theories during that time supposed the skies to be composed of a series of crystal spheres which carried the heavenly bodies around in cycles and epicycles. The earth stood still at the center of all this motion.

One of the basic problems from the beginning was the matter of explaining the fall of objects on the earth. Not only the question "Why do bodies fall?" but also "What is the velocity of a falling body?" stirred storms of controversy for many hundreds of years.

This seems rather silly to us today. We wonder why the ancients, instead of arguing about how fast bodies fell, didn't try making measurements to settle the argument. It was not until the beginning of the seventeenth century that this was actually done.

The Greek philosophers, though undoubtedly men of high intelligence, were hobbled by what seemed to them the "natural way of thinking," which did not include experimenting and measuring the phenomena they were thinking about. Democritus (460 B.C.), one of the earliest to play with the idea that matter was composed of atoms, had some thoughts about how these atoms moved under the influence of gravity. It seemed "natural" to him that in a vacuum the heavier atoms would fall faster than the lighter ones.

Aristotle found his way to a completely different conclusion, by means of a delightfully twisted piece of logic. He believed that when a body moved through a medium that resisted its motion (such as the air), its velocity equalled the force divided by the resistance. However, this leads to the conclusion that where there is no resistance, or no air, the velocity must be infinite. Since this was inconceivable, Aristotle argued that a vacuum could not exist!

Aristotle's overwhelming influence led men to believe for nearly two thousand years that a vacuum was impossible. When they said that "Nature abhors a vacuum," they meant it strictly. They accepted a false conclusion because they could not bring themselves to question Aristotle's equation.

One of the first to break away from this purely deductive kind of thinking was that genius in many fields, Leonardo da Vinci (1452–1519). He recognized that science must begin with observation, and that "those sciences are vain and full of errors which are not born from experiment. . . ."

In the science of mechanics he recognized the principle of inertia, which was later verified by Galileo. Leonardo wrote: "Nothing perceptible by the senses is able to move itself; . . .

every body has a weight in the direction of its motion." He meant that every body in motion resists being stopped, and behaves as if it continues to be pulled in the direction of motion. This "weight in the direction of motion" we now call inertia.

Unfortunately, Leonardo published very little on his philosophical ideas. They did not become known until many years later, when historians discovered and studied his private notebooks.

It was therefore left for Galileo Galilei (1564–1642) to initiate the modern era in physics by making the first respectable set of measurements that showed how bodies actually move.

ᕦᕤᕦᕤ GALILEO

Galileo was not actually the first to test the Aristotelian notion that bodies fell with different speeds according to their heaviness or lightness (because they "sought their natural places" with varying power). In 1586 (nearly 100 years after the discovery of America) a Dutch military engineer named Simon Stevin got the bright idea of actually dropping some weights to see whether Aristotle was right. In a book entitled *Weeghconst* ("Art of Weighing") Stevin told of an experiment in which he dropped two pieces of lead, one weighing ten pounds, the other one pound, from a height of 30 feet. When they hit the wooden floor, the sound of impact of the two weights could not be separated. Evidently they had both fallen with the same speed.

At this point, Galileo, a young man of 22, had not yet experimented with falling bodies. At 24 he became a professor of mathematics at the University of Pisa. His ideas at the time were an odd mixture of truth and error. He would have agreed with Stevin's conclusion: one pound of lead should fall with the same speed as ten pounds, because both bodies had the same density. But Galileo believed that the speed of fall would vary with density: ten pounds of lead would fall faster than ten pounds of wood, because lead was denser than wood.

He learned that this was a mistaken idea after getting down

to a serious study of just how bodies fell. He started by trying to write a mathematical formula which would tell how far a body had fallen or how fast it was going after a given time had elapsed. He could see by experiment that the farther a body fell, the faster it went. His first conjecture was that the velocity therefore depended upon the distance the body had fallen. However, this resulted in an absurdity. At the beginning, when a body has traveled zero distance, it has zero velocity. Since it cannot travel a distance until it acquires a velocity, and it cannot acquire a velocity until it travels a distance (according to the hypothesis), the body cannot even get started.

Therefore Galileo abandoned this idea and assumed that the velocity of a falling body increases simply in proportion to the duration, or *time,* of its fall. According to this hypothesis, the velocity of a falling body that starts from rest would be expressed by the equation:

$$v = gt$$

Here g is the acceleration produced by gravity, a number which describes how fast the velocity increases. Since the body starts from rest and ends with a velocity v, its *average* velocity is $\frac{1}{2}v$. The distance traveled is the average velocity multiplied by the time, so that one could say that the distance was equal to $\frac{1}{2}vt$, or $\frac{1}{2}gt^2$.

Here was a result that Galileo could check by actual experiment. He realized that it was too difficult to measure the speed of freely falling bodies, especially with the primitive instruments at his disposal. However, by rolling balls down an inclined plane (slowing up their fall) he was able to measure their speed. His time-measuring apparatus consisted of a vessel of water equipped with a stopcock at the bottom. By weighing the amount of water that flowed out of the vessel while a ball rolled down a measured distance, he could make comparisons of time which were accurate enough to test his hypothesis. The experiments confirmed that it was essentially correct.

By present standards Galileo's measurements were crude, for he ignored many sources of error. But the important point is that he set up a hypothesis, deduced results from it by means of mathematics, and then made measurements to see whether the actual objects moved as he had predicted they would.

Later experimenters, using more advanced instruments, could repeat the tests, could make measurements precise to a dozen decimal places, and could verify the hypothesis as accurately as they pleased. Yet Galileo, with his crude instruments (and a sharp instinct for a good theory), had the right answer.

His experiments established a number of important principles:

1. The velocity of a falling body increases at a constant rate. (A modern experimenter, with modern precision, would have to correct this to take into account the change in the gravitational force as the body falls toward the center of the earth.)

2. The acceleration of the body is produced by the action of a force. The effect of a force acting on a body is the same whether the body is at rest or in motion.

3. If there is no force acting on a body already in motion, it will continue to move forever. (The principle of inertia.)

4. The acceleration of gravity is the same for all bodies, regardless of their weight or density.

The first three points were later to be incorporated into Newton's laws of motion. It was Galileo who saw for the first time that a force acting on a body produces not simply a velocity but a *change* of velocity.

The supreme importance of the fourth point was not fully recognized until three centuries later, when Einstein used it as the basis of part of his theory of relativity.

While Galileo was the first to understand the importance of inertia, his conception of it was very limited. He thought the natural form of motion was circular, rather than in a straight line. Therefore, if a body started to roll on the surface of the earth, it would just naturally continue to roll in a circle around the surface. He believed that the planets moved in circular orbits, even after Kepler had shown that the orbits of planets were elliptical, not circular.

With this point of view, Galileo was not ready to discover the law of gravity. That was left for Newton, who finally cleared away the remainder of the mystical and unscientific notions left over from the Middle Ages and put the science of mechanics on a more logical basis.

〰〰 NEWTON

Sir Isaac Newton (1642–1727) was born the year Galileo died. The jump from the ideas of Galileo to the ideas of Newton was not a direct one; Tycho Brahe and Johann Kepler, who lived at the same time as Galileo, formed a bridge between Galileo and Newton.

Tycho Brahe was strictly an observer. His passion in life was to observe the motion of the planets and the stars. He spent his entire life in his observatory, building the most accurate instruments possible at that time and recording the positions of each planet (as well as the moon) from day to day.

Kepler, on the other hand, was a theorist. He took the observations of Tycho Brahe and tried to find some sort of order in them. His motives were not what we would consider good scientific reasons. He was a numerologist. He believed that God had constructed the universe according to certain harmonic patterns, and therefore one should be able to discover interesting numerical relationships in the orbits of the planets. He did not have the idea of discovering natural laws as we conceive them.

Whatever his reasons, Kepler did uncover certain patterns in the great mass of data that Tycho Brahe had stored away. These became known as Kepler's laws of planetary motion:

1. The orbit of each planet is in the form of an ellipse, with the sun at one focus of the ellipse.

2. A line drawn from the sun to a planet passes over equal areas in equal times.

3. If T is the time of a planet's travel around the sun, and r is

the average radius of its orbit, then the quantity r^3/T^2 is the same number for all the planets. (This last rule was really a delight to Kepler's numerological spirit.)

These observations became building blocks for Newton's theory of gravitation. Other important building blocks were Newton's own three laws of motion, which Newton considered to be the basic postulates by which all motion could be described:

1. Every body perseveres in its state of rest or of uniform motion in a straight line, unless it is compelled to change that state by impressed forces.

2. Change of motion (*i.e.*, the rate of change of momentum) is proportional to the impressed force and takes place in the direction in which that force is impressed.

3. Reaction is always equal and opposite to action; that is to say, the actions of two bodies upon each other are always equal and directly opposite.

The first law is really included in the second law, for if the impressed force is zero, then there is no change of motion and the body continues to travel in a straight line with a constant velocity. Perhaps Newton felt it important to emphasize the first law because there had been so much confusion about the matter previously; Galileo, for instance, had supposed that the "natural" motion of a body was circular.

Newton saw clearly that a planet should travel in a straight line unless deflected by some force. Since the planets did not travel in straight lines, there must be some force operating between the sun and the planets (and between the earth and the moon) which caused the elliptical orbits.

Newton pondered what happens when a projectile is shot in a horizontal direction from the top of a hill. Inertia tends to keep the projectile going in a straight line, while gravity pulls it down. The projectile compromises by moving in a curved path; at ordinary projectile speeds, the path eventually meets the earth's surface. If the speed of the projectile is increased, it strikes the earth farther away; given a high speed, it may not hit the earth until it has traveled around to the other side. And at a certain high speed the projectile may keep going around the earth in a circular orbit, never touching the earth at all.

We see from this picture that the projectile is always falling, even in the case where it never hits the earth. The direction of the projectile is always changing toward the center of the earth. This is the acceleration caused by gravity. When the direction of the projectile's path changes at the same rate as the earth's surface—that is, when the curvature of the path is the same as the curvature of the surface—then the projectile always remains at the same distance above the surface.

Newton now asked whether the same type of description could show how the moon circled the earth, and how the planets circled the sun. Could it be that the moon was constantly falling to the earth under the influence of gravity, while its velocity was just enough to keep it in an orbit? If this were true, then could he assume that the acceleration of the moon in its falling was the same as the acceleration of an object falling at the surface of the earth? Clearly, he could not assume this. However, the moon's acceleration could easily be measured from its known velocity.

Newton had been able to show mathematically that when a body travels in a circle with a given velocity, it must constantly be accelerating toward the center of the circle. If the radius of the circle is r, and the velocity of the object is v, the acceleration is related to these quantities by the equation:

$$a = \frac{v^2}{r}$$

(This is simply a question of geometry, and says nothing about the physical cause of the acceleration. It is another way of saying that if a body travels in a path other than a straight line, it must be accelerating in some direction. If the path happens to be a circle, then the acceleration is always toward the center of the circle.)

The velocity of the moon is known because we know the dis-

tance from the earth to the moon and the time it takes the moon
to make one revolution around the earth. Using the equation
above, Newton could calculate the acceleration of the moon
toward the earth. This turned out to be only about 1/3600 of the
acceleration measured for bodies falling at sea level.

Therefore the gravitational force exerted by the earth must
be much weaker out where the moon is located than it is near
the earth's surface. The question to be answered was: Exactly
how did the force vary with distance from the earth?

Newton needed some comparative measure of bodies at various distances from the center of attraction. For this, he turned to
the sun and its planets.

Tycho Brahe and Kepler had amassed all the information
necessary—the distance of each planet from the sun and the time
it took for each planet to travel around the sun. It simply remained for Newton to take the final step in logic, which was to
assume that the gravitational attraction between the sun and
the planets was of the same nature as the attraction between the
earth and the moon. By mathematical reasoning, he was able to
demonstrate that the force of attraction between two celestial
bodies followed a very simple mathematical relationship. If M_1
is the mass of one body and M_2 the mass of a second body, while
r is the distance between their centers, then the gravitational
force is related to these quantities by the equation:

$$F = \frac{GM_1M_2}{r^2}$$

This is the well-known inverse-square law of attraction as developed by Newton. G is a number which relates the strength of
the force to the amount of mass in the bodies. It is known as the
"universal gravitational constant." It is a very important number
indeed; once this constant was measured in the laboratory, it
became possible to calculate the amount of gravitational force
between any two objects in the universe.

A great deal of information is hidden in this simple equation, and a complex course of logical reasoning. Newton's intricate, step-by-step reasoning from astronomical observations to mathematical deductions is a prime example of modern scientific method. His law of gravity was a magnificent achievement, not merely in the final result but also in the creation of new thinking methods. These methods served as a model for all present thought concerning forces between elementary particles.

The essential features of the law of gravitation are these:

1. The force depends upon the product of the two masses.

2. The force depends on the numerical value of a universal constant which tells us the "strength" of the force.

3. The amount of force depends on the distance between the two masses according to a definite rule.

4. The force is exerted in a straight line between the two masses.

5. The force exerted on the first mass is equal in strength and opposite in direction to the force exerted on the second mass. (This is required by Newton's Third Law of Motion.)

6. If we divide the equation above by the mass M_2, we find that

$$\frac{F}{M_2} = \frac{GM_1}{r^2}$$

Now F/M_2 is simply the acceleration of the second mass toward the first mass, and if we look at the right-hand side of this equation, we see that the acceleration depends only on the mass of the first body. For example, if M_1 is the mass of the earth, then the equation gives the gravitational acceleration of all objects on the surface of the earth. This shows that Newton's law of gravitation agrees with Galileo's observation that all objects fall to the earth with the same acceleration, regardless of their masses.

Newton described his ideas about motion and gravitation in his book *Philosophiae Naturalis Principia Mathematica,* more commonly known as *Newton's Principia,* which was first published in July 1687. That book is now recognized as one of the great landmarks of science. In it, Newton not only presented the three laws of motion and the law of gravity, but described his invention of the calculus and used it to work out many of the problems concerning motion under gravity.

Newton's ideas did not meet with immediate and enthusiastic acceptance by all scientists. Even some of the most important scientists of the day, such as Leibniz and Christian Huygens, attacked Newton's theory of gravitation as "unphilosophical," because it did not attempt to explain the *cause* of gravitation.

At that time everybody was used to thinking of forces as being transmitted by direct contact. Either one body pushed another body directly, or else the force was transmitted by means of a fluid which filled all space, as in the vortex theory of Descartes.

Newton's theory seemed to require "action at a distance." He spoke of the gravitational force passing through the vacuum of space, with nothing between the attracting objects. How could this be? It seemed quite mystical and supernatural.

Newton took pains to explain that he was merely describing the end result of the gravitational attraction, and was purposely ignoring the question of what caused the attraction. By becoming less philosophical, he was able to take a great practical step forward, for he was now in a position to solve real problems concerning the motions of planets, satellites, projectiles, etc.

For more than 200 years Newton's law of gravity went unchallenged. But at the turn of the twentieth century it became apparent that the gravity concept contained complications and subtleties which called for a rethinking of the subject. We shall come to this later in the chapter on relativity.

⁓⁓⁓ FURTHER DEVELOPMENTS IN MECHANICS

Newton, of course, was not the only one to work on problems of mechanics. Many other men made contributions during

Newton's lifetime, and in the following two centuries the science of mechanics was elaborated by many important scientists.

Huygens (1629–1695) is now most famous for the "Huygens principle," describing how light propagates through space. However, he made many other discoveries and inventions important in their day, including the pendulum clock. Huygens, like Newton, used Kepler's third law to deduce the inverse-square law of gravity. Perhaps most important, he was the first to use the law of conservation of kinetic energy as a method of solving many problems, although at that time the term kinetic energy was not yet in use. (Leibniz originally applied the term *vis viva* to the quantity mv^2, which is twice our kinetic energy. It was not until later that the factor ½ was added to make the kinetic energy equal to the work done in setting the object into motion.)

Huygens' interest in *vis viva* became aroused when, in 1668, the Royal Society of London set a number of its members to investigate the problem of what happens when two bodies collide with each other. Huygens went into the problem most thoroughly and arrived at a large number of conclusions, most of which we would now recognize as particular examples of conservation of energy and momentum. Perhaps the most important conclusion was the one he expressed as follows:

"In the mutual impact of two bodies, the sum of the products of the masses into the squares of the respective velocities is the same before and after impact."

Impenetrable language such as this reminds us that if a picture is worth a thousand words, an equation is worth at least a paragraph. This paragraph, as a matter of fact, simply states that, when two bodies collide elastically,

$$m_1v_1^2 + m_2v_2^2 = m_1v_3^2 + m_2v_4^2$$

The left side of the equation represents the total amount of *vis viva* before the collision, and the right side is the amount of *vis viva* in the two bodies after the collision. Here we have the earliest expression of the law of conservation of kinetic energy.

At the time of Huygens and Newton this conservation law was not considered as important as it is now, although it was a useful tool for solving certain problems. Its full importance was not recognized until the nineteenth century, when people began to understand how the various forms of energy were completely interchangeable, so that kinetic energy could be connected with heat, electrical energy, and so on.

Newton's three laws of motion provided the first complete method for calculating the path that bodies take under the action of forces, and they still remain among the simplest ways of describing these motions, but they are by no means the only way to describe how things move under the action of forces. During the eighteenth and nineteenth centuries, it seemed that every major mathematician tried his hand at expressing the laws of motion in a new way. These, of course, were just different ways of describing the same thing, but some turned out to be more useful for solving many problems.

In the 200 years after Newton, the idea of *energy* gradually took on more and more importance. Eventually, it became possible to solve all the problems of physics without putting the symbol for *force* into the equations at all—energy was all that was necessary. From this point of view, energy seemed most fundamental.

Actually, force and energy are simply concepts we have created so that we may conveniently describe what happens in nature. To say that one is more fundamental than the other is merely playing with words. When, for example, two elementary particles interact and change their positions and velocities, we may say that they have exerted forces upon each other, but we can also describe the event by saying that the kinetic and potential energies of the particles have changed.

The idea of potential energy is a great unifying principle which has extended the power of scientists in solving problems. The connection between force and potential energy was worked out in 1777 by Joseph-Louis Lagrange (1736–1813), probably the greatest mathematician of the eighteenth century.

Lagrange showed how the gravitational field of the earth can be treated as a potential field. Near the surface of the earth, the gravitational force changes very little. To simplify the picture, imagine a flat world consisting of a perfectly plane surface spreading out indefinitely in all directions. On this flatland the force of gravity is perfectly vertical and does not change with height. An object weighs the same on the ground as it does at some high altitude. This is the kind of world experienced by an ant, for example.

The potential energy associated with a body in this world is defined as the work required to move the body from the plane surface to some position above or below the surface. (We do not say "the potential energy *of* the body," because, as we explained earlier, the energy should be considered as belonging to the gravitational field, rather than to the body itself.) Since the weight of a body never changes in this world, the potential energy is simple to calculate. If the body is raised from the ground to a height h, the work done is the weight, w, times the height, h. Since the weight of a body represents its mass times g (the constant acceleration of gravity), the work done equals mgh. For one unit of mass, this quantity is simply gh.

We call the quantity gh the *potential* of the gravitational field at the height h; it is conventionally designated by the letter V. Inserting a number for h, we can calculate a value of the potential for every point in the space above our flatland. This concept of a potential belonging to every point in space is called a *potential field*.

For every force field there is a corresponding potential field. If we know the force existing at every point in space, we can calculate the potential. This is true not only for the simple situation we have described, but for the most complicated situations in nature. Conversely, if we know the potential in a given region of space, we can calculate the force acting on a body located in that region, and so we can predict how the body will move. For most problems in advanced realms of science, this latter method turns out to be the most convenient, and so it has been developed to a great degree of sophistication.

For example, the force exerted by one electric charge on another charge follows the inverse-square law just as the gravitational force does. The force is directed between the centers of the two charges, and it is simple to calculate its magnitude if we know the distance between the charges. However, if we want to calculate the force on an electric charge exerted by two or more charges, then immediately the problem gets complicated, because we must add up the forces taking their *directions* into account.

On the other hand, potential fields are simple to add up. Potential energy has no direction: it adds up in the same way that ordinary numbers add up. Therefore, to find the potential at a given point in space, we simply add up the potentials contributed by the charges in its neighborhood. A charge located at that point will experience a force. The magnitude and direction of the force can be calculated by a simple rule:

The magnitude of the force on a body is found by asking how fast the potential energy changes when the body moves in a given direction. If the potential energy changes rapidly, the force is great. In other words, the amount of force is directly proportional to the rate of change of the potential. The direction of the force is always such as to make the body accelerate toward the place where the potential energy is lowest.

A roller-coaster gives an excellent picture of potential energy in operation. The potential energy of the roller-coaster is proportional to the height of the track. The car always accelerates toward the lower parts of the track, and the steeper the incline, the greater the acceleration.

A number of important basic principles arise from this picture of potential energy. We notice that the roller-coaster car moves faster at places where the track is lower. The lower the potential energy, the greater is the kinetic energy. In fact, it turns out that the potential energy and kinetic energy of the car always add up to the same amount of *total energy*, if no energy is added from a motor and none lost by friction. This is conservation of energy in its simplest form.

Another important principle is this: Since the force experienced by an object in a given direction depends on the *change* of potential energy in that direction, it follows that in the absence of any change of potential energy in a particular direction there is no force in that direction. If there is no force, there can be no acceleration, or change of momentum, in that field.

Take, for example, the flatland situation, where the potential energy depends only on the height above the ground, not at all on the place where a body happens to be in the horizontal plane. A body moving under the influence of this field (with no other forces acting) can change its momentum only in the vertical direction. In the horizontal direction its momentum is always constant. We see that this is a new way of expressing the law of conservation of momentum. Furthermore, it enables us to see immediately the kinds of conditions where momentum will be conserved.

The new rule is this: If the potential energy is constant along a certain direction, then the momentum in that direction will be unchanged.

The momentum in this particular direction is called a "constant of the motion." In the flatland example, the momentum parallel to the ground is a constant of the motion, while the momentum vertical to the ground keeps changing. If we turn the flatland into a spherical planet, and take into account the fact that motion parallel to the ground is now motion in a circle around the center of the planet, we find that the potential energy depends only upon the radius—the distance between the center of the planet and the object whose motion we are studying. The potential does not depend on the latitude or longitude of the body (if the planet is a perfect sphere). Thus we find that *two* kinds of momentum connected with the orbital motion of the body are constant. First, the angular momentum of the body while circling (or ellipting) the planet will always be unchanged.

Secondly, the plane of this orbit will never change (relative to the distant stars).

ᵕᵕᵕᵕ MODERN MECHANICS

Lagrange not only showed how to find the force on a body if the potential energy is known, but he also devised a very powerful method for solving many problems in mechanics, using the idea of the potential. The beauty of the method lies in the fact that once you write down a formula which describes what the potential energy is at every point in space (for the particular situation you are interested in), then the problem is solved in theory. You merely turn the crank through a series of mathematical manipulations, which Lagrange described, and you come out with the answer. (The answer is an equation which describes where all the objects in the system are at any point of time.) These manipulations are built into what are called "Lagrange's Equations."

In practice, the trouble with these equations is that in complicated situations it becomes impossible to work through all the steps required to solve them. Furthermore, the case does not have to get *very* complicated to produce such an impasse. For example, while we can readily calculate the gravitational interaction of two bodies (such as the earth and the moon), the problem becomes extremely difficult when we consider three bodies (*e.g.*, the sun, the earth, and the moon). This problem has not yet been solved to the satisfaction of mathematicians. (You can always get numerical answers as accurately as you like on a computing machine, but that is not the same as deriving an equation which gives the *exact* position of each of the three bodies at every instant of time.)

The science of dynamics (the study of the motion of bodies under the action of forces) reached its ultimate development in the equations of Sir William Rowan Hamilton (1805–1865), probably the greatest man of science Ireland has produced. Hamilton carried forward the work of Lagrange, and among his important discoveries were two which must be mentioned here.

We again picture our usual situation of one or more bodies moving around in space under the influence of various forces. At each point in space we write down the kinetic energy ($\frac{1}{2}mv^2$) of all the bodies, and we subtract from this their potential energy. This gives us a mathematical expression called the Lagrangian: it is defined as the kinetic energy minus the potential energy, or, in the symbols commonly used, $L = T - V$.

Now as a body (or bodies) moves around, the Lagrangian takes on various values from one moment to the next. If we plot a curve showing the value of L at each successive instant of time as the body moves from one place to another in a given time interval, the curve has a certain area below it (see Figure 9). Now suppose we start all over again, and set up the same

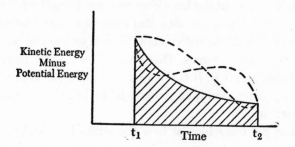

FIGURE 9. Hamilton's principle: a body under the influence of a field of force must follow a path which at all times keeps the value of kinetic energy minus potential energy at the smallest possible figure (shaded area). It cannot move in paths such as are represented by the dotted lines here.

body in exactly the same situation, and suppose that this time it travels over some other path in space during the same time interval. Along the new path, L has different values, so that we now get a curve with a different shape and a different area from the first one. If we did this for all possible paths we would get all sorts of different curves.

Now this is what Hamilton was able to prove: If left to itself, to go through space in its natural way, a body will actually travel only along the path that gives the *least* area under the Langrangian curve. This rule is known as Hamilton's principle. Hamilton proved his principle in a rigorous manner, and he made it a very powerful method of solving problems which is still being used, developed, and extended to this very day.

Hamilton also developed another extremely important set of equations known as the canonical equations. In this method, instead of using the Lagrangian (kinetic energy minus potential energy), he used another quantity called the Hamiltonian, which is simply the kinetic energy *plus* the potential energy (written mathematically according to special rules).

As Hamilton proved, if you can write down an expression which tells you what the kinetic energy plus the potential energy is at every point in space, then that expression—the Hamiltonian—includes in it all the information there is to know about a system of masses and forces. This sounds like a most remarkable convenience, and it is. It is the kind of thing a physicist loves to do—to combine everything there is to know into one concise equation.

We can get some idea of how the method works by looking at a simple example. Once again, we imagine our flatland with the constant gravitational force, and we consider an object which is moving above the ground under the influence of this force. The first thing we do is to set up a three-dimensional set of axes so that we can measure the position of the moving body from some basic frame. We use the customary x, y, and z coordinates. Along the ground are the x and y axes, while z sticks straight up in the air. The height of the body is now called z (see Figure 10).

The kinetic energy of the body is $\frac{1}{2}mv^2$, which we expect will vary with time. In writing down the Hamiltonian, the rule is to express the kinetic energy in terms of the momentum (mv), rather than the velocity, and the momentum is usually called p. Thus T (the kinetic energy) $= p^2/2m$. The potential energy (called *V*) is *mgz*, so that for this particular situation the Hamiltonian is:

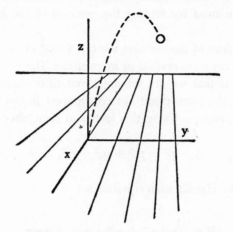

FIGURE 10. In Flatland, the potential energy of a moving body depends only on its height (*z*).

$$H = T + V = \frac{p^2}{2m} + mgz$$

First of all, we recognize that this is the total energy of the system, and we know that the kinetic energy plus the potential energy is always a constant if no energy is supplied from outside the system. Therefore, wherever the body moves, the Hamiltonian has a constant value. To find this value it is only necessary to know the kinetic plus the potential energies at one point in space. This fixes the total energy for all other locations.

If, for example, we know that the momentum is p_0 when the object is on the ground (where $z = 0$), then we can say that

$$\frac{p_0{}^2}{2m} = \frac{p^2}{2m} + mgz$$

In other words, from the known momentum at one height, we can calculate the momentum at another height. This is the kind of situation that exists when we shoot a missile into the air. With this equation we can immediately compute what the momentum (or velocity) will be at any height (z). Hamilton's equations also give the rules for finding the position of the body at any given time.

Another piece of information we can wring out of the Hamiltonian concerns conservation of momentum. The way we do this is to note first that we are talking about three-dimensional motion, so that the momentum has components in the three directions: p_x, p_y, and p_z. Using this fact, and remembering that

$$p^2 = p_x{}^2 + p_y{}^2 + p_z{}^2,$$

we rewrite the Hamiltonian equation as:

$$H = \frac{1}{2m}\left(p_x{}^2 + p_y{}^2 + p_z{}^2\right) + mgz$$

One of the things Hamilton proved is that, if one or more of the coordinates is absent from the Hamiltonian, the momentum in the missing directions is constant. In the equation just cited, we see that z is present as part of the potential energy, but not x or y. Therefore we can say immediately that p_x and p_y are constant. This is really identical with what we have already said: Where the potential does not depend on x or y, then the momentum in the x and y directions is unchanged during all the motions that go on in the system.

Now all this sounds as if we might arrive at the same conclusions just by looking at Newton's laws of motion. And of course, that is true. Hamilton's equations contain nothing really new: the information is all given in Newton's laws.

However, when we start dealing with more complicated systems than the one described above, systems where we must use spherical or cylindrical coordinates and where we become involved in various kinds of fields, such as electromagnetic or nuclear fields, then Hamilton's equations show their power as an organized method of solving problems. Once you are able to write down a mathematical expression for the potential energy at every point in space, then almost by inspection you can write down what types of conservation laws to expect in this situation. For, as we have seen, there are many different kinds of momentum that can be conserved.

Hamilton's method of solving physical problems consists of two separate steps. First, one must determine the potential energy everywhere within the system and learn how to express this properly in mathematical form. The second step is to apply the rules of Hamilton's equations and solve the problem. Solving the problem means to predict what the positions and velocities of all the bodies in the system will be at any given time.

The various types of problems handled by these methods range all the way from nuclear physics to space navigation. The motion of a space vehicle in the gravitational fields of the earth, the moon, and the sun is, of course, a problem of great interest at present. The motion of charged particles in magnetic fields is of importance in building everything from magnetrons to cyclotrons. The motion of protons, neutrons, or other elementary particles when they collide with atomic nuclei is the basis of all experiments performed with particle accelerators.

The most basic work in physics makes use of the methods devised by Hamilton. In recent years, the frontier regions of science have become divided into two main areas. One area consists of the many situations where the potential energy of a system is known, so that the problem is to solve the equations of motion. In other words, we already know the forces operating between all the objects reacting with one another, and we want to know what the objects do once they start moving. This kind of problem arises when we study the structure of atoms and molecules, the behavior of matter at very high and very low temperatures, and questions such as why some materials are electrical conductors and others are insulators or semi-conductors, how gases and liquids flow through pipes or around wings and other obstacles, what produces the magnetic field of the earth, and what produces the magnetic field of a little horseshoe magnet. All of chemistry, biochemistry, and biophysics belong in this area, when these sciences are studied in terms of atoms and molecules interacting under the influence of force fields.

The second area has to do with the behavior of single elementary particles within the nucleus. When we get down into this extreme microworld, we find that we don't even know what kind of potential energy equations to write. We do not know exactly what kind of force exists between a neutron and a proton, or what makes a pi meson change into a mu meson. Here the first step in the problem is still to be accomplished: finding the correct potential energy to describe the system. We are not even sure that this method is a valid one to use when we deal with the interactions between certain elementary particles.

∿∿∿ SYMMETRY

During the past few decades the conservation laws have taken on increased scope and power. This has been especially true in the field of nuclear physics and the study of elementary particles, where we are forced to extract the greatest meaning from the least amount of information. For example, we would like to understand how neutrons combine in various combinations with protons to form the nuclei of the elements, and we would like to understand why some nuclei are more stable than others. We are handicapped by the fact that we do not know exactly how the force between two neutrons (or a neutron and a proton) varies with the distance between them.

However, if we can assume that the strength of this force is the same in all directions, so that the potential energy of the two particles depends *only* on the distance between them, then immediately we know a great deal. We know that the angular momentum of the two particles as they circle each other is a "constant of the motion" and remains unchanged until something else comes along to alter the situation. As we have seen, this kind of knowledge is of great importance in solving many problems, and often is the only information necessary.

What makes us think that the strength of the force between two objects is the same in all directions? We learn it by observation. We know, for example, that the strength of the earth's gravitational field is about the same in Bombay as in New York. If there are any small differences in the field from place to place, we can explain them by variations in elevation, by different densities in various parts of the earth's crust—in other words, by some lack of symmetry in the earth's shape or density. If the earth were perfectly symmetrical, perfectly uniform, and perfectly smooth, there would be no way of identifying one's location on its surface. Every point would be exactly the same as every other, and there would be no references from which to mark latitude and longitude (if we ignore the earth's spin). On this perfectly symmetrical sphere, the gravitational force would be the same everywhere on the surface, always pointing straight toward the center of the sphere.

We have already seen that if an object's potential energy does not change when it moves from one place to another, its momentum remains constant. If the energy does not change in moving from A to B, then we really cannot tell the difference between locations A and B, just as we cannot tell the latitude and longitude on a sphere that is absolutely symmetrical and featureless.

So we may state the various conservation laws in this way: If, on moving from point A to point B, we can observe no difference between the two locations, there is no change in the momentum of any object moving along this path.

This is a very general kind of rule and includes within it all the conservation laws we have discussed up to this point, plus many others. Stating the conservation laws in this way seems to give an insight into something very fundamental about the universe. It tells us that whenever we observe symmetry in a physical situation (such as the interaction between two bodies), we can take this as confirmation of a conservation law. We can illustrate the point by a number of examples.

Suppose that an observer is in a region of space where his potential energy remains constant no matter where he goes. As he moves from one place to another, he experiences no force. His momentum remains constant. (This means that he must have been in motion before he entered the force-free region.) Here is perfect symmetry: in every direction space is unchanged and linear momentum is conserved.

We can conceive only two conditions that might produce such a situation. One would be the complete absence of matter outside the observer, so that there were no gravitational fields. This does not correspond at all to the actual universe. The other possible condition of perfect symmetry would be absolutely uniform distribution of the matter in the universe around the observer. In that case, all the gravitational fields would cancel one another out. As a result, there would be effectively no force acting on the observer, and his momentum would be forever unchanged.

Now imagine the flatland situation, with a gravitational field in one direction only. In vertical motion, the potential energy will change when the observer moves from one height to another. But in the horizontal plane there is perfect symmetry: neither the potential energy nor the observer's momentum ever changes as he moves about in that plane.

If we now go to the situation of the perfectly smooth planet we have already described, we find that in this realm of spherical symmetry, again, the angular momentum is always constant. Since the symmetry is two-fold (latitude and longitude are two dimensions), two components of angular momentum are conserved. An object moving in an orbit around the planet has a constant angular momentum in the plane of this orbit, while at the same time the position of the plane always stays fixed.

Where do we experience such conditions of perfect spherical symmetry? Not on our planet, for it is slightly unspherical. We can measure latitude and longitude on it, because it spins on its axis and has landmarks we can use to fix locations. And because of its variations in gravity, the angular momentum of a satellite traveling around the earth is not perfectly constant. The deviations from perfection, to be sure, are small—not enough to disturb Newton's calculations.

When we deal with the world of atoms and elementary particles, one of our major problems is to decide what kinds of symmetry these particles possess. Is the neutron a perfect sphere? It turns out that it is not. The force between two neutrons is not the same in all directions. This is connected with the fact that a neutron spins on its axis like a top, so that you can describe a "north" and "south" pole on each of these particles. Because of this, when two elementary particles circle around each other in orbits, they are only allowed to take certain paths—those paths that permit the angular momentum to be constant.

It is very useful to treat the dimension of time in the same manner that we treat the three dimensions of space. This is both a mathematical convenience (simplifying certain equations) and satisfying to our sense of esthetics, because it brings out more clearly certain symmetries existing in the universe.

Suppose we say that an observer remains fixed in the same position in space but moves from A to B in *time*. If his potential energy stays constant while this is going on, his total energy also remains unchanged. In other words, if position A is no different from position B as you move along in time, then your total energy is constant. Symmetry in time is thus connected with the law of conservation of energy. Energy, in this treatment, is the fourth-dimensional counterpart of momentum. This must be the situation in dealing with elementary particles, where the force fields between the particles do not change with time.

There are many other kinds of symmetries in nature, each connected with a conservation law. Many are rather subtle and abstract. One symmetry that has recently become important in the study of elementary particles, and also attracted much public attention, is called *mirror symmetry*. The name comes from the fact that when you hold your right hand up to a mirror and look at its reflection, the image looks like a left hand. Physicists have long wondered whether there is a right hand–left hand symmetry in the universe: whether our world would look exactly the same if we could see its reflection in a mirror. All the evidence seemed to suggest that it *was* symmetrical—no detectable handedness—but in the behavior of certain elementary particles this idea was recently overturned. We shall consider this development in the chapter on elementary particles.

The concept of symmetry has a danger hidden in its beauty. It seems extremely reasonable to assume, for example, that "the force exerted by a uniform sphere is the same in all directions." It seems so reasonable that we begin to consider this postulate to be one that is self-evidently true and can be taken for granted. But that is the kind of thinking that led Aristotle astray. We can never take anything permanently for granted.

We must remember that the concept of symmetry grew out of innumerable experiments in which momentum *was* conserved, energy *was* conserved, and so on. The observations came first; the concept of symmetry followed. But the moment we find experiments that disagree with our ideas of symmetry, we must be prepared to revise those ideas.

CHAPTER 7

Forces and Fields

In elementary physics courses students are tormented with a long catalogue of forces: gravitational, electrical, magnetic, mechanical, elastic, frictional, cohesive, adhesive, hydraulic, pneumatic, centrifugal, centripetal, and so on. These names originated when scientists had no idea how the various effects were produced. For every kind of force observed, a new name was coined.

It was not until the second half of the nineteenth century, when the idea of atoms and molecules began to be understood, that progress was made toward simplifying the picture—toward showing that there were not really so many different kinds of force. It turned out that many which seemed distinct could be explained in a unified way in terms of the behavior of atoms.

Some eminent scientists held on to the belief that atoms were only convenient "constructs"—mental pictures that simplified the explanation of physical happenings but did not necessarily have any "truth" behind them. But after the invention of the cloud chamber by C. T. R. Wilson in 1911, it became very difficult to dismiss elementary particles as simply "constructs." The cloud chamber made it possible to see the actual tracks of particles, in the form of droplets of water produced in the path of a particle passing through the chamber. Atomic particles then took on a very real character. Physicists plunged into intensive studies of the particles, and as they learned more about their behavior, it became more and more evident that interactions among atoms and elementary particles could account for all the phenomena observed in nature.

I am sitting at a typewriter hitting its keys with my fingers. A scientist of the nineteenth century, watching me, might have said that a psychic force emanating from my brain was passing down the nerves to the muscles of my arms and fingers, causing them to contract and thereby converting the psychic force into a mechanical force.

Today we can interpret such large-scale effects—nerve impulses, mechanical force, etc.—on the basis of the concerted action of billions of atoms in the biological and mechanical systems involved. When we get down to that kind of analysis, we find that there are just four kinds of force: gravitational, electromagnetic, "strong" nuclear, and "weak" nuclear. Everything that happens in nature, as far as we can tell, can be explained by means of one or more of these four forces.

ᴡᴡᴡ GRAVITATIONAL FORCE

The most familiar of the forces is gravity. It holds us down to the earth and resists our efforts to leap into space. It also operates within the atom—in fact, between any two particles that possess mass, even including photons, the particles of light. We do not normally think of light as being affected by gravity, but one of the important predictions of Einstein's Theory of Relativity is that photons of light actually do respond to this force. When photons fall to the earth, their energy increases by a small amount, as very precise measurements of the wavelength of the light show. (More about this in the chapter on relativity.)

When you fall down a flight of stairs, or stand for several hours, you have an acute sense of the potency of gravity. Nevertheless, gravity is an extremely weak force—by far the weakest of the four kinds. It seems strong to us because we have the entire mass of the earth pulling on us. But between two masses of one kilogram each, separated by a distance of one meter, the gravitational force, calculated from Newton's equation, is only 6.7 billionths of a dyne, which is roughly 7×10^{-12} of a gram. When we remember that the common chemical balance can barely measure one ten-thousandth of a gram (10^{-4}), we see that this is indeed a small force.

To visualize the weakness of the force in another way, suppose we have two spheres floating in space. Each sphere weighs 1,000 kilograms (about 1.1 tons), and they start at rest, ten meters apart. They move toward each other under the force of their mutual gravitational attraction (we assume no other forces are acting). If each sphere is one meter in diameter, it will take them about 25 minutes to travel the ten meters and come together!

We can see that there is little danger of a space vehicle pulling meteors to itself by its gravitational field.

The weakness of the gravitational field makes it very difficult to do anything with it in the laboratory. The gravitational force exerted by objects small enough to fit inside a room is so tiny that only an extremely sensitive apparatus can detect it. Nonetheless, such instruments have been built. As far back as 1781, Henry Cavendish in England determined the gravitational constant by measuring the force of attraction between two balls in a torsion balance.

The fact that the force of gravity is always an *attraction* has important physical consequences. There has been much speculation recently about the possible existence elsewhere in the universe of "anti-matter" which would be repelled by our kind of matter. So far there is no evidence that such matter exists, and there is some preliminary evidence for believing that it cannot exist. Be that as it may, we get into real trouble when we try to think of a way to cancel the attractive force of gravity. The idea of a shield against gravity is as old as science fiction; it is one of the wonderfully tantalizing dreams of getting something for nothing (like perpetual motion). Unfortunately, we know of no way even to approach the problem. Gravity penetrates through a vacuum and through the densest material, all the way to the center of the heaviest star. There is just no stopping it.

Some people say: If we can make shields or screens against electrical forces, why not against gravitational forces? The answer is quite simple. An electrical field, like a gravitational field, goes right through matter, but in electricity we have two opposite kinds of charge—positive and negative. The field of a negative charge "neutralizes," or cancels, the field of a positive charge.

For example, the nucleus of an atom consists of positive charges. The field of these charges spreads out in all directions according to the inverse-square law. But the nucleus is surrounded by a cloud of negative electrons, whose fields exactly cancel the field of the positive nuclear charges. Consequently no outside electron is attracted to the nucleus. From the outside, the atom as a whole is an uncharged, neutral body.

The same is true of events on a larger scale. If you put a positively charged object inside a metal can and connect the can to ground, the positive charge within will attract electrons from the ground onto the surface of the can. These spread themselves around in just enough quantity so that the fields of the electrons exactly cancel the field of the positive charge. The can then appears neutral to any measuring instrument on the outside. The can acts as an electric shield.

You cannot do this with a gravitational field, for our world has only one kind of gravitational "charge." Unless we find "anti-matter," or "negative" matter, there is no possibility of neutralizing this gravitational field.

There are those who have proposed building some kind of "anti-gravity generator" to counteract the weak force of gravitation. At least two important facts argue against such a scheme.

The first fact: You cannot create a field from nothing; you can only use fields that already exist. These fields always originate in elementary particles. All our operations with electromagnetic fields are based on the manipulation of positive and negative charges which are already part of matter. We "create" electric fields by separating positive charges from negative charges. We "create" magnetic fields by running electrons through wires. The word "create" is put in quotation marks because the fields were there to begin with. We simply arrange matters so that the fields in which we are interested become organized instead of being scattered around at random.

The second fact: Because the gravitational force of matter is very weak, it takes a large amount of mass to produce an appreciable amount of force. You could make a small object weigh a tiny bit less by suspending a mountain above it, exerting a pull on the object away from the center of the earth. But that pull would be insignificant. What about other possibilities not using mass? Well, you cannot produce a gravitational field large enough to be of any use by running matter through a pipe in the way we "create" a magnetic field by passing electrons through a wire. There is, in fact, no known way to produce a gravitational field without the presence of mass.

In short, as far as we can tell at the present time the idea of anti-gravity seems to be a will-o'-the wisp. To produce anti-gravity would require basic changes in our ideas about force fields. It would require, perhaps, a knowledge of how to produce fields which do not originate in elementary particles. There is no hint that such a thing can be done.

⟿ ELECTROMAGNETIC FIELDS

It used to be assumed that electric fields and magnetic fields were two separate things. According to that simple picture, an electric field was a force field surrounding an electrically charged body; a magnetic field, something surrounding a magnet.

Let us start by describing the fields in these simple terms. The strength of an electric field is known to obey the inverse-square law, just like the gravitational field. If we have two electric charges represented by e_1 and e_2, and r is the distance between the charges, the force between them is:

$$F = k \ \frac{e_1 e_2}{r^2}$$

The letter k here stands for a constant, whose value depends on what system of electrical units is used. In electrostatic terms, the unit of electric charge is the charge that will repel a similar charge with a force of one dyne when the distance between them is one centimeter. Take note that the equation above applies both to the force of repulsion between like charges (both positive or both negative) and to the attraction between opposite charges (positive and negative). That is, the force of repulsion is of the same magnitude as the force of attraction. This is usually indicated by putting the "plus-or-minus" sign ($\pm$) before the right-hand side of the equation.

The magnetic field situation is more complicated. To calculate the strength of a field around a magnet we must start with two magnetic poles—positive and negative (or north and south). We find the strength and direction of the field from each pole, using the inverse-square law. Adding up these two fields, we can get the total magnetic field at any point in space around the magnet.

Why must magnetic poles always come in pairs? Why can we never find a single magnetic pole all by itself? This used to be a bit of a mystery, until we learned the cause of the magnetic poles.

As every student of physics knows, in the nineteenth century Michael Faraday, James Clerk Maxwell, and other physicists discovered that electric and magnetic fields are inseparably connected. We can illustrate this in a simple way.

Suppose you have two positively (or negatively) charged spheres and measure the force of repulsion between them. The force proves to be exactly what the equation given above predicts. Now suppose you put the two spheres in a transparent box of some kind and send the box flying. If you measure the force of repulsion between the spheres now (as you can by measuring the rate at which they move apart), you will find that the force, mysteriously, seems to be weaker this time! What is the difference between the two situations? The only difference is that in the first experiment the two spheres were at rest with respect to you, the observer, whereas in this experiment they are in motion (via the flying box) with respect to you. Something connected with their motion must be counteracting the force of repulsion.

That something turns out to be a magnetic field, produced by the motion of the electric charges. Since the magnetic field tends to draw the two bodies together, it has the effect of reducing the repulsion.

The direct and intimate relation between electric and magnetic fields led physicists to conclude that they could think of them as one field: the electromagnetic field. The electric part is the field observed when the particles are at rest with respect to the observer; this field obeys the simple inverse-square law. The magnetic part is noticed only when the charges are in motion, and its strength depends on their velocity and distance in relation to the observer.

This picture allows us to explain everything observed about magnetism. All magnetic fields arise from the motion of electric charges—and in almost all practical cases the charges in motion are electrons. Even "permanent" magnets are the result of tiny circulating currents within the atoms of the magnet. In fact, in the case of iron magnets, the circulating currents are thought of as existing in the individual electrons, and the "spin" of each electron creates a tiny magnetic field. In a permanent iron magnet, the atoms within the iron crystals are aligned so that many millions of them aim their electron magnets in the same direction. In total, these little elementary fields add up to a strong, large-scale field which makes the chunk of iron magnetic.

These ideas have arisen out of numerous experiments over a long period. A conclusive experiment was performed by H. A. Rowland in 1876. He mounted a metal disc on an insulator, charged it with electricity, and whirled it around rapidly; the motion produced a slight magnetic field which he was able to detect.

It is well known that two parallel wires carrying current in the same direction are attracted to each other by magnetic forces. Actually, wires are not necessary to set up a magnetic field. Mere beams of electrons (like those in a cathode-ray tube) traveling in the same direction produce a magnetic field which would pull the beams together if its effect were not hidden by the stronger electric repulsion between the electrons.

When an electric current is passed through a tube containing a suitable gas (such as hydrogen at low pressure), the rapidly moving electrons knock some of the orbital electrons away from the atoms of the gas. This leaves the atoms positively charged; we say that they are *ionized*. Now the positively charged ions move in one direction and the negatively charged free electrons move in the opposite direction. In other words, we have a current in the gas. This produces magnetic forces. On the other hand, the repulsive forces of the electric particles are neutralized, because there are just as many positive charges as negative charges in the gas. As a result, the magnetic forces are able to push the streaming electrons together. In this manner the current passing through the gas tends to squeeze itself into a narrow cylinder. If the current is very large (in the millions of amperes), the constricting force is enormous, so that a broad column of gas is drawn into a thin filament of electric current. This "pinch effect" can be used to heat a gas to extremely high temperatures (millions of degrees) for brief periods (millionths of a second).

In comparison with gravitational fields, electromagnetic forces are extremely strong. We can get some idea of their strength by returning to the example of the two one-kilogram spheres one meter apart. If the spheres are iron, there are roughly 10^{25} atoms in each sphere. Suppose that we remove just one electron from each million atoms. The electric field between the two positively charged spheres will then be so strong that the force of repulsion will amount to about 27 million kilograms, or some 30,000 tons!

Matter tries very strongly to balance the electric charges—to maintain the same number of positive and negative charges in each region. When we separate positive and negative charges, this work stores energy in the electromagnetic field. The situation is unstable: the positive and negative charges tend with great force to come together again. Thus the energy stored in the field is returned to us as kinetic energy.

〰〰 COHESIVE AND ELASTIC FORCES

What holds a solid body together? What is the force that resists efforts to pull a bar of iron apart, and causes a rubber band to snap back after we have stretched it?

Think of the bar of iron as a collection of atoms, tightly packed together. The atoms are neutral in charge, so offhand we might suppose that the only force holding them together is that of gravitation. But obviously that force is far too weak to explain why atoms cling together as fiercely as they do in a piece of iron.

The true explanation is complicated; we can do little more than give an oversimplified sketch of the story as it is understood. We start by looking at two atoms some distance apart, as they are in a gas. There is no appreciable force between them, and they come together only by chance collisions.

Now let us see what happens when two atoms are close together, as in a solid, or when they collide in a gas. In this situation the atoms are so close that their outermost electrons intermingle. Electrons, as we have seen, are like little bar magnets, as a result of their spin. The direction of the electron's spin determines the poles of its magnetic field. When the spins of two neighboring electrons are "parallel" (in the same direction), the electrons repel each other strongly; when they are anti-parallel (in opposite directions), the electrons are less strongly repelled. So in the case of two close atoms whose outer electrons have opposite spins, the electrons are drawn to the interface between the two nuclei, because each electron is under the attractive force of the positive nucleus of the opposite atom. There is essentially a sharing of the two electrons by the two atoms. The net result is an attraction between the atoms. The attraction is effective up to the point where the atoms come so close together that the repulsion between their positively charged nuclei becomes as strong as the attractive force. At that point, the atoms cannot come any closer together.

This description explains a great deal about the behavior of matter. In elements such as helium (where the atom's outer shell of electrons is filled up) there is very little attraction between the atoms. Therefore helium atoms do not join together under ordinary conditions; they do not normally form molecules. Other atoms, such as those of hydrogen or oxygen (which have an unfilled shell, leaving "valence" electrons available for sharing between atoms) tend to pair up very quickly to form two-atom molecules. Once this attraction is satisfied, there is less tendency for other atoms to be drawn to the molecule (but hydrogen may occasionally form molecules of three atoms, and under certain conditions oxygen combines in the three-atom form called ozone). In these gases it is the molecule, rather than the atom, that acts as a unit, moving about and colliding with other molecules.

In a solid, such as a bar of iron, the attractive forces are not so easily satisfied. After two iron atoms join together, there still remains enough attractive force to bind other iron atoms to them. In fact, many millions of atoms will line up together in an orderly pattern, forming a crystal. When we stretch a bar of iron, what we are doing is moving the atoms apart beyond their normal distance of separation. If we succeed in this, the attractive forces tend to pull the atoms back to their original positions; this is what we call the force of elasticity. On the other hand, if we try to compress the iron bar, we run into the repulsion between the nuclei, which resists all attempts to squeeze the atoms closer together. The strength of the repulsive force increases enormously as the distance between the nuclei is reduced.

In view of the strong attraction between iron atoms, why can't we join two pieces of iron together simply by pressing one against the other? The answer is that it is very difficult to bring two metal surfaces together close enough so that the attractive force of the atoms takes over; this force extends only as far as the diameter of an atom. The surface of a metal or other material, no matter how highly polished, has little ridges and bumps (which can be seen in a powerful microscope). Furthermore, the surface of a metal attracts gas atoms from the air, and these form a coat over it. If you prepare an absolutely clean iron surface in a vacuum chamber, the moment you expose the surface to air it becomes covered with layers of oxygen and nitrogen atoms. The effect is known as *surface adsorption*.

When the atoms of a liquid are adsorbed on the surface of a solid, we say that the liquid *wets* the solid. Whether this will happen depends on the atomic properties of both materials. For instance, mercury cannot wet a wooden surface (it rolls around on the surface in little globules), but it will wet a copper surface, spreading over it evenly. Most solids cannot come into close enough contact with each other to wet or stick to each other; to make them stick together we have to employ a material such as wax or glue, which fills in all the little crevices and improves the closeness of the contact.

With this picture of atomic behavior, we can understand the various mechanical forces much better. The pressure of a gas on the walls of its container, for instance, is the sum of all the tiny electric repulsions exerted by the atoms of the gas on the atoms of the wall as they collide with it. Friction boils down essentially to the effect of collisions between atoms of the two bodies in contact. (Bodies of gas or liquid show friction, as well as solids.) In the case of metals these collisions set the atoms vibrating faster than before in their crystal lattices—this we observe as an increase in temperature. Kinetic energy of the solid body as a whole has been transformed into kinetic energy of the individual atoms.

Thus electromagnetic interactions can explain all the large-scale effects we see in the behavior of matter, aside from purely gravitational phenomena. The happenings within the nuclei of atoms, however, are another story, and this we will save for the chapter on elementary particles.

~~~~ INERTIAL FORCES

A few words must be said about two familiar forces we have not yet discussed: the centripetal and centrifugal forces. Actually, there is nothing very special about the idea of centripetal force. It is just a name we give to any kind of force that causes a body to depart from straight-line motion and travel in a curved path. Usually we speak of centripetal force in connection with motion in a circle. When we swing a bucket on the end of a rope, the centripetal force is the force exerted by the rope on the bucket. The direction of the force is inward toward the center of the circle. Ultimately this force is due to electromagnetic attractions and repulsions between the atoms of the rope and the atoms of the bucket handle, all adding up to a mechanical force which keeps the bucket from continuing in a straight line. In the case of a satellite circling the earth, the centripetal force is the gravitational interaction between earth and satellite.

Of centrifugal force, we might say that it is the reaction of the bucket on the rope: just as the rope pulls the bucket in, the bucket pulls the rope out. Newton's third law says so. There seems to be nothing profound about this. However, when we think about it carefully, we must ask: Why does the bucket prefer to go in a straight line? Why does it resist being pulled in a circle?

The reciprocal effect here is akin to that in all other forms of acceleration. When you step on the gas in your car, you feel yourself pushed backward against the seat. The astronaut in his capsule feels himself pressed downward when the rocket is accelerating him upward. Similarly, while the whirling bucket is being accelerated inward toward the center of the circle, it goes on pulling outward—away from the acceleration.

When your car accelerates, a stationary observer might say you are not really pushed *back* against the seat but the seat is pushing you *forward.* He would say that the forward push is the primary force, while the backward "force" you exert on the seat is just an illusion produced by your acceleration. Likewise the centrifugal force is often called a "fictitious" force which only seems to be present: the "real" force is the centripetal force that is accelerating the bucket in a circle against its tendency to move in a straight line.

Well, let us try to explore the problem further by picturing another situation. Here is a group of people traveling in a wheel-shaped spaceship which is made to rotate (so that they will not be disturbed by weightlessness). The passengers will feel a force holding them to the outer wall of the ship, which naturally, they will call the floor. If there are no windows, they will not have any sense that the ship is rotating (provided the rotation is at a constant speed). All they will know is that they feel something pulling them to the floor, and that when they drop something, it falls. To them this is indeed a real force—and in fact it is a force which cannot be distinguished from gravity.

If we say that this force is fictitious because it results only from the rotation of the ship, then we should also call the magnetic force fictitious, because that shows up only when charged particles are moving. It is better to accept the fact that the centrifugal force is real, and to label it an *inertial* force—a force connected with the inertia of the object undergoing acceleration.

Inertial forces appear literally every time we move. As we have pointed out, the "g-force" that presses the astronaut into his seat on take-off is an inertial force. The force that plunges you into the windshield of your car when you make a sudden stop is an inertial force. The force that pushes you against the ground when you fall on it is inertial. (As is well-known, it's not the fall that kills you—it's the sudden stop.)

There is a type of inertial force connected with rotation which is known as the *Coriolis* force. A familiar example of its effect appears when you move from the outside edge of a merry-go-round toward the center. As you run inward, you feel a force pushing you sideways (see Figure 11). This force increases your angular

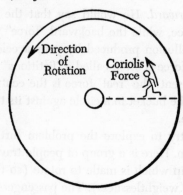

FIGURE 11. The Coriolis force on a merry-go-round.

velocity and so keeps your angular momentum constant as you move toward the center. The Coriolis force produced by the rotation of the earth is of considerable importance. When an airplane drops a bomb from a great altitude, the bombsight must compensate for the fact that the falling bomb tends to be deflected from west to east because of the earth's rotation. The Coriolis force also accounts for the fact that winds traveling in a north-south direction are swung around into large circles—the familiar cyclone pattern of the weather maps.

The origin of these inertial forces used to be a great mystery. In recent years some progress has been made toward describing how such forces originate. They appear to be connected with gravitational fields, and the reason we have had so little understanding of inertial forces is that we have known very little about gravitational fields. Because the study of the deeper aspects of gravity comes under the theory of relativity, we shall have more to say on inertial forces in the chapter on relativity.

~~~ CHANGING FIELDS

So far we have been dealing with fields of force primarily in their constant aspects. Now we must consider how fields change.

We have seen that an electric charge at rest is surrounded by an electric field whose strength is ruled by the inverse-square law. If the same charge moves with respect to the observer, it generates a magnetic field which accompanies the electric field. We now ask what will happen when a charged body moves with changing velocity. In other words, what sort of field does an accelerated charge produce? Is it different from the field of a charge moving with constant speed?

Before we can answer, we must backtrack for a moment and think again about the interaction between two motionless charges. We have said nothing about the time it takes for the force to travel between the two charges. All the inverse-square law tells us is that there is a force existing between two charges located a certain distance apart. It cannot tell us, for example, what would happen if the two charges were suddenly brought into existence a mile apart. Would they start attracting each other instantly, or would it take some time for the force to travel between the two bodies?

The question can be stated more generally this way: If a body is suddenly placed in a certain location, does its field extend out through all space instantly, or does it take time for the field to spread out? (This form of the question implies that a body can be placed at a given point *instantaneously,* which is not quite possible, but it does not alter the essential problem we are considering.)

Suppose we start with an electric charge at rest in position *A* and move it to position *B* (see Figure 12). What happens to the field as seen by an observer at point *P?* To determine the direction of the field at every moment as the charge moves from *A* to *B,* he watches a second charge, which he has placed in the field to show the direction of the force exerted on it.

At the beginning of the experiment, the observer sees the force acting in the direction of the arrow *a.* We say there is a line of force extending outward from *A* to *P.* Now we move the first charge to *B.* If the influence of the field is felt instantaneously, then the direction of the force must change instantly from

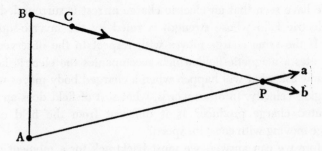

FIGURE 12. Change in direction of force after the source
is moved from A to B.

a to *b*. If there were an observer at *C*, somewhere between *B* and
P, he too would see the force acting in the direction *b*.

On the other hand, suppose the action of the force takes some
definite time to travel through space. Then the situation must
look like the picture in Figure 13. When the charged body has

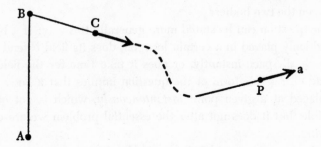

FIGURE 13. Effect of a time delay in travel of the
force from A to P.

moved to *B*, the observer at *C* sees the force in the direction of
arrow *c*, while the observer at *P* still sees the force in the original
direction, *a*. *P* has no way of knowing that the charged body has
moved from *A* until the disturbance, or change, in the field gets
out to his location. Therefore between *C* and *P* the line of force
must curve in some manner, as shown by the dotted line.

How can we test this question and find out whether the actual
situation is represented by Figure 12 or Figure 13? We might

try the physical experiment, taking a station at *P* to observe what happens when *A* is moved to *B*. But the effect of this single move would take place too quickly to measure. A better method is to move the electric charge rapidly back and forth between *A* and *B*. If the force does take time to travel through space, the lines of force will wiggle back and forth rapidly, producing a picture something like Figure 14. This looks very much like what hap-

Figure 14. Time lapse shown by moving the source of the force back and forth.

pens when you wave the end of a rope back and forth vigorously, sending ripples down to the far end.

Vibrating electric charges back and forth is a very easy accomplishment. Every radio transmitter, for example, performs this feat in various parts of its circuit. An alternating current consists of electric charges shuttling back and forth. When such a current is fed into a transmitting antenna, it sets up a train of waves which travels through space away from the antenna. The velocity of such waves has been measured many times with great accuracy. The fact that they have a definite speed proves that it takes a certain amount of time for a change in the electromagnetic field to get from one place to another.

We now have a rather elaborate picture of an electromagnetic field. We said originally that a charged body at rest is surrounded by an electric field, and that when the charge is in motion it has, in addition, a magnetic field. Now we add a third field—one that belongs to the charge when it undergoes acceleration. This field is rather complicated, but Figure 15 illustrates it schematically. Here we see a charge being accelerated in the downward direction. The field associated with the acceleration consists of a magnetic field pointing in the *x* direction, at right

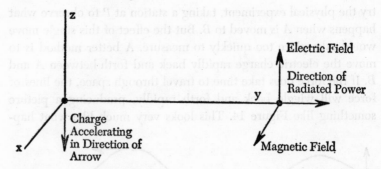

FIGURE 15. Fields associated with an accelerated electric charge. It produces radiation in the *y* direction.

angles to the acceleration. At the same place the electric field points in the *z* direction, opposite to the direction of acceleration and at right angles to the magnetic field.

The most striking feature of the field associated with acceleration of a charge is that its strength varies inversely with the distance from the source instead of inversely with the *square* of the distance. In other words, this field weakens with distance less rapidly than the static electric field. Its influence reaches over a greater distance; it is a longer-range force than the simple electric field of a stationary charge.

The electromagnetic field arising from an accelerated electric charge is by no means an esoteric or unimportant phenomenon. It transmits energy away from the source in the form of radiation, and therefore it is called a *radiation field*. This may consist, as we have seen, of radio waves: the oscillating charges in a transmitting antenna set up an oscillating radiation field which carries energy out in all directions. But of course radio waves (which also give us television) are not the only kind of electromagnetic radiation. And all the other kinds, including infrared, visible light, and ultraviolet, consist of oscillations in the electromagnetic field originating in accelerated electrons.

In every situation where an electron changes its speed or direction, radiation is given off. We see this in the production of X-rays. Here a very rapidly moving electron collides with an atom, is swung around by the nucleus (like a comet swinging around the sun), and then flies off in a new direction. In so doing it gives off radiation which can be detected far away. Commonly we produce these collisions by bombarding a target of tungsten, or other dense material, with a beam of electrons at an energy of several thousand electron-volts. The result is an intense beam of X-rays—radiation whose wavelength is so short that it passes through matter much more readily than visible light.

The production of radiation by the acceleration of charged particles is one of the commonest events in the universe. In the vastness of interstellar space, there are magnetic fields which accelerate the wandering electrons and ions so that they give off radiation, which can be measured with highly sensitive radio receivers. We are just beginning to learn something about such radiations coming to our planet from the distant regions of space.

⌐⌐⌐ HOW DO WAVES TRAVEL?

An electromagnetic field has certain things in common with a violin string. You pluck the string at one spot, and the disturbance spreads along the string in both directions with the speed of sound. Pluck an electromagnetic field by moving an electron suddenly, and the disturbance in the field will spread in all directions with the speed of light.

This little analogy brings up a profound question. What carries the vibrations, or oscillations, or waves, of light and other electromagnetic radiations? If light is a disturbance, traveling with finite speed, doesn't it require some kind of medium to transport it? What is it that is being disturbed?

For hundreds of years physicists, from Newton on, wrestled with this question. Space must be filled, they decided, with a transparent substance, which came to be known as "the ether." To account for the great speed of light, the "ether" must be extremely stiff, for vibrations travel fastest in a rigid medium.

The trouble is that this concept demands something with impossible properties. The ether must be highly rigid and yet absolutely frictionless, for otherwise it would slow up the earth, for example, in its travel around the sun. The more scientists thought about it, the harder it was for them to understand how the ether could do what it was supposed to do.

Toward the end of the nineteenth century they were startled by the discovery of another paradox in the travel of light. "Common sense," and the behavior of all known vibrations (such as sound waves), suggested that the speed of light should depend on the motion of the source. In 1887 the physicists A. A. Michelson and E. W. Morley, seeking to find out how the earth's motion through the "ether" affected the speed of light, set up an experiment in the basement of the Case Institute of Technology in Cleveland. To their great surprise, and the surprise of nearly everybody, they discovered that the speed of light was always exactly the same, regardless of the motion or direction of the source! Michelson and Morley, and other physicists, repeated the measurements at various places and under various conditions, and the results were invariably the same: in all circumstances, the velocity of light was constant. Their proof of this fact turned physics upside down.

To understand the reason for all the excitement, let us look in more detail at how this result differed from the behavior, say, of sound waves.

We know that sound is transmitted by means of mechanical vibrations in the medium: air, water, a solid body—any elastic material. That the speed of sound is affected by the motion of the source can be shown by a simple experiment. We send a pulse of sound from point *A* to point *B* 1,000 feet away, where a reflector sends it back to *A*. In round numbers, let us say the pulse takes two seconds for the round trip; that is, its average velocity is 1,000 feet per second. Now suppose we place points *A* and *B* in two airplanes, flying exactly 1,000 feet apart. Let the airplanes travel at a speed of 999 feet per second relative to the air (we assume the air is still—no wind). Airplane *A* sends a sound pulse to airplane *B*, flying 1,000 feet ahead, and measures the time for the reflected signal to return. The observer in *A* will find that as far as he is concerned the sound has traveled at the rate of only about two feet per second. This is understandable, for the plane in front is traveling almost as fast as the sound pulse that is pursuing it, so it takes a long time for the sound to overtake it. Thus the measured speed of sound depends on the speed of the observer.

If the two planes were flying 1,000 feet apart but parallel to each other (neither ahead of the other), the sound pulse would now seem to travel at about 22 feet per second in making the round trip because again the pulse would have to travel considerably more than 1,000 feet to reach the moving plane. This shows that the observed speed of sound depends not only on the velocity of the observer but also on the direction in which the measurement is made.

We can see now why physicists were so surprised that the speed of light was the same no matter how it was measured. As long as they supposed that light was transmitted through an "ether" in the same way that sound was propagated through the air, it was natural to expect that the velocity of light should vary with the relative motion and direction of the observer. On this reasoning, the speed of light as measured in the direction of the earth's motion through the ether should be different from the speed measured at right angles to that direction.

Michelson's and Morley's demonstration that actually the speed of light was the same in both directions killed the idea of the ether. It did more than that: it forced physicists to look for some new theory of the behavior of energy and matter which would be consistent with the constant velocity of light.

Several physicists, notably George Fitzgerald of Ireland, Hendrik Lorentz of the Netherlands, and Henri Poincaré of France, came up with brilliant ideas which showed the way to a solution. But it took the radical mind of Albert Einstein, stripping away all the preconceptions of classical physics, to propose a completely new way of looking at nature. He took the constant velocity of light as a basic postulate, and on this foundation he built his Theory of Relativity.

The picture of light as consisting of waves in the electromagnetic field is a useful one, and is, for many purposes, entirely accurate. The speed of light is now defined as the velocity of propagation of an interaction between charged particles through the field in free space. What the relativity theory emphasizes is that this velocity, called c, is the fastest speed with which *any* interaction may propagate.

This means that the gravitational and nuclear forces cannot travel faster than the speed of light. There is reason to believe that the speed of all four of the basic forces is the same. If that is the case, then we have a great simplification of nature, for now we can say that *all interactions propagate with the speed of light,* regardless of the source or observer.

Since the speed of light is the maximum velocity for the propagation of any interaction, it follows that no signal of any kind, no energy, and no material object can travel through space faster than light—namely, 186,000 miles per second. This is a frustrating fact for those who wish to travel to the distant stars, but there is no getting around the limitation.

~~~~ THINGS THAT GO FASTER THAN LIGHT

Having said this, we now have to reckon with the seeming paradox that actually there are phenomena which *do* travel faster than light. For example, very-high-frequency radio waves (microwaves) go faster than light when traveling through a waveguide. Light itself slows down when it moves through glass —again an apparent contradiction of our basic law that its speed is constant. How come?

The answer is that the statments about the constant speed of light and the maximum speed apply only when we talk about propagation through a vacuum—through free space with no matter in it or nearby. When light travels through glass, or when microwaves travel through a waveguide, the electromagnetic fields interact with the electrons in the material medium and produce an effect making it look *as if* the waves were going either slower or faster than the speed of light in free space. In a sense we can call the effect an illusion.

To understand this, we must first define clearly what we mean by the velocity of a wave. If we fix our attention on the crest of a single wave, we can see that the wave velocity is simply the speed with which the crest travels through space. We might measure the velocity by noting how many crests pass a given point per second. We can easily do this with water waves, but light travels much too fast to see the crests. It turns out, however, that a simple formula enables us to calculate the velocity of any wave. The velocity is just the length of one wave (the distance from one crest to the next) times the number of crests passing per second. In other words, it is the wavelength (L) times the frequency (f), or fL.

The frequency of a given wave never changes: it is set by the oscillating charges that originated the wave. But we can see from the formula that if the wavelength were changed somehow during the wave's travel, its velocity also would change.

What could cause a change in wavelength? Let us look at the case of an electromagnetic wave passing through a waveguide. (This is simply a metal tube, usually rectangular in cross-section, used for transmitting short radio waves.) A wave that is much shorter than the width of the tube travels with the speed of light straight down the tube, just as it would in free space. But waves whose wavelength nearly spans the width of the guide bounce back and forth across the tube (see Figure 16).

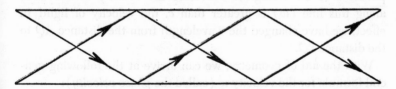

FIGURE 16. The paths of waves reflected from the walls of a waveguide. The arrows show the direction of travel of the wave crests.

Let's take a closer look at one of these waves (Figure 17). Rebounding from one side of the tube to the other, the wave crest (p) is traveling at the speed of light (c). When it hits the wall, it is reflected, just as a beam of light is reflected by a mirror, and the wave crest is turned in the direction shown by the arrow q. On the next bounce it takes the direction r. The angle of its reflection is determined by the wave's length; it travels in a zigzag path such that the distance between crest p and crest r is exactly one wavelength.

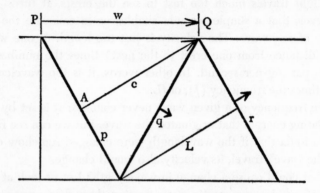

FIGURE 17. Illustration of the phase velocity (w) of a wave reflected in a waveguide.

Now, while crest p travels from A to the point Q at the tube wall (a distance of one wavelength), the phase of the wave at P on the tube wall must also move to Q. The distance from P to Q is longer than from A to Q (since, as we can see, it is the hypotenuse of the triangle). Therefore the velocity of the wave along this line (w) is greater than c, the velocity of light! In effect, we have changed the wavelength from the distance AQ to the distance PQ.

With the aid of geometry, we can arrive at the following general formula for the velocity w (called the *phase velocity*):

$$w = \frac{c}{\sqrt{1 - (L/2D)^2}}$$

The letter L stands for the original wavelength, and D for the width of the waveguide. Note that the bigger the number L (that is, the longer the wavelength), the higher is the velocity w (because c is divided by a smaller number). When L is twice D (that is, the wavelength is twice the width of the guide), then the quantity $L/2D$ becomes 1, and $1 - 1 = 0$. Since any number divided by zero becomes infinity, this means that the velocity w would be infinite! The formula also tells us that when the wavelength is more than twice the width of the guide, the quantity under the square-root sign becomes a negative number, which simply means that such a wave cannot travel through the waveguide.

What can we make of all this? Well, we note that the point P (or Q) is a place where two lines intersect, and we are simply talking about the motion of that point. The situation is something like the closing of a pair of scissors: as the blades are closed—that is, as the angle between the blades approaches zero—the point where they intersect moves forward faster and

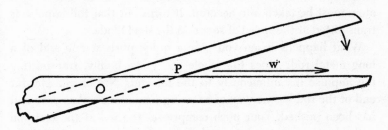

FIGURE 18. Closing of a pair of scissors. The intersection point (P) moves faster and faster as the angle between the blades gets smaller.

faster (see Figure 18). If the scissors were long enough, the intersection point could actually reach a velocity faster than the speed of light, even though the blades themselves would be moving at a much lower speed.

We have here two clear examples which seem to violate the law that nothing can go faster than the speed of light—the radio waves in the waveguide, and the intersection of the scissor blades. What is wrong? Have we overlooked something?

We notice, first of all, that we have been talking about steady situations. We have considered a long, continuous train of radio waves, of constant frequency and amplitude (strength), and a pair of scissors closing at a constant rate. We have said nothing about how these motions start, stop, or change.

What if we suddenly changed ("modulated") a wave in some way—how fast would this *change* be transmitted along the wave-train?

Consider the scissors, to begin with. The instant you start closing the handle, the blade tip begins to move at the far end.

Or does it?

Your eyes deceive you. Any motion you give to the near end of the blade must be transmitted atom to atom down the length of the blade. And this change cannot be transmitted faster than the electrical forces between the atoms allow. This is certainly no faster than the speed of light. As a matter of fact, it is considerably slower than the speed of light, for the inertia of each atom must be taken into account. It turns out that the impulse is transmitted at the speed of sound in the steel blade.

What happens when you give a quick push at one end of a long metal rod? Does the whole rod move bodily, transmitting the impulse instantaneously to the far end? Not at all. The far end of the rod has no way of knowing immediately that your end has been pushed. Your push compresses the rod at the end you strike; a compressional wave then travels down the rod; and the far end learns that the rod has been pushed only when this wave reaches it. The velocity of the wave depends on the elastic properties of the material, just as in the case of the scissors.

The result is the same with radio waves in the waveguide. If we suddenly start pouring a train of waves into one end of a long waveguide, we find that the front end of the wave train always travels down the tube slower than the speed of light, even though the individual wavelets may travel faster than light.

The mathematical theory explaining this behavior is quite

complicated; we can do no more than sketch the logic. We have seen that more than one kind of velocity is involved in the transmission of electromagnetic waves. The speed of each wave crest is called the *phase velocity*, as we have mentioned. This velocity is equal to the speed of light (c) when the wave travels through empty space. When light waves pass through a transparent material such as glass, the phase velocity is less than c. An unchanging train of radio waves passing through a waveguide may have a phase velocity greater than c. But when we modulate a wave to carry a message, the modulation usually travels at a speed different from the phase velocity—in most cases at a slower speed.

This speed is called the *signal velocity* or *group velocity*. The usual way of measuring the speed of light is to break up a beam of light into short pulses and measure the time it takes for these pulses to travel a known distance. Radar operates on the same principle. These pulses of electromagnetic radiation travel with the signal velocity. It is calculated that the signal velocity should differ from the phase velocity whenever the light travels through a material where the index of refraction varies with the wavelength. (In other words, the same process of refraction that spreads light out into its spectrum of colors in a prism also produces a change in the speed of a signal impressed upon a wave.) The signal velocity must always be less than c.

The distinction between phase velocity and group velocity clears up the mystery of "things that go faster than light." There is no law of nature that says *nothing* can go faster than light. Many phenomena may have *phase velocities* greater than c. It remains true, however, that no signal, energy, or material object can be transmitted faster than c.

The existence of phase velocities greater than c is not merely a bizarre curiosity of no practical importance. Without this phenomenon we could not have long-range radio transmission, for it is the speeding up of radio waves when they hit the layer of ionized gases in the upper atmosphere that causes their reflection from the ionosphere back to the earth.

CHAPTER 8

~~~~~~~~~~~~~~~~~~~

The Laws of Relativity

~~~~~~~

When you describe the motion of an object, you must relate its position and speed to some reference point. If you say that a plane is traveling at 1,000 miles per hour, you should specify whether you are relating its motion to the ground or to the air; when we say that the earth travels at 18 miles per second, we mean that this is its speed of motion around the sun. Without such a reference, a statement about motion is meaningless.

There is nothing new in this idea. Newton knew it, and early in the eighteenth century the philosopher Bishop Berkeley put it in terms which we recognize today as a remarkably advanced point of view. He wrote: ". . . motion cannot be understood . . . except in relation to . . . some other body. Up, down, right, left —all directions and places are based on some relation, and it is necessary to suppose another body distinct from the moving one. . . . Therefore if we suppose that everything is annihilated except one globe, it would be impossible to imagine any movement of that globe. Let us imagine two globes and that besides them nothing else material exists—then the motion in a circle of these two globes round their common center cannot be imagined. But suppose that the heaven of fixed stars [is] suddenly created —[then we are] in a position to imagine the motion of the globes by their relative position to the different parts of the heaven."

Berkeley was well beyond the point of view of Galileo and Newton. Although they had recognized that the *velocity* of a body had to be related to some other body, they had thought there was something special about acceleration. The effect of the force of acceleration can be observed without reference to anything else. Newton illustrated this with a problem that has perplexed scientists ever since—the famous case of the bucket of water in a closed room.

When a bucket of water is rotated, the surface of the water shapes itself into a parabola (see Figure 19). If you did not rotate the bucket yourself but stood in a closed room which was rotating as a whole (including you and the bucket), you would

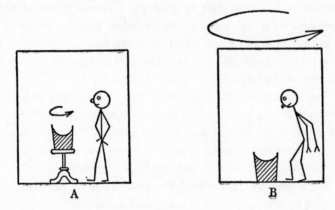

FIGURE 19. Water rotating in a bucket in a stationary room (A) and a rotating room (B).

not see the water moving, yet its surface would be hollowed out in the parabolic shape. Thus you could tell that the room was rotating, even though you could not look out to observe your motion with respect to an outside object.

Newton concluded from this that there must be some "absolute frame of reference" by which you could measure the acceleration of an object even if no other object existed in the universe. Therefore there must be "absolute motion" and "absolute acceleration." Berkeley disputed this idea. He believed that the water in the rotating bucket was subject to a centrifugal force whose existence depended on the presence of the stars in the heavens. If there were no stars, he contended, there could be no centrifugal force.

For all practical purposes, Newton's point of view prevailed. This point of view accepts as a basic property of matter the idea of inertia—the resistance of bodies to acceleration. But the question remains: What causes inertia? Why does a mass resist being accelerated? Why does centrifugal force appear when a body rotates?

Bishop Berkeley's idea of relativity was not taken seriously by scientists of his time. But in 1872 the German physicist Ernst Mach revived it. He argued, like Berkeley, that the behavior of the bucket of water must result from the fact that it had a rotation relative to the distant stars. He went further: he contended that you might equally well say the bucket was standing still and the stars were rotating around the bucket! The two statements were simply two ways of describing the same thing, for all you were speaking of was relative motion. You could not say that anything was *absolutely* at rest. There was no center of the universe you could point to and say: This is at rest.

Mach's principle got about the same kind of reception that Berkeley's idea had had a century and a half earlier: the whole thing smacked of black magic and astrology. But one man on whom it made a deep impression—a generation later—was a young patent examiner in Switzerland named Albert Einstein.

Einstein started thinking about the problem of relativity by examining the situation of observers on two bodies, each moving at a constant velocity. A convenient example would be two spaceships somewhere out in space. Suppose you are in one ship (S) traveling at a constant speed. Because the speed is constant, you consider your ship essentially at rest. Along comes another ship (S_1) moving with a certain velocity (v) relative to you. The observer in S_1 also traveling at constant speed, is convinced that *he* is at rest and *you* are in motion relative to him. As a matter of fact, you are both right: the only important fact is the relative motion.

In this situation, how does each observer describe what he observes? Can they both find a common frame of reference?

The way Galileo and Newton handled this problem (perhaps visualizing boats rather than spaceships) was to set up two co-ordinate systems—the familiar x, y, z graphs used to locate points in three-dimensional space—and relate them to each other. Call ship S's coordinates x, y, z, and S_1's coordinates x_1, y_1, z_1 (see Figure 20).

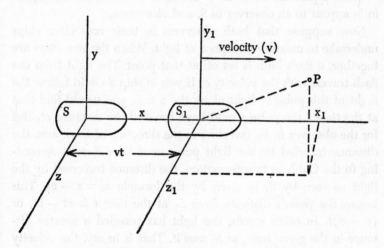

FIGURE 20. Coordinate systems of two ships—Ship S and Ship S_1, moving with velocity v relative to Ship S.

Let us say that at a given moment both ships are at the point S in our picture. At this point the two coordinate systems coincide: x, y, z and x_1, y_1, z_1 are the same. Now the ships move apart with the velocity v in the direction along the x axis. After a certain time, t, the distance between them will be vt. The center of ship S_1's coordinate system is now at the point S_1 on the diagram. Suppose the observers in the two ships both see a third ship at point P. Can each observer describe its location to the other, and both agree in fixing the location?

According to the reasoning of Galileo and Newton, they can. Let's say that v is ten feet per second and t is 20 seconds; then the distance vt between S and S_1 is 200 feet. If P is 50 feet ahead of S_1 on the x_1 axis, then it must be 250 feet from S on the x axis.

This operation is called making a *transformation* from one system to the other. It is known as the Galilean transformation, and its general formula is $x = x_1 + vt$ if we transform from the S_1 system to S, or $x_1 = x - vt$ if we transform from S to S_1. The transformation equations also stipulate that $y = y_1$ and $z = z_1$.

These equations allow us to calculate how motions of objects in S_1 appear to an observer in S, and *vice versa*.

Now suppose that both observers in their respective ships undertake to measure the speed of light. When the two ships are together, a flash bulb is set off at that point. The light from the flash travels with the velocity c. If you in ship S could follow the flight of this pulse of light along the x axis, you would find that at the time t the pulse would have traveled the distance ct. But for the observer in S_1, traveling in the direction of the x axis, the distance traveled by the light pulse must be different. According to the Galilean transformation, the distance traversed by the light as seen by S_1 is given by the formula $x_1 = x - vt$. This means the pulse's distance from S_1 at the time t is $ct - vt$, or $(c - v)t$. In other words, the light has traveled a shorter distance in the given time, as S_1 sees it. That is to say, the velocity of light is not the same for both observers, if the Galilean formula is correct.

In all our ordinary affairs it doesn't really matter whether this formula is 100 per cent correct or not. When you travel in a rowboat, or even in a swift airplane, any difference in the speed of light, if it existed, would be much too tiny to be noticeable. The Galilean equation works perfectly well in all problems not involving extremely high speeds. It was not until Michelson and Morley measured the speed of light with very high accuracy that the basic truth was discovered: the velocity of light, in fact, is exactly the same for all observers, no matter how fast they are moving.

Toward the end of the nineteenth century many important scientists worked on the problem of understanding this paradox. Fitzgerald hit upon a way out of the dilemma. Suppose, he suggested, that all moving objects are shortened—including yardsticks and measuring devices of every kind. They are shortened by just the right amount so that the measured velocity of light always comes out to be the same.

Fitzgerald had no idea how or why this shortening came about, but his suggestion turned out to be correct. The effect is sometimes called the Fitzgerald contraction and sometimes the Lorentz-Fitzgerald contraction, giving credit to the Dutch physicist Lorentz, who developed certain equations which later became part of Einstein's theory of relativity. Einstein's theory did not emerge out of a vacuum, as our brief review of the history makes amply clear. It was in the air. Henri Poincaré was so close to developing the theory of relativity that if you read his writings you may wonder what Einstein did that was so remarkable.

What Einstein did was simply to follow through, to its utterly logical conclusion, the basic assumption that the motion of any object must be measured relative to some other object. In doing this, he threw overboard some preconceived ideas which other scientists had not been willing to let go. For this reason Einstein gets credit for putting physics on a new foundation with a new kind of logic.

Like Mach, Einstein adopted the view that, in considering two objects in relative motion, it is futile and meaningless to try to decide which object is in motion and which at rest. If you are in a spaceship traveling at a speed of 1,000 miles per second relative to the earth, it makes no difference whether somebody says you are moving at that speed or the earth is moving. In either case, the operation of physical laws in your ship and on the earth will be the same. As far as you are concerned, you can consider yourself at rest. There is no *absolute frame of reference* that can contradict you.

The result is that if the occupants of spaceship S consider the ship at rest (that is, its relative motion is constant), and those in ship S_1 also consider themselves at rest, then any experiment done in S must give exactly the same results as the same experiment in S_1, even though the two ships are moving at a speed of thousands of miles per second relative to each other. For instance, the rule that force equals mass times acceleration must be true both in S and in S_1. The form of this equation never changes. Therefore, a mass of one kilogram, as measured in S, will still be one kilogram if it is transferred to S_1 and measured there. After all, the mass is at rest in each ship while the measurement is made. Why should it behave differently in S than in S_1?

This does not mean, however, that the mass will necessarily appear the same if an observer in S is somehow able to measure it while it is moving along in S_1. In short, Einstein discarded the preconception that the mass of an object is sacred and unchanging.

He also abandoned the equally sacred notion that time was unchanging—that it had to run at the same rate in both S and S_1. In the Galilean transformation it was assumed that a clock in S would always tick off time in exactly the same way as a clock in S_1. This meant that two events which were simultaneous in S would also be simultaneous in S_1.

Einstein's rejection of this assumption was perhaps his most original new idea. It required the discarding of concepts everybody had taken for granted for thousands of years. The new Einsteinian idea seemed ridiculous. How could two events be simultaneous in one place and not simultaneous in another place?

~~~~ THE LORENTZ TRANSFORMATION

Let us follow Einstein's reasoning. Here is a body in space moving with a velocity V_1 as measured by an observer in S_1. What is its velocity as measured by somebody in S? According to the Galilean idea, the observer in S would see the object traveling with the velocity $v + V_1$, because the relative velocity between the two ships would have to be added (assuming they were going in the same direction as the moving object). If this were so, a pulse of light sent out from S_1 would move with the velocity c as measured from S_1 but with the velocity $v + c$ as measured from S. But this directly contradicts the demonstrated fact that the speed of light is always constant. Its velocity must be c whether it is measured from S or S_1. Therefore the Galilean transformation cannot be quite correct.

Einstein started out afresh, using the constant speed of light as one of the two basic postulates which are the foundation of the special theory of relativity. These postulates can be stated this way:

1. *The laws of nature are always found to be the same in any frame of reference moving with constant velocity.*

2. *The speed of light is always found to have the same value, no matter what is the motion of the source or the observer.*

From these two postulates Einstein deduced a number of surprising results which would have been totally unacceptable to a more conservative mind. (Einstein was only about 25 when he announced them).

I shall merely summarize the results here. (See Appendix 2 for the mathematical details.)

The most basic result is that we find a new set of transformation equations which allows us to write down what an observer in ship S sees when he looks at ship S_1, and *vice versa*. These equations are known as the Lorentz transformation, because it was Lorentz who first found that they could explain how it was that the speed of light was constant, though he still clung to the idea of the "ether." Einstein did away with the ether and obtained the same transformation in a much simpler and more basic manner.

The Lorentz transformation can be written as the following set of equations, one side representing transformation from the S_1 system to S, and the other side *vice versa*:

$$x = \frac{x_1 + vt_1}{\sqrt{1 - v^2/c^2}} \qquad x_1 = \frac{x - vt}{\sqrt{1 - v^2/c^2}}$$

$$y = y_1 \qquad\qquad\qquad y_1 = y$$

$$z = z_1 \qquad\qquad\qquad z_1 = z$$

$$t = \frac{t_1 + x_1 v/c^2}{\sqrt{1 - v^2/c^2}} \qquad t_1 = \frac{t - xv/c^2}{\sqrt{1 - v^2/c^2}}$$

Like the Galilean transformation equations, these equations (in which the symbols mean exactly the same things) allow us to compare what two different observers see, even though they are traveling with different velocities. When an observer in S_1 sees an object at the position x_1, y_1, z_1, t_1, an observer in S sees it at the position x, y, z, t. Notice the important feature: the *time* must be given as well as the position, because the respective clocks in S and S_1 will cease to read identical times after they have parted from each other. This is the meaning of the fourth equation in the set above. The fact that time is given the same importance as the space positions means that time is raised to the stature of a dimension. There is nothing mystical about this; we are not going to travel in the fourth dimension. Thinking of time as a fourth dimension is little more than a convenience in the mathematics.

At this point we might step back to survey the scene and ask what we have done. Why do we make such an important issue out of the act of looking across from one spaceship to another, an event which is somewhat rare at the present time? Of course, we have used this only as a colorful illustration. Instead of talking about spaceships we could be discussing trains, airplanes, or any frame of reference. In other words, when we learn to interpret them, these transformation equations tell us what is happening whenever we look at *any* moving object.

While the equations look somewhat formidable at first glance, we notice that when the velocity is very small compared to the speed of light (that is, when v/c is a very small fraction), these equations become practically identical with the simpler Galilean

Transformation. After all, if v is 186 miles per second (one-thousandth the speed of light), then $1 - v^2/c^2$ is very close to the number 1—it is only 50 millionths less than 1. When the number is this close or closer to 1, there is practically no difference between the numbers $\dfrac{x - vt}{\sqrt{1 - v^2/c^2}}$ and $x - vt$. Consequently most relativity effects are not noticeable when we look at bodies moving at ordinary speeds.

Nevertheless, the relativity theory has most important consequences, at least one of which has profoundly affected our daily lives—it led to the atomic bomb. Let us examine some scientific results of the theory.

⌐⌐⌐ THE TIME DILATATION

Suppose there is a clock located in S_1. An observer in S sees this clock moving with the velocity v, and at any time, t, the position of the clock with reference to his system is given by $x = vt$. If the length of time between two ticks of this clock is T_1 in the S_1 system, the transformation to the S system (assuming that $x_1 = 0$) makes the time between ticks appear, as S sees it, to be:

$$T = \frac{T_1}{\sqrt{1 - v^2/c^2}}$$

Since T is a longer time than T_1, it seems to S that the clock is running slower than it does to S_1. This, of course, applies not only to the clock but to all the physical happenings in S_1 that depend on time: the vibrations of electrons in their atoms, the rate of chemical reactions, and the living processes of the human occupants of S_1.

In short, it appears to the observer in S (call him George) that his counterpart in S_1 (call him George I) is living at a slower rate than he is. George I doesn't realize this, because as far as he is concerned, it is George who is moving and living at a slower rate. George I says that the clocks in S are running slow, while George says that the clocks in S_1 are running slow.

This is quite a paradoxical situation, but we can't escape it if we carry relativity through to its logical conclusion. As long as the two ships have a constant relative motion, we cannot say that one is moving and the other standing still. George says that George I is moving and George I says that George is moving. It is a perfectly symmetrical situation.

Furthermore, if the ships keep moving apart, the two men can never get together for a reunion to compare notes on who it was who "really" grew older more slowly. They are gone from each other's ken forever.

To bring about a reunion we would have to create a very different situation. Let us say that George and George I are moving at a constant speed, and George I is then accelerated to some higher speed so that he moves away. (Such is the case when a man takes off from the earth in a rocket for a space voyage.) To come back to George, George I at some point will have to slow down, or decelerate (physically, deceleration is equivalent to acceleration), then speed up again to overtake George, and finally change his speed again to fall in step with George's pace. All this time George has not experienced any acceleration; he has just gone on at his constant, normal pace.

What effect has all the acceleration had on George I? It turns out that time has passed more slowly for him and he has aged less than George. If they were twins to begin with, George is now older than George I.

This consequence of relativity is the basis of the science-fiction stories that tell of space explorers traveling around the galaxy at great speeds and coming back to earth after having aged only a few years (according to their clocks) to find that generations have passed on the earth and that all their friends have died. The idea is perfectly consistent with all the principles of relativity; from a practical point of view the only difficulty with this scheme is the fact that we don't know how to attain such great speeds.

The relativistic time effect has been observed in a number of physical phenomena. One example is afforded by mesons, the particles that are produced when atomic nuclei are smashed by cosmic rays or by the particles in a high-energy beam from an accelerator. Mesons live only a small fraction of a second before they decay into other particle forms. It has been found that mesons moving very rapidly have a longer average lifetime than mesons not in motion. This shows that time runs at a slower rate for the rapidly moving mesons.

Another example is connected with the well-known Doppler effect. Any radiation (light, radio, sound) changes in wavelength and frequency as the source moves toward or away from the observer. The Doppler rule tells us exactly how this change should vary with velocity. But when we make very accurate measurements of the change in frequency of light emitted by atoms moving very rapidly relative to the observer, we find that the change does not agree precisely with Doppler's original formula. The atom's little "clock," meaning the oscillators that regulate the frequency of the light waves it emits, runs slower when the atom is moving rapidly. This results in a small, but measurable, relativistic time effect.

ᨃᨃᨃ THE RELATIVISTIC ROTATION

Having seen what happens to clocks in Einstein's relativistic world, let us now return to the Lorentz-Fitzgerald contraction. We said that high-velocity motion shortens yardsticks. How would you go about measuring this shortening?

We resort to our convenient two spaceships, S and S_1. A camera is set up in ship S. As ship S_1 whizzes by, with its yardstick lying lengthwise in the direction of motion, the camera makes an instantaneous picture of it. The distance between the rays of light coming from the two ends of the yardstick is its length as seen from S.

If the length of the yardstick as measured in S_1 is L_1, and it is moving with the velocity v relative to S, then according to the contraction formula its length as recorded by the camera in S should be:

$$L = L_1 \sqrt{1 - v^2/c^2}$$

(See Appendix 2 for the derivation of this formula.)

The equation means that when v (the velocity of the yardstick) is nearly equal to c (the velocity of light), the observer in S finds L (the length of the yardstick) to be very short.

Some writers have concluded that to passengers traveling at almost the speed of light the stars and planets they passed would look like flattened spheroids. Oddly, this question was not examined mathematically in a serious way until many years after Einstein formulated the theory of relativity. In 1959 James Terrell of the Los Alamos Laboratory did so, and he found, to everybody's astonishment, that if you looked at a bulky body (rather than a long, thin rod), the body would not appear shortened but instead would appear to be *rotated!*

This new interpretation of the Lorentz-Fitzgerald contraction does not change the basic theory at all. And its only practical consequence is to suggest to science-fiction writers that they should revise their picture of space travel: travelers whizzing by a star at relativistic speed will see not a foreshortened spheroid but a sphere, which will seem to be rotated so that they can briefly see its far side!

～～～ THE MASS INCREASE

From the time of Newton until the end of the nineteenth century, the mass of a body was considered to be absolutely constant. Conservation of mass was regarded as a fundamental law of nature. But when physicists began to experiment with atomic particles, they found mass playing a peculiar trick.

The oddity cropped up first in the behavior of electrons. The experimenters had learned that a magnetic field would deflect the flight of electrons into a curved path, and the amount of deflection depended on the velocity of the electrons: if you doubled their velocity (*i.e.*, their momentum), the magnetic field deflected them only half as much. The surprise came when physicists did this experiment with electrons already moving fairly fast; they noticed that, with further increases in speed, the electrons showed more resistance to deflection than the formula had led them to expect. Apparently, as the speed of electrons increased, they increased in mass!

It was Einstein's theory of relativity, once again, that cleared up this mystery. He showed that the mass increase was a necessary result of the Lorentz transformation. To understand his demonstration, we must think further about the nature of velocity and momentum.

Let us start by examining how velocities add up in the Newtonian system and in the relativistic system. In Newton's system, 100,000 miles per second added to 100,000 miles per second is simply 200,000 miles per second. Not so in the Einstein way of figuring. If a spaceship traveling at 100,000 miles per second relative to the earth (call this speed v) fires a missile in the same direction at 100,000 miles per second (call this u_1), then the resulting speed of the missile (u) must be calculated by the formula:

$$u = \frac{u_1 + v}{1 + \dfrac{u_1 v}{c^2}}$$

The missile's speed relative to the earth turns out to be not 200,000 but 155,000 miles per second!

Now this way of looking at things must have important consequences when we come to consider the momentum of bodies in relativistic terms. Suppose we try to describe the collision of two perfectly elastic spheres in a spaceship moving with constant speed relative to the earth. The laws of conservation of energy and momentum tell us that the total momentum and energy of two bodies after the collision must be equal to the total before the collision, and Einstein's first postulate says that these laws must be just as true in the spaceship as here on the earth. We have just seen, however, that in describing events on the spaceship from our frame of reference on the earth, we cannot add up velocities there in the simple Newtonian way. We must use the transformation equations.

When we do that (see Appendix 2), we discover that the values for the total momentum of the colliding spheres before and after the collision do not balance *if we assume that the masses of the two spheres remain constant.* Momentum is not conserved unless we allow the masses to change. We find, in fact, that the mass of any body in motion must vary according to the formula:

$$m = \frac{m_0}{\sqrt{1 - v^2/c^2}}$$

Here m_0 is the mass the object has when it is at rest relative to the observer, and v is its velocity relative to the observer. For obvious reasons, m_0 is called the *rest-mass,* and this is a constant number assigned to each object. The quantity m is the variable mass of a body that is actually observed as it enters into reactions and is placed in various real-life circumstances. This quantity represents the inertia of the object.

We can see from the equation above that as v gets larger, m also gets larger. At ordinary speeds the increase in mass is imperceptible, but when v approaches the speed of light, the mass increases very rapidly. If the velocity of a body ever equaled the speed of light, its mass would become infinite.

We discover even more interesting results when we look into what happens when v is very much smaller than c. If we expand the equation by means of the binomial theorem, we get a formula which runs as follows: $m = m_0 + \frac{1}{2}m_0 v^2/c^2 + \ldots$. (The terms represented by the dots on the right are omitted because they are insignificant when v is very small compared to c.) Multiplying both sides of this equation by c^2, we get:

$$mc^2 = m_0c^2 + \tfrac{1}{2}m_0v^2 + \ldots\ldots$$

The second term on the right is, we notice, the kinetic energy of the moving body. As in all such equations, this implies that the other terms in the equation also must represent energy. The first term on the right, then, is the energy the body has when it is at rest—in other words, the energy equivalent of the rest-mass. The left side of the equation, since it is the sum of the rest-mass energy and the kinetic energy, represents the total energy. In short, $E = mc^2$.

That is how Einstein arrived at the now-famous connection between mass and energy.

Just as mass contains energy, so kinetic energy has mass. As a body goes faster (meaning that kinetic-energy mass is added), the mass increases until, at a velocity approaching that of light, it approaches infinity.

Since it would take an infinite amount of energy to make a body travel at *exactly* the speed of light, this is impossible to accomplish. An accelerator in the billion-volt range can speed up an electron to almost the speed of light, but not all the energy in the galaxy could make it reach that speed.

From all this we must conclude that no material object could possibly travel as fast as light. And the only objects that can attain light's velocity are particles which have no rest-mass, such as photons and neutrinos.

ᰛᰛᰛ GRAVITATION

If you were in a ship being blasted by rockets into interplanetary space, you would feel the inertial force caused by the acceleration pressing you down against the seat. If the rocket was closed up tight so that you did not see what was happening outside, you would not be able to tell the difference between this acceleration force and the force of gravity. It would feel just as if a gravitational force was pulling you down to the seat.

The basic reason you would feel this way is that all the objects in the ship would be pulled to the floor with the same acceleration. The whole situation would be exactly equivalent to being in a gravitational field.

Einstein first expressed the idea in 1911, calling it the Principle of Equivalence. An immediate result is the conclusion that photons of light, like everything else, must be affected by gravitational fields. This is easy to illustrate by imagining how two observers, one inside a rocket and the other outside, would see a beam of light crossing a room in the rocket. The light beam is directed straight across the room toward a spot at the same level on the opposite wall (see Figure 21).

If the room is moving upward with constant velocity, the observer inside feels that the room is at rest, and of course he is not at all surprised that the beam of photons travels straight across (he would be astounded if it didn't). The outside observer, however, sees that during the time the photons are crossing, the room moves upward, so that the spot they hit has risen to a higher level with reference to the earth. In other words, the straight path of the light beam slants upward, as he sees it.

Now suppose the room is accelerated at a high rate. The outside observer still sees the light traveling in a straight line, but because the spot travels a greater distance upward during the time the photons take to travel across the room, the light now strikes the wall at a point below the spot it hit before. The observer inside sees it striking this same point, but because the upward acceleration makes him feel he is drawn down by gravity, it seems to him that the light beam curves downward under the same influence. Both observers see the same result, but each gives it a different cause. The person inside says the photons are attracted by gravity; the one outside says the photons are simply moving in a straight line in a room undergoing upward acceleration.

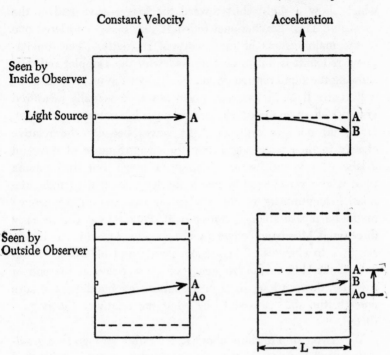

FIGURE 21. Light crossing a moving room, as seen by an inside observer and by an outside observer, when the room moves with constant velocity (*left*) and when it is accelerated (*right*).

According to relativity concepts, the two explanations are completely equivalent.

In the case of light shining straight down on the earth, the photons are falling in the gravitational field. Because of this they gain energy. The added energy cannot increase their velocity, for they are already moving at the speed of light; what it does is shorten the wavelength of the light. Conversely, a photon traveling up from the surface of the earth loses energy and increases its wavelength.

The effect is extremely small and hard to measure. However, it has been detected in the spectra of light from heavy stars, which show a slight shift toward the longer-wave end of the spectrum. This "gravitational red-shift" has been considered one of the major proofs of the theory of relativity. (The gravitational red-shift is not to be confused with the Doppler red-shift showing the rapid motion of galaxies away from us.)

Recently R. V. Pound, a Harvard physicist, actually measured gravity's effect on radiation by means of a laboratory experiment. He could not use ordinary light waves because the relative change in their wavelength over the short distance of travel in a laboratory would be far too small to detect. But with gamma rays, whose wavelength is much shorter than that of light, the relative lengthening of the waves (or decrease in frequency) might be measurable. To measure it, Pound used the recently discovered Mössbauer effect (see Appendix 3), which is highly sensitive to changes of frequency. Pound and his associates recorded the shift in the frequency of gamma rays at the end of their fall down a long shaft in the laboratory building, and sure enough, the shift proved to be what the relativity theory predicted.

When you stop to think about it, it's rather strange that gravitation produces exactly the same acceleration of all bodies and packets of energy, regardless of their mass or density. Einstein decided that this must reflect a basic property of the gravitational field. To explain this, he worked out a new method of describing the gravitational field which did not use the word "force" at all. Instead, he said the space around a body (such as a star or planet) is "curved" so that an object travels along a path dictated by this curvature. In other words, this is the object's natural path of travel in the gravitational field, just as in "flat" space an object naturally travels in a straight line unless some force deflects it. In Einstein's curved space there are no forces; the curvature of the space itself causes things in the region to travel along paths which we *interpret* as being caused by a gravitational force.

This idea is the core of Einstein's general theory of relativity, which deals with systems undergoing acceleration, whereas his special theory deals only with systems moving at constant velocity. The general theory is one of the most complicated and abstract branches of physics. Part of the reason is that the gravitational field is really very complex—much more complex than the electromagnetic field.

We have seen that in the case of an electric field the force between two charged bodies is expressed by the formula:

$$F = \frac{kq_1q_2}{r^2}$$

with q_1 and q_2 representing the quantities of electric charge on the bodies, r the distance between them, and k a constant. This expression tells us that the electric force varies inversely as the square of the distance and directly with the amount of charge. Thus if we double the amount of charge on one of the bodies, we double the force between them. Because of this one-to-one correspondence, we call the electric field a *linear field:* plotting the force against the amount of charge on a body, you get a straight line.

This is not true of gravitational fields. That may come as a great surprise, for Newton's law of gravity looks exactly like the equation above:

$$F = \frac{Gm_1m_2}{r^2}$$

But there are unsuspected depths in this innocent equation. What happens if we double one of the masses?

To do that we have to bring in the additional mass from somewhere far off (where it did not previously influence the gravitational field between m_1 and m_2). Now this added mass, call it m_3, had a potential energy with respect to m_1 before it was brought in to join m_1. It loses this potential energy, the loss amounting to Gm_1m_3/a (a is the distance between masses m_1 and m_3 after they are brought together). Thus m_1 and m_3 together now have less energy, gravitationally speaking, than they had when they were separated. Consequently their total mass must be smaller, for energy is equivalent to mass. The lost mass, m, is measured by the formula $m = E/c^2$.

The lost potential energy is called the *binding* energy: this is the amount of energy that would have to be supplied to separate the two masses. (Exactly the same situation exists in the nucleus of the atom. When a neutron and a proton join to form a nucleus of heavy hydrogen, deuterium, the mass of the deuterium nucleus is less than the sum of the proton and neutron masses; this lost mass becomes the binding energy holding the nucleus together.)

Subtracting the mass that has gone into binding energy, the combined mass of m_1 and m_3 (call it M) is:

$$M = m_1 + m_3 - \frac{E}{c^2}$$

Since the binding energy E is Gm_1m_3/a, the equation becomes:

$$M = m_1 + m_3 - \frac{Gm_1m_3}{ac^2}$$

Now if we substitute these terms in Newton's equation, the gravitational force between m_2 and M is:

$$F = \frac{Gm_2(m_1 + m_3)}{r^2} - \frac{G^2m_1m_2m_3}{ac^2r^2}$$

The first term on the right side of this equation is the classical Newtonian force of gravity; the second term is the small quantity that must be subtracted to take account of relativity. Under ordinary conditions this quantity is very small indeed—too small to measure. But its existence adds a complication to the gravitational field which is not present in an electric field.

Whereas electric fields can be added together in linear fashion, we see that gravitational fields do not add up in a simple way.

We are forced to say that the gravitational field is *non-linear*. This is a fancy way of saying that if you double the mass, you don't quite double the field.

Yet gravitational fields have certain similarities to electromagnetic fields. Changes in a gravitational field are propagated with the speed of light, just as in an electromagnetic field. This suggests that there may be such a thing as gravitational waves. If so, they are very weak. How are we ever going to detect them?

We might try to catch gravitational oscillations emitted from a collapsing or exploding star (a nova). Or from a pair of stars revolving around each other. Or from a pair of weights vibrating on the end of a spring. The recent great refinements in electronic amplification of small signals of various kinds may make detection of gravitational waves possible. At least one experiment has been set up for this purpose (at the University of Maryland).

⬝⬝⬝ INERTIA

Early in this chapter we raised the question: What causes inertia? How does the force of inertia originate? Let us return to that question.

The inertial force comes into play whenever a body undergoes acceleration; it is the "reaction" mentioned in Newton's third law of motion. Even when you fall freely under the acceleration of gravity, an inertial force acts on you in the upward direction. You do not "feel" this force, because in free fall there is a balance between the gravitational force downward and the inertial force upward. In this condition you have no sensation of force at all: you are weightless.

The downward gravitational force between the earth and a falling object is given by the Newtonian equation:

$$F = \frac{GMm_g}{r^2}$$

Here M is the mass of the earth and m_g is the mass of the object. We use the subscript g to indicate that this mass represents a source of gravitational attraction (just as an electric charge is a source of electrical attraction). This we call the gravitational mass.

The downward acceleration by gravity is the force divided by the mass being accelerated. This mass represents the inertia of the object, so we call it the inertial mass (m_i):

$$a = \frac{F}{m_i}$$

For the moment, let us make a distinction between the two kinds of mass: the gravitational mass gives the strength of the force, and the inertial mass determines the acceleration resulting from the force.

Combining the two equations above, we find that

$$a = \frac{GM}{r^2} \cdot \frac{m_g}{m_i}$$

Now, as Galileo first showed, the acceleration of gravity is the same for all bodies, regardless of mass or density. The most painstaking experiments (which are going on to this very day) have failed to show that gravity acts differently on bodies of different density. The result of this is that m_g/m_i must be a constant. In fact (by defining G properly) we say that the gravitational mass *equals* the inertial mass always.

We now ask why these two masses should be identical; so far we have seen no theoretical reason to make them so. Let us see if we can find a reason.

Taking a cue from Mach's principle, we start with the hypothesis that the inertial force arises from the gravitational interaction between the accelerating body and the mass of all the distant stars. How might such an interaction arise? Newton's law of gravitation says nothing about the forces between accelerating bodies —but we know that Newton's law is only an approximation to the truth. When we deal with masses in motion, we must ask

whether special forces arise as a result of the velocity or acceleration of these bodies. We know that when a charged body accelerates, the electromagnetic field acquires a new component.
There is reason to believe that gravitational fields behave the
same way, so we may expect new forces to appear when a mass
accelerates. These may be extremely weak, but the enormous
mass of all the distant stars can add up to give an appreciable effect—an effect just large enough to account for the existence of
inertia.

The magnitude of this force is proportional to the gravitational
mass of the accelerating body as well as to the amount of the
acceleration. If we call the constant of proportionality K, then

$$F = Km_g a$$

The value of the constant of proportionality must depend on the
universal gravitational constant G, and also on the mass and
density of all the stars in the universe.

Now we know that the acceleration, the force, and the inertial
mass have this relation:

$$F = m_i a$$

Comparing this with the equation above, we see that $m_i = Km_g$.
Since $m_g = m_i$, then it must be true that $K = 1$.

This suggests that the strength of the gravitational field depends directly on the density of the entire universe. One possible
test of this theory, proposed by R. H. Dicke of Princeton University, would be to see whether the earth's gravitational field is
slowly changing as the universe expands. The change, of course,
must be exceedingly small and slow, so it will not be easy to
detect.

If the explanation of inertia just described is correct, we must
reconsider some of the hypothetical experiments that relativists
are fond of making. The "closed room" has been a favorite device
for thinking of isolated systems, but it seems now that when our

experiments involve inertia, we shall have to make the walls of our room porous to the free entrance of the gravitational fields responsible for inertia.

If the inertial force is an effect arising from all the matter in the universe, we can arrive at another interesting conclusion. The direction of the inertial force does not depend on the direction of acceleration. For instance, the inertia of a spaceship is the same whether we fire it in the direction of the North Star or in the direction of Andromeda: it takes the same force to accelerate the mass to a given speed either way. That means the gravitational field must be symmetrical throughout space, which in turn means that the stars and galaxies are spread out evenly in the universe as a whole. On the average, there are no more stars in one direction than in another if we go out to the farthest reaches of the universe.

CHAPTER 9

~~~~~~~~~~~~~~~~~~~~~

The Laws of Probability and Entropy

~~~~~~~

The real world in which we live seems so different from the ideal world of the scientist. His is a world in which the laws of nature rule with rigid finality; our workaday world appears to be governed largely by the whims of chance. The scientist can predict the exact moment at which the sun will rise tomorrow morning, but when he sets out to drive to his laboratory, he will not venture to predict precisely how long it will take to get there. The world of everyday life is vastly more complicated than the orderly world of the laboratory.

Or is it? Is everything predictable in the "simple" realm of stars and atoms? Does chance play no part in their observed behavior?

We shall see that atoms and "elementary" particles are not as simple or elementary as they once seemed. When physicists get down to measuring and describing the behavior of particles, they find that they are dealing not with certainties but with probabilities. They cannot predict the behavior of any single particle but only the *average* behavior of a group of particles.

The concept of probability has become a foundation-stone of modern physics. It has its own laws and mathematical system. These are just the laws that operate in any game of chance. In fact, the theory of probability sprang out of a dice game.

It all began when a professional gambler asked the great seventeenth-century mathematician Blaise Pascal how one should bet on throws of the dice. Thinking about the odds involved in this simple game, Pascal became absorbed in the mathematics of various problems of the same nature. He exchanged letters on the subject with another brilliant French mathematician, Pierre de Fermat, and together they launched the new branch of mathematics that has become known as the theory of probability.

The theory is best and most simply illustrated by the tossing of a coin. If the coin is symmetrical, we expect heads to come up as often as tails. In other words, there are two possible results, and both have equal probability. The probability of heads (or tails) is one out of two, or ½.

It's easy to see that we can expand this into a general rule: if there are three possible results of some action, all equally probable, the probability of each is ⅓, and so on. The general formula for any number of equally probable results (R) is:

$$P = \frac{1}{R}$$

Of course, in practice we don't usually know in advance whether two possible results of an action are equally probable. For instance, looking at a fork in a road, we may not be able to tell *a priori* whether the next car that comes along is as likely to turn right as left. The only way to assess the probabilities in that case is to watch and count a large number of events. If we observed 1,000 cars and found that about half took the right fork and half the left, we would conclude that the probability of each event was roughly ½.

In general, if we try something N times, and we get a particular result in a certain number (say H, for heads) of these N trials, then the probability of obtaining that result is:

$$P = \frac{H}{N}$$

This means, of course, that a probability is always some fraction between zero and 1 (zero meaning that the event never occurs, and 1 that it occurs every time the trial is made).

What is the probability of picking the ace of spades out of a thoroughly shuffled deck of 52 cards? Our formula says it is $\frac{1}{52}$. What we mean is that if we had 52 million decks of cards and blindly drew one card out of each deck, about one million of our draws would be the ace of spades. Not every 52nd card—but about one out of every 52 *as an average.* In any single draw, there is just no predicting what we would get. The draw from each pack is completely independent of all the others, so it gives us no information whatsoever about the next draw.

If you flip a coin and it falls heads, what is the probability of getting heads on the next toss? Exactly the same as before the first—that is, $\frac{1}{2}$. Even if you happened to toss 100 heads in a row, the chance of heads on the next throw would still be $\frac{1}{2}$ (assuming that your fingers had not somehow discovered the trick of controlling the coin).

This fact is very hard to accept; after a run of heads, almost everybody will start betting on tails, on the theory that the worm must turn sooner or later. So it must, but not necessarily on the next trial—or the one after that, or the one after that. This illustrates what we mean by independent action. Each throw is completely independent of all those that have gone before.

This being so, what is the probability of getting two heads in a row—that is, obtaining two desired results which are independent of each other?

If we flip a coin twice, there are four possible results of the pair of throws: heads-heads, heads-tails, tails-heads, and tails-tails. We see that heads on the first throw can be followed by one of two sequels (heads or tails), and tails on the first likewise offers two possibilities (heads or tails on the second). Therefore the number of possible combinations in two throws can be calculated as $2 \times 2 = 4$.

We also see that two heads in a row is one of four equally probable combinations, so its probability is $\frac{1}{4}$. (Tails-tails, naturally, has the same probability.) Heads *and* tails, however, can occur in two ways (*H-T* or *T-H*), and its chances are therefore two out of four, or ½.

Tossing a coin three times, we have eight possible sequences ($2 \times 2 \times 2$, or 2^3). Of the eight, only one is three heads in a row; this probability, then, is $1/2^3$, as against $1/2^2$ for two heads in a row. And so it goes as the number of throws is increased: the probability of throwing any number (*H*) of heads in a row is $1/2^H$. For ten heads in a row the probability is $1/2^{10}$—that is, the odds are 1,024 to one it will not happen.

In general, the probability of getting any particular sequence of results (say ten heads followed by ten tails) is $1/2^N$ with *N* standing for the total number of throws. Thus the odds on getting eleven heads in eleven throws are $1/2^{11}$. What are the odds on ten heads followed by tails on the eleventh try? Exactly the same: $1/2^N$, or $1/2^{11}$. This little equation shows why it is hard to make money by laying odds against a continuation of a run of luck.

The formula amounts to saying that if *P* is the probability of one event taking place, and *Q* is the probability of another independent event, then the probability of *both* things happening together is the product *PQ*.

ᜒᜒᜒ THE RANDOM WALK

Now this kind of reasoning and the mathematical rules we have stated become very useful whenever we consider any phenomenon of nature involving a large number of events. A classic example is the diffusion of molecules in a gas or liquid.

Suppose we blow a puff of yellow gas into a container of colorless gas, or put a drop of blue ink in a glass of water. How will the colored molecules behave? To simplify the situation, let's fix our attention on a single molecule and assume it may move with equal probability either to the left or to the right (as if it were a coin falling heads or tails).

The molecule keeps colliding with other molecules, and each time it is knocked to the right or left. (Each collision corresponds to the toss of a coin.) After N collisions, where will the molecule be?

On the average, such a molecule should be just about where it started, because it is knocked back and forth—to the right about as often as to the left. There is a certain definite probability, however, that it will have taken more steps to one side than to the other, just as in 1,000 tosses of a coin you would be very unlikely to get exactly 500 heads and 500 tails. So the molecule moves through the gas or liquid in what is called a "random walk."

After a time—a fairly short time, because all the molecules are milling around rapidly—the random walks of the molecules in the puff of yellow gas or the drop of blue ink will spread them all around and mix them thoroughly throughout the container.

~~~~ FREQUENCY DISTRIBUTIONS

The theory of probability enables us to predict what might be the outcome of situations where chance controls the results. Here we come to the heart of the nature of observation and experimentation in science. Measurements are never perfect, nor are the conditions of an experiment ever perfectly controlled. There are unavoidable variations in results each time we perform a given experiment. Therefore we must have some way of deciding whether these variations are due to the errors in the measurement, or whether they are caused by real random variables in the thing we are measuring.

In the case of coin-tossing, we can calculate the chance of getting any given number of heads out of a certain number of throws (using for this purpose the formulas of permutations and combinations). We assume that the results are determined strictly by chance. If this is so, the most likely single result in any test of 1,000 tosses is 500 heads and 500 tails. But many other results are possible, ranging all the way from 1,000 heads in a row to 1,000 tails. The highest probabilities, however, will be around the 500:500 ratio. If we plot a curve giving the mathematical probabilities of all the possible outcomes, we get the bell-shaped form shown in Figure 22.

This famous curve is known by various names, most often as the "normal distribution curve" or the "Gaussian distribution." It depicts an ideal situation: the perfect operation of chance. A curve like this is obtained when you plot the number of people grouped according to their height in a normal population. The curve shows a spread, or distribution, around some average height. Of course, no real distribution matches this ideal curve exactly, but it serves as a standard for comparison.

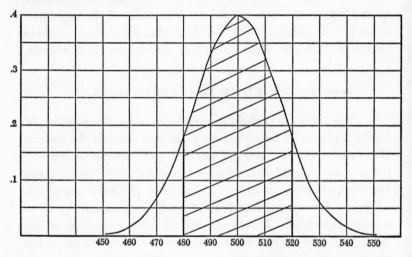

FIGURE 22. The normal distribution curve (*e.g.*, for 1,000 throws of a coin).

The curve here is a mathematical statement of the assumption that tosses of a coin will fall strictly according to chance. Just as you might test any hypothesis by experiments, you may sit down and start tossing coins to see whether your results agree with this curve. Each time you complete a test of 1,000 tosses, you mark down how many heads turned up. When you have finished numerous tests, you find out how many times you came up with 500 heads, how many times you got 501 heads, and so on through the entire range. You use these numbers to plot a curve, which you then compare with the normal distribution curve obtained from theory.

If you do *not* get something close to the normal distribution with a large number of tests, you can conclude that the coin is not falling according to chance. Some factor is causing one side of the coin to come up more often than the other. In other words, the hypothesis you are testing turns out to be wrong.

Very often you do not want to know the probability of coming up with *exactly* 500 heads (for that probability will be rather small). Instead, you would like to know the probability that in a thousand throws the number of heads will fall within a reasonable range—say between 480 and 520 heads. The theory allows you to calculate this readily, and this is a very useful bit of information—not because tossing coins is so important, but because the same mathematics is used in many situations where chance is involved.

In any experiment where you measure or count something repeatedly, you can describe the results by means of a *frequency distribution* curve. (The normal distribution described above is one kind of frequency distribution.) For example, a plot of the number of children getting various grades in an exam is a very common frequency distribution. In physics, an experimenter will plot in this form the number of gamma rays emitted from a radioactive source per second, for this is found to fluctuate from one second to the next. The number of cosmic-ray particles bombarding a certain area of the earth per day will follow such a curve. Such curves usually take the shape of a normal distribution. Others are asymmetrical, or "skewed," as the statisticians say. For instance, the distribution of family incomes in the United States is bunched at the lower end, with a peak at about $5,000, but has a long tail extending all the way up to millions of dollars a year.

A distribution curve conveys far more information than a bare average. To say that the average person does this or that has almost no meaning, for it gives no hint about the tremendous variety of things people actually do. When we say, "The average man in Centerville is a Republican with 2.36 children and a salary of $5,395 per year," we are concealing the broad range of political opinions in the city's population and the fact that some people have no children while others have ten. A distribution curve can portray the city's people far more accurately and meaningfully. The ability to think in terms of distribution curves is an important asset, not only in science but also in everyday life.

The normal distribution curve is characteristic of all events that seem to occur in a purely random manner: the flipping of coins, the emission of gamma rays from a radioactive source, the number of babies born in the United States at a given hour of the day, and so on. Yet none of the laws of nature we have discussed allows for anything happening by chance. Einstein liked to say that he could not believe God played dice with the universe. According to his deterministic point of view, if we knew exactly how all the natural forces acted on a coin at each toss, we should be able to predict how it was going to land.

Why, then, do we assume that the coin falls according to chance? The reason is that the combination of forces acting on it is highly variable and unpredictable. Your fingers never flip the coin exactly the same way from one toss to the next. Each time the toss is influenced by differences in the nerve impulses coming from the brain and changes in muscle tension, as well as many other influences, all acting independently. The result is that the coin falls *as if* at random.

This, indeed, is a basic principle of nature: Whenever an event is subject to a great many independent influences, it occurs *as if* according to chance. Even when we measure something perfectly constant, such as the speed of light, we find that each time the measurement is slightly different, because tiny and unavoidable imperfections in our measuring apparatus introduce random variations. Of course, in this case the range of differences in the measurements (that is, the width of the distribution curve) is very, very small.

PROBABILITIES AND UNCERTAINTIES

Naturally, we want to know what margin of error we should expect in any particular measurement or experiment. One way of describing this error is the *standard deviation*. For instance, the average value we get for the speed of light with the best techniques is 299,793 kilometers per second, and the standard deviation from that figure is 0.3 of a kilometer per second. That represents the degree of uncertainty in our measurements. Two-thirds of all the measurements are expected to fall within this range around the average.

The standard deviation will depend, of course, on the number of measurements or tests you make: the more tests, the smaller the standard deviation (conventionally symbolized by σ—the Greek sigma). In the coin-flipping game, the standard deviation is found to be:

$$\sigma = \tfrac{1}{2}\sqrt{N}$$

This means that if you toss N coins, there is a probability of about 0.66 that the number of heads will fall somewhere within the range $\tfrac{1}{2}N - \sigma$ to $\tfrac{1}{2}N + \sigma$. (Recall that $\tfrac{1}{2}N$ is the most probable number of heads.) The total spread, defined in this way, is just twice the standard deviation, or $2\sigma = \sqrt{N}$.

For example, if you toss 1,000 coins, there is a two-out-of-three chance that the number of heads turning up will be greater than 484 and less than 516, because $\sqrt{N}$ is about 32. You can predict, then, that in any such test the odds are two to one you will get between 484 and 516 heads.

You can make your prediction safer by widening the spread; for instance, if you say that the number of heads will fall between 474 and 526, the probability of winning your bet is raised to 90 per cent. This spread is called the *90 per cent confidence range*. The formula for finding this range for any number of throws (N) is $1.65\sqrt{N}$.

What we are usually more concerned about in science, however, is the size of our probable error *in proportion to what we are measuring*. For instance, if we are ten miles off in our measurement of the diameter of the earth, this is a far bigger error, percentagewise, than a ten-mile mismeasurement of the diameter of the earth's orbit around the sun. In mixing chemicals, an error of one gram in 100,000 may be insignificant, but an error of one gram in ten grams could be catastrophic.

In the case of coin-throwing, we calculate the proportional uncertainty as the ratio of the range of error ($1.65 \sqrt{N}$) to a perfect result ($\frac{1}{2} N$), multiplying this ratio by 100 to make it a percentage:

$$Percentage\ uncertainty = \frac{1.65 \sqrt{N} \times 100}{\frac{1}{2} N}$$

$$= \frac{330}{\sqrt{N}}$$

We have seen that for 1,000 throws there is a 90 per cent probability of getting between 474 and 526 heads. The *percentage uncertainty* for 1,000 throws, therefore, is:

$$\frac{330}{\sqrt{1000}} = \frac{330}{31.6} = 10.4\%$$

If the number of throws is increased to 10,000, the percentage uncertainty becomes:

$$\frac{330}{\sqrt{10,000}} = \frac{330}{100} = 3.3\%$$

By making a larger number of throws, we have improved the accuracy of the prediction on a percentage basis. Of course, that is what common sense would lead us to expect. In fact, this is the way we tend to judge the reliability of a public-opinion poll: the bigger the sample of the population polled, the more accurate we expect the results to be. But take note of the pitfalls. It does no good to increase the size of the sample unless the sample is a truly representative cross-section of the entire population. Furthermore, before you bet on an election on the basis of what the pollsters predict, it would be wise to find out the margin of uncertainty in their predictions. Unfortunately, the pollsters do not usually publish this figure (*i.e.*, the confidence range).

⚡ PREDICTIONS IN SCIENCE

We are now in a position to appreciate the important role that the rules of probability play in investigations of the laws of science. As we have seen, in many situations, especially when we come to atomic particles, it is impossible to predict how a single individual will behave: all we can do is foretell the *average* behavior of a group.

This can be illustrated with a familiar example. Out of the United States population, about 300 persons are killed each day in auto accidents. Although we can say confidently that the toll will be close to that figure as an average, no one can possibly predict which 300 individuals in the population will be the victims.

That is exactly the situation we have when we observe a collection of radioactive atoms—say radium atoms. Looking at any one atom, there is no way of telling precisely when it will break down and give off a gamma ray. We cannot even tell the exact number of the atoms in the group which will break down. Experiment tells us what the average number per second will be.

The number of gamma rays we actually count depends on the number of atoms emitting gamma rays, on the distance between the atoms and the counter, on the efficiency of the counter, and on the duration of the experiment. If we get 100 counts in one second, we may say that there is a 90 per cent probability the average per second under the same conditions will be within the range between 83 and 117, or 100 plus or minus 17. We can refine this estimate ten-fold by counting for 100 seconds instead of one second; if we record 10,000 counts in 100 seconds, our 90 per cent confidence range is narrowed to 100 plus or minus 1.65 *per second*. By counting for 10,000 seconds we could get another ten-fold improvement in precision. Improvements can also be obtained by increasing the efficiency of the counter and by moving it closer to the radioactive source.

There is a limit to the possible precision of any measuring device. With the most delicate balance we can make, we may never get exactly the same reading twice in a row of the weight of a piece of platinum. We can repeat the measurement as often as we like to narrow the probability of error, but there comes a point where the accuracy can be increased no more. Air molecules bombarding the balance will make it fluctuate; if we remove the air, there will still be other sources of error, such as the gravity of the moon, the pressure of the light required to read the balance, and other minute perturbations. All these influences conspire to give a tiny uncertainty to our prediction of what the metal will weigh the next time we weigh it.

Surely there must be some predictions we can make with absolute confidence. According to our fundamental laws, energy must always be conserved. The universe will exist tomorrow; could anybody possibly doubt that?

Predictions like these seem 100 per cent safe, but they depend on the assumption that the laws of nature will be the same tomorrow as they were yesterday, which we cannot prove. The eminent scientist and philosopher Hans Reichenbach argues that even the most basic laws are simply *probability statements*—that is, predictions that something will happen with a very high degree of probability. Nevertheless, this need not bother us particularly: you could bet a million dollars that momentum will be conserved tomorrow with very little fear of losing.

~~~~ THE LAWS OF THERMODYNAMICS

Our reflections on probability lead us to an extremely interesting case of conservation that we have not yet considered. Everybody knows that, between two bodies at different temperatures, heat always flows from the hotter body to the cooler one, never from the cooler to the hotter. The temperature of a body depends on the average kinetic energy of its molecules. What prevents kinetic energy from moving from a cool body to a warmer one?

We are dealing here with the motion of molecules. We know that all motions are completely *reversible:* the earth would have exactly the same orbit around the sun if it traveled in the opposite direction; two colliding molecules would trace out exactly the same paths if their before-and-after directions were reversed. There are no one-way streets under the laws of motion; all traffic is allowed to travel in either direction. Therefore, when we think of the molecules in a gas, for example, we should expect all their motions to be reversible. Why, then, should a net kinetic energy be transferred in one direction and not the other?

Well, think of a container of gas divided into two compartments, A and B. The gas in A is hotter, meaning that its molecules are moving faster, on the average, than those in B. We now open a hole in the partition and allow the two gases to mix. Molecules will move through the hole in both directions. As A's faster molecules collide with B's slower molecules, the fast molecules tend to be slowed down and the slow ones to be speeded up. The intermingling and sharing of energies eventually equalizes the temperature in the two compartments at a level somewhere between the two original temperatures.

Now a reversal of this process—heat flowing back to A although it is not cooler than B—would require that those molecules in both compartments which happen to be faster should collect again in A, while the slower molecules segregate themselves in B. What is to prevent this? Nothing but the probabilities of the situation.

When you shuffle a new deck of cards, the suits gradually get mixed and the arrangement becomes more and more random. True, it is possible that after repeated shuffling you might deal four perfect hands around the table—each consisting of the 13 cards of one suit. But the extreme rarity of this event indicates how highly improbable it is.

So it is with molecules of gas in a box, except that the improbability is more extreme because there are billions upon billions of molecules.

The probability concept tells us something else. Suppose our box starts out with all the molecules in one compartment and none at all (a vacuum) in the other. If we open a hole in the partition, the molecules will quickly distribute themselves uniformly throughout the volume of the two compartments. Thereafter, the probability that all the molecules will collect again in compartment A by chance and leave B empty is so small that for all practical purposes we can say it will never happen. In fact, it is extremely unlikely that there will ever be any appreciable difference between the numbers of molecules in the two compartments, if their volumes are equal.

The important point here is that after the molecules are mixed we have less information about each molecule than we had before we opened the hole. Before, we knew that we could find any given molecule in compartment A; now it may be in either A or B. Likewise, in the case of the two compartments at different temperatures, we knew that if we were looking for a fast molecule, we had a better chance of finding it in compartment A; when we let the contents of the two compartments mix, the situation became more disorganized and we were less well informed than before.

This is true of all organized systems that are free to mix or change. We can state the rule as a fundamental law of nature: *In a closed system, there is a tendency for organization to change into disorganization, or for the amount of information available about the system to become smaller as time goes on.*

There is a short name for this property—*entropy*. The less we know about a situation (that is, the more disorganized it is), the higher is the entropy. Entropy, therefore, is a measure of our ignorance about a system. And in the physical universe, the tendency is for the entropy to increase. Every time we burn fuel for heat, every day that the stars shine and emit heat, the universe runs downhill toward greater entropy.

It was a German physicist, Rudolf Clausius, who coined the word entropy and also first stated the rule that heat cannot be transferred from a cold body to a warmer body without the aid of some outside source of energy. That rule became known as the second law of thermodynamics, one of the most basic laws of nature. (What is the first law of thermodynamics? Why that is simply the law of conservation of energy under a fancy name.)

The second law of thermodynamics governs all our devices for converting energy into work, from engines to refrigerators. Every machine that converts heat into mechanical energy must have two essentials: a hot place and a cold place. In a steam engine the hot place is the boiler, and the cold place is the condenser. In a gasoline engine the hot place is the cylinder, and the cold place is the exhaust.

The second law explains why the dream of drawing heat from the oceans or the atmosphere remains only a dream—sometimes called a perpetual-motion illusion of the second kind (after the second law). To take heat out of the ocean you would have to pump it out in some manner, which would require more energy than you got in return. We might, however, use the difference in temperature between the warm surface and the cold bottom of the ocean. Wherever there is a natural *difference* in temperature, some of the heat may be put to work as it flows from the hot region to the cold.

The interesting thing about the second law of thermodynamics is the fact that it arises from the laws of chance. We do not say that it is impossible for heat to go uphill or for mixtures to unmix; we simply say that the improbability of these events is so fantastically great that they cannot be expected to happen in the many billions of years of the earth's history.

∿∿∿ THE DIRECTION OF TIME

Perhaps the most fascinating aspect of the laws of chance has to do with the question of the "direction" of time. What enables us to distinguish between the past and the future? What is there about two events that allows us to say one comes "after" the other?

As we have pointed out, there are many types of situation where there is really no difference between past and future. If you say the earth travels around the sun in the clockwise direction, this is no different from saying it moves in the counterclockwise direction: in both cases its path will be exactly the same. Backward or forward, the earth would give us the same cycle of seasons. Whenever motions or events are perfectly reversible, we cannot distinguish between a "forward" or "backward" direction of time.

On the other hand, all irreversible events do have a direction. When you put a drop of ink in a glass of water, there is a before and after: the ink mixes with the water and it is extremely unlikely that it will ever unmix, even if you wait millions of years. When you burn a piece of wood, it is very improbable that the wood will later unburn. A living body ages; the chances that it will ever grow younger are infinitesimal.

What distinguishes such situations from the motion of the earth is the fact that we are dealing not with one body but with billions and billions of atoms, all reacting with one another in a way that makes it much more probable for the reactions to go in one direction than in the other. Our awareness of these irreversible changes provides us with signposts facing from past to future. Unmixed comes before mixed. Unburned comes before burned. This awareness arises from the laws of probability, not from any absolute, hard-and-fast law which says: THIS WAY TO THE FUTURE.

These arguments are not easy to accept. You may say, for instance, that when you drop a ball and it bounces back to your hand, there is no question that the drop came before the bounce.

Well, let us see. If the ball is perfectly elastic, it will come back up to the height from which you dropped it. Suppose we make photographs just as the ball leaves your hand and just as it is returning to your hand (see Figure 23). To another observer

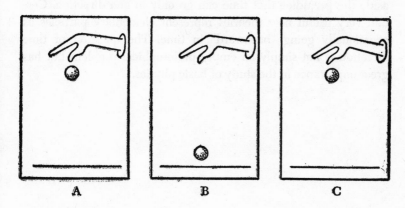

FIGURE 23. Positions in the fall and rebound of a perfectly elastic ball.

there is no difference at all between these pictures. You say you *know* that you dropped the ball *before* it hit the ground. But this knowledge is itself the result of irreversible actions in your brain. As far as the objective observer is concerned, it doesn't make a particle of difference whether the downward or the upward motion of the ball came first. He sees the motions as completely symmetrical.

However, if the ball is not perfectly elastic, it will not come back all the way to your hand on the rebound. Now we can agree with you that there is no question the drop came before the bounce. The situation is not symmetrical, and the reason is that irreversible reactions intervened. When the ball struck the ground, some of its kinetic energy was converted into heat (random motion of the molecules inside the ball), and the entropy therefore increased.

Thus the example confirms the fact that our awareness of the direction of time is caused by the action of irreversible processes, and these are irreversible because of the operation of the laws of chance.

Scientists now working in the more advanced and esoteric realms of modern physics are finding that it is convenient to lay aside the prejudice that time can go only in one direction. Certain very useful new theories represent elementary particles as occasionally going "backward" in time. The question of time direction is not simply an empty philosophical problem but has great importance in the study of basic physics.

CHAPTER 10

~~~~~~~~~~~~~~~~~~~~~~~~

The Laws of Quantum Physics

~~~~~~~~

When James Clerk Maxwell discovered the electromagnetic nature of light (just a century ago, in the 1860s), physics began to look like a finished structure. His theory explained the connection between electricity and magnetism. It apparently settled the age-old argument over whether light consisted of waves or particles—he showed that it definitely had the nature of waves. And his idea that any disturbances of the electromagnetic field propagated as waves with the same speed as light proved to be a great unifying principle.

Maxwell's theory was brilliantly confirmed in 1887 by Heinrich Hertz. His experiments produced radio waves—previously unknown but predicted by the theory—and showed that they did indeed travel with the speed of light. With this proof of the Maxwellian concepts, physicists felt that they were at last in a position to form a simple and orderly picture of the physical universe. It seemed that all the basic laws of nature had been discovered, and it was now possible to understand the whole scheme of things.

But nature refused to remain simple and understandable. Within just a few years after Hertz put the roof on Maxwell's system the whole structure of physics began to fall apart. In quick succession physical experimenters came upon a series of mystifying discoveries—peculiarities of light radiated from solid bodies, X-rays, radioactivity, the nucleus of the atom, and the photoelectric effect—none of which could be explained by Maxwell's equations. Perhaps the most revolutionary of these discoveries was the photoelectric effect, for to explain it you had to think of light as being composed of a stream of particles, rather than waves. Ironically, it was Hertz who first detected this effect, though he did not know what it meant.

The next 30 years became a period of turmoil in physics. The investigators entered a strange new world which became known as the realm of quantum physics. In this new realm our familiar images disappear. It becomes impossible to make a clear-cut distinction between waves and particles. We can no longer speak of sharply defined bodies and locate them in a definite place; if we must picture elementary particles, we may think of them as tiny patches of fog, located not at a particular point, but only within a region of space.

Many of the ideas in quantum physics can be understood only as mathematical abstractions. But this need not bother us too much, because it is possible to understand the main concepts and much of the reasoning behind them without going into such higher mathematics.

Let us start with Hertz's experiments. He generated his radio waves with a simple apparatus (see Figure 24). It consisted of an induction coil with a gap, across which crackled a spark discharge produced by the high-frequency electric current. This discharge emitted radio waves, and Hertz picked them up some distance away with a loop of wire which was tuned to the wavelength: the radio energy picked up by the loop caused sparks to jump across a gap in the wire.

Hertz happened to notice that when the receiving loop was exposed to the light of the sparks in the transmitter, the receiver produced an unusually big output of sparks; this effect stopped when he put a screen or sheet of glass between the transmitter and the receiver. He decided, correctly, that the metal receiving loop was affected in some way by ultraviolet light (which does

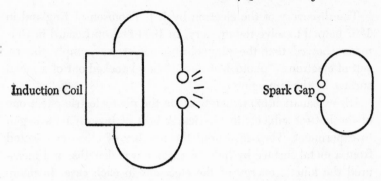

FIGURE 24. Hertz's apparatus for generating and detecting radio waves.

not go through glass) so that it sparked more easily. Hertz reported this as a curious fact in a paper entitled "An Effect of Ultraviolet Light upon the Electrical Discharge." Having thus done his duty to his fellow physicists, he washed his hands of the observation and concentrated on his primary investigation of the electromagnetic waves. (Which was really a proper thing to do.)

The phenomenon came to be known later as the *photoelectric effect* (meaning electricity produced by light). A number of other scientists fastened onto this odd effect as something worth investigating. In 1888 Wilhelm Hallwachs, a German physicist, reported that when a polished zinc plate was struck by ultraviolet light, the plate acquired a small amount of positive charge. Another way of putting it would be to say that it lost negative charge. (This means, of course, that it lost electrons, but the existence of the electron was not known at that time.) It was soon discovered that the photoelectric effect could be produced more easily in some metals than in others, and that the alkali metals (sodium, potassium, rubidium, cesium) were sensitive to visible light as well as to ultraviolet. Most remarkably, it was found that the impact of ultraviolet light could *cause a current to flow* between two electrodes in a tube from which most of the air was evacuated.

The discovery of the electron by J. J. Thomson of England in 1897 helped to solve the mystery. In 1900 Philipp Lenard in Germany showed that the photoelectric effect was simply the result of electrons ("photoelectrons") being knocked out of a metal surface by the impinging light.

His explanation immediately made the photoelectric effect one of the hottest subjects in physics. A host of investigators began to experiment. They measured the number of electrons ejected from a metal surface by light of various wavelengths, and measured the kinetic energy of the electrons in each case. In many different ways, they tried to find out how the photoelectric effect was related to the nature of the light.

Their findings finally boiled down to two general rules, one of which was a shocking surprise. In the first place, it turned out that the *number* of electrons knocked out of the metal by light of a given wavelength always depended on the intensity (*i.e.*, the amount) of the light. This, of course, was to be expected: the stronger the light beam, the greater should be its effect. But the second finding was that the *energy* carried by each ejected electron depended only on the frequency (or wavelength) of the light, not at all on its intensity! You could make the beam as intense as you liked, and the electrons still came out with the same kinetic energy.

This was a complete puzzle. How did it happen that the energy input represented by the intensity of the light added nothing to the energy of the electrons? And in what way did the *frequency* of the light determine the electron's energy?

Again it was Albert Einstein who solved the puzzle. This time the groundwork for his solution was laid by the German physicist Max Planck.

Planck had studied a paradox that had to do with radiation from the famous "black body" of physical theory (a body that would completely absorb all the electromagnetic radiation striking it). According to the then current interpretations of the wave nature of light when a black body is heated so that it is incandescent, it should radiate energy over a broad spectrum of wavelengths. Unfortunately, this calculation showed that a body heated to a temperature of a few hundred degrees should radiate mainly ultraviolet rays (and in infinite amount!). Of course, it does no such thing; a body at a few hundred degrees' temperature radiates mostly infrared rays (*i.e.*, heat).

Planck puzzled over this contradiction and finally decided that the only way to explain it was to suppose that the energy radiated from the body was in the form of small, separate bundles, not continuous waves. He called these units of energy *quanta*. For each radiation frequency, the unit of energy was different: the higher the frequency, the larger the quantum. He wrote the relation in this form:

$$E = h\nu$$

E stands for the energy of the quantum; ν (the Greek nu) is the symbol for frequency; and h is a number, a constant of proportionality, which relates the units of energy to the units of frequency. As every student of physics knows, h is now called *Planck's constant*. By measuring the heat radiated from solid bodies, Planck found that the value of h was about 6.6×10^{-27} erg-seconds.

It was Planck's quantum theory that gave Einstein the clue to the photoelectric effect. Einstein reasoned: if a body emits radiation in the form of quanta, then it must absorb radiation in the same form. Suppose a quantum of light striking a metal surface is absorbed by an electron. The energized electron will then jump out of the metal. Part of the quantum of light energy will have gone into freeing the electron from the solid, and the rest will be carried off by the electron as its kinetic energy. That is, the total energy of the quantum can be calculated as the energy of the emitted electron plus the energy required to get the electron out of the metal surface.

Now the size of the quantum, as Planck had shown, depends on the frequency of the light. At low frequencies (*e.g.*, red light) the quantum of energy is not sufficient even to free an electron, and so this light shows no photoelectric effect. At somewhat higher frequencies, the quantum is just barely enough to release an electron, and in that case the emitted electron has little or no kinetic energy. At still higher frequencies (toward the blue portion of the spectrum of visible light and through the ultraviolet frequencies and beyond) the quantum provides enough energy not only to knock out the electron but also to give it considerable kinetic energy. That is why the energy of photoelectrons depends on the frequency of the light.

This interpretation also explained why the *number* of electrons knocked out depends on the intensity of the light beam. The greater the amount of light, the more quanta there are striking the metal, which means that more electrons will be energized.

Einstein's theory accounted for all the results the investigators had observed in their experiments on the photoelectric effect. It had been impossible to explain how energy in the form of waves could be concentrated enough to energize single electrons. But if you thought of light as coming in little packets, or quanta, then the whole process became understandable. The new theory pictured light as consisting of tiny, weightless particles, and these came to be called *photons*. (The name "photon" comes from the Greek word for light, but in modern physics it is applied to the units of all forms of electromagnetic radiation, not only visible light. We can speak of photons of heat, of radio energy, of X-rays, and so on.)

Einstein published his theory of photons and the photoelectric effect in 1905. That was a big year for him, as we have seen; it was the same year in which he announced the special theory of relativity. Curiously, when he received the Nobel Prize in 1921, the award was made not for his relativity theory but for his explanation of the photoelectric effect.

At the time, the concept of the photon created as great a stir in the world of physics as did relativity. It wrapped the nature of light in mystery again. There was plenty of unshakable evidence that light acted like waves. Yet here was equally firm evidence that it behaved like particles. The wave-particle paradox became one of the deepest problems in physics, and it has absorbed the attention of theoretical physicists ever since.

~~~~ QUANTA

Let us look further into the meaning of the photon. Because it is pictured as a little bundle of energy, there is a temptation to suppose that it can be reduced to a fundamental unit of energy, just as there is an ultimate unit of electric charge, represented by the electron. This would mean that each photon would have one, two, or three, or some other whole number of units of energy, since there is no such thing as a fraction of a unit (not in electric charge, anyway). The fact of the matter, however, is that photons have a continuous range of sizes, for their sizes are determined by the frequencies of the continuous spectrum of radiation.

In other words, photons are indeed bundles of energy, but these bundles come in all sizes.

The range of sizes is tremendous. We can get some idea of the range if we examine the energies of photons representing three widely separated portions of the radiation spectrum—radio (at the frequency of one megacycle), green light, and X-rays. How many photons of each of these does it take to carry a given amount of energy?

Let us say the amount of energy to be used as our yardstick is one erg per second passing through a hole of one square centimeter area a meter away from the source. (This is roughly the amount of energy that would come from a one-watt light bulb at that distance.)

The table below gives the comparative energies of the three photons. The information bearing on our experiment is in the last column. It shows that when one erg of energy in the form of radio waves passes through the hole, this is equivalent to 1.5×10^{20} (150 billion billion) photons per second. This means, of course, that each radio photon carries an exceedingly small

THE ENERGY OF A PHOTON

FREQUENCY	WAVELENGTH	ENERGY PER PHOTON		No. OF PHOTONS PER CM.^{2} PER SEC.
		Ergs	*Electron-volts*	
1 megacycle (radio waves)	300 meters	6.5×10^{-21}	4×10^{-9}	1.5×10^{20}
6×10^{14} (green light)	5×10^{-5} cm.	3.9×10^{-12}	2.5	2.5×10^{11}
2.4×10^{20} (X-rays)	1.2×10^{-10} cm.	1.6×10^{-6}	1 million	6.25×10^5

amount of energy—much, much less than a photon of light and still less compared with a photon of the X-ray frequency.

The radio photons come along at intervals of less than a billionth of a billionth of a second. No known counter could count particles arriving at that rapid rate. The photons, in other words, cannot be separated. That is why a beam of radio waves seems to be a continuous flow of energy. To the best of our observation, radio waves behave only like waves; we have no way of resolving them into particles.

The photons of light are a different matter, as the table shows. Each photon of green light carries 2.5 electron-volts of energy. It still takes 250 billion photons per second to deliver one erg per second per square centimeter, and the flow of photons is too fast to count by any ordinary means. But if the light is passed through a small pinhole, a good fast counter could detect individual photons.

The photons of light are in a borderland: they can be observed behaving like particles (through the photoelectric effect) and also like waves (through diffraction gratings which cause them to produce the typical interference patterns of waves).

When we come to the X-rays, the photon is easily detectable as a particle. Arriving at the rate of about 625,000 per second per square centimeter, the photons can be counted without difficulty by a fast scintillation counter (a block of material that gives off a tiny light flash as each particle hits it). Each X-ray photon of the frequency in the table above carries one million electron-volts of energy—millions of billions of times more than a long-wave radio photon and hundreds of thousands of times more than a photon of visible light. X-rays can pass through matter because their wavelength is much shorter than the diameter of an atom. This is why they can be used to photograph the inside of a metal object or to kill cancer cells deep in the body.

〰〰 PROPERTIES OF THE PHOTON

The photon is often pictured as a "wave packet"—a bunch of waves traveling through space. Wave packets are not uncommon in everyday experience. You produce a packet of sound waves when you tap a drum or crack a whip. If you turn a flashlight on and off rapidly, you produce a train of light waves that has a beginning and an end. This is a wave packet of a sort, although it contains many photons. When a single atom emits light, it is like a flashlight that is turned on and off so rapidly that only a single photon comes out. This wave packet cannot be subdivided into smaller packets.

The mass of a photon is related to its energy by the familiar formula $E = mc^2$. This energy, in turn, is related to the frequency of the wave by Planck's formula: $E = h\nu$. Thus the photon mass is related to the frequency by the following equation:

$$m = \frac{E}{c^2} = \frac{h\nu}{c^2}$$

Since the frequency (ν) is equal to the speed of light (c) divided by the wavelength (λ, or lambda), we can relate the mass of the photon to the wavelength:

$$m = \frac{h}{c^2} \cdot \frac{c}{\lambda} = \frac{h}{c\lambda}$$

The momentum of a photon, like that of any particle, is its mass multiplied by its velocity. But the interesting thing about a photon is that it can have only one velocity—the speed of light. This is one of the basic things that make a photon different from the other elementary particles. All the other particles (except the neutrino) have a definite rest-mass and can travel at any speed up to but not including the speed of light. The photon (like the neutrino) has no rest-mass and can travel only at the speed of light. Its mass, then, comes entirely from its kinetic energy, mc^2. Since the velocity of the photon is always c, the momentum (p) can be written:

$$p = mc = \frac{E}{c} = \frac{h\nu}{c} = \frac{h}{\lambda}$$

This has been an extremely important equation in the study of elementary particles. With its help, the physicist Arthur Holly Compton was able to show in 1923 that a photon behaved just like a solid body, obeying the law of conservation of momentum. Compton observed that after X-rays of a certain wavelength were scattered from various materials, some of the scattered X-rays had an increased wavelength. There was no possible way of explaining how scattering could change the length of a wave if one thought of it simply as a wave. Compton conceived the bold idea that the X-ray photons had collided with electrons in just the same way that billiard balls collide!

The picture of the Compton effect is this: The X-ray photon, slamming into the solid with an energy of a million electron-volts, collides with an electron orbiting around its nucleus and knocks it completely out of the atom. The photon recoils at some angle, while the electron goes off at another angle. Since the photon has given up some of its energy to the electron, the photon must drop to a lower frequency, because we know that the smaller the energy, the lower the frequency (or the longer the wavelength). The change of frequency that Compton observed agreed with calculations of what was to be expected on the basis of the conservation of momentum and energy.

Notice that this phenomenon is quite different from the photo-electric effect. In the latter, the photon disappears completely, giving up almost all its energy to the electron, whereas in the Compton effect the photon simply makes an elastic collision with the electron.

Both the photoelectric effect and the Compton effect are very useful for detecting and measuring X-rays; in fact, they are the basis of X-ray detection by Geiger counters, scintillation counters, and photographic films. But visible and ultraviolet light do not produce a Compton effect: their wavelengths are so much larger than the diameter of the atom that their photons do not enter into Compton collisions with electrons.

～～ THE SIZE OF A PHOTON

When we talk about the size of a photon, exactly what do we mean? It is hard to say—exactly. A wave packet inevitably has fuzzy edges (see Figure 25). Furthermore, the wavelength connected with a packet of waves also is rather indefinite. In order to put a beginning and an end on the wave train, you have to put in "sidebands" of different wavelengths. Every radio ham knows what this means. To transmit the dots and dashes of the Morse code by radio, you turn the transmitter rapidly on and off. The frequency carrying the message is called the "carrier frequency." When you chop the wave into dots and dashes, you automatically produce a narrow group of other frequencies (sidebands) on each side of the carrier.

Similarly, a photon of a certain frequency, which we can think of as a single dot being transmitted through space, must be accompanied by sidebands—frequencies both higher and lower than the carrier. The wave packet thus consists of a mixture of waves having different wavelengths and frequencies. If the packet is spread out broadly in space, then the sidebands are narrow. In other words, the bigger the spread in space, the

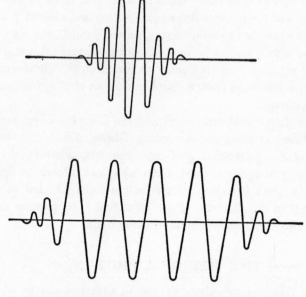

FIGURE 25. Wave packets—narrow and broad.

smaller the spread in frequencies. On the other hand, a very wide range of frequencies must be mixed together to produce a short wave packet consisting of only a few wavelets.

This is very similar to certain problems in radio communication. Consider, for example, an AM radio broadcasting station that has a bandwidth (or frequency spread) of 20,000 cycles (20 kilocycles) per second to transmit voice and music. We now ask: What is the shortest pulse of waves that can be transmitted by this station? The formula that has been found to apply is this: if W is the bandwidth available (in cycles per second), and T is the duration (in seconds) of the shortest pulse which can be transmitted, then

$$T = \frac{1}{2\pi W}$$

In the case being considered, the answer is $1/(2(10)^4 \times 2 \times 3.14)$, or about eight millionths of a second. This is the shortest-duration pulse the station can transmit. To broadcast a pulse one microsecond long, a station would need a bandwidth of 160 kilocycles (which is why television transmission requires such high frequencies).

At this point we encounter a strange situation. If there is a spread in frequency and wavelength, there must also be a spread in the energy and momentum of the photon. We can understand how a wave packet may be spread out over a region of space. But what does it mean to say that a photon has a range of energies or a spread in momentum?

This is a deep question, and it forces us to realize that up to now we have not really explained the meaning of the wave packet. To make the situation a little clearer, we try to visualize what happens when light strikes a photographic film. The photons produce black grains in the film after it is developed, and the more photons hit a given area, the darker that part of the film will become. Now suppose we have the light come through a narrow slit. It has been known for a long time that light passing through such a slit produces a pattern of light and dark stripes on a photographic film (see Figure 26). Before the discovery of the quantum, the effect was attributed to interference of the light waves with one another: that is, bright lines on the picture (dark on the negative) were supposed to represent places where the waves reinforced each other, and the undeveloped stripes places where they canceled each other.

This theory assumed that the waves carried a continuous flow of energy through the slit onto the film. But the odd fact is that the same effect is produced when photons come through the slit one at a time! We can arrange this by using a very weak source of light. What happens? We find that the photons land erratically, unpredictably, at various points on the film; yet in the end we get a pattern of light and dark stripes exactly like the one formed by a bountiful supply of light pouring through the slit. That is to say, single photons filing through the slit can still produce the interference effect.

We do not know what sort of path each photon follows; all we

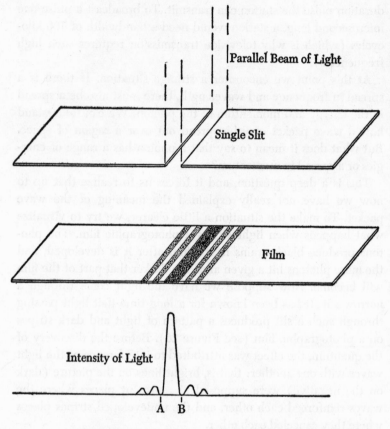

FIGURE 26. Diffraction of light by a slit. Most of the light falls in the stripe A-B, but the beam is spread out, and many photons form bands at the sides.

know is that they do not pass through the slit in a straight line. Some of the darkened grains are off to the side, out of the direct line of the light beam. The explanation we give is that each wave packet somehow spreads out after passing through the slit. It "interferes with itself." Then a photon represented by this wave packet suddenly transfers its energy to a grain of silver when it strikes the film.

What decides which grain will be chosen for blackening when

a certain photon passes through the slit? We have absolutely no idea. We can merely predict, from the theory of these wave packets (using the proper equations and the proper algebra), that the film will be darker along one strip and lighter along another strip. We can tell what a great many photons will do on the average, but we are powerless to predict exactly which grain will be darkened at any instant.

This is exactly the kind of situation we discussed in the chapter on probability. We are dealing with random events, and we can draw a distribution curve which shows how a large number of photons will behave. Although we cannot make absolute predictions, our mathematics allows us to predict the *probability* that a photon effect will be detected in any given spot on the film.

This leads us to say that a photon is represented by a *probability wave packet*. We can depict it as a shaded blob, denser in the center than around the edges (see Figure 27). Then we can

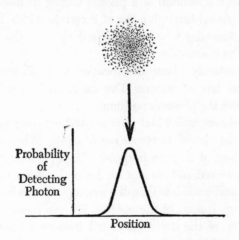

FIGURE 27. Diagram of a probability wave packet.

say: The intensity of the shading at a given spot in this picture represents the probability of finding the photon in that location. Where the shading is darkest, there is the greatest probability of locating the photon. When the blob hits a photographic emulsion, one of the silver grains located somewhere within the area covered by the wave packet will be blackened. The probability of this happening will be greatest where the shading of the packet is most intense.

The waves that make up the packet are sometimes called *probability waves*. We may think of the photon traveling through space as a particle following a path laid out for it by the probability waves.

The photon has been boiled down to a rather abstract, intangible thing. We are not permitted to inquire about its appearance, or about its precise path through space. In this it is like any other elementary particle. In dealing with these particles we can talk only about things that can be observed (directly or indirectly). We can observe the energy of a photon, its momentum, its approximate location, the strength of the electromagnetic fields connected with it, and a number of other properties. But we cannot pinpoint the location of a photon during its motion. We can say that it passed through a slit of a certain width, but we have no way of knowing whether it passed close to the edge of the slit or right in the middle.

This uncertainty about the location of a photon leads to a fundamental law of nature. The uncertainty applies to other things besides the photon's position.

We can detect individual photons and measure their energies only when they knock electrons out of atoms. When a large number of photons of a given frequency hit a piece of material, the electrons knocked out do not all have the same energy. Some have more and some less than the average. This is what we mean by the energy-spread of the photon. We can speak of its energy only in terms of the statistical distribution of a large number of photons, and this distribution of energies depends on the width of the wave packet (see Figure 28). The average energy of the electrons they knock out may be 100 electron-volts, with a standard deviation (spread) of 0.01 of an electron-volt on each side, which means that two out of three electrons will have energies

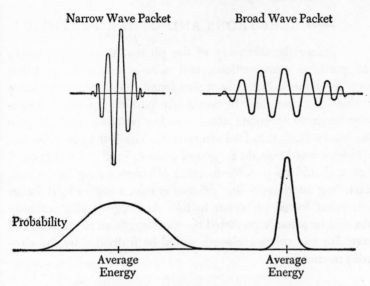

Narrow Wave Packet   Broad Wave Packet

Probability

Average Energy   Average Energy

Energy of Electron Knocked out of Atom by Photon

FIGURE 28. How the spread of energies of photoelectrons depends on the width of the wave packet.

in the range between 99.99 and 100.01 electron-volts. There is no way of predicting the exact amount of energy that any one photon in the beam will give to an electron. Putting it conversely, there is no way of selecting one photon with an exactly known energy.

Therefore we must say that there is an uncertainty in the energy of the photon. As we have seen, there is also an uncertainty in the position of the photon. Thus we are faced with the fact that we cannot measure the energy and position of a photon with perfect accuracy, no matter how we try. This uncertainty has nothing to do with imperfections in the measuring equipment; it is the unavoidable result of the fact that the wave packet itself has a spread in position, energy, and momentum.

Photons are not the only thing subject to uncertainty, as we discover when we go on to study other elementary particles.

~~~~ ELECTRONS AND OTHER PARTICLES

Before the discovery of the photon, waves were waves and particles were particles, and nobody supposed the twain could ever meet. But after it was found that light waves led a double life, sometimes behaving like particles, physicists naturally began to speculate about whether particles might behave like waves (scientists love symmetry!). The first to propose this wild idea was Louis de Broglie of France. In 1924 he suggested that it should be possible to catch electrons acting like waves, producing interference and diffraction effects just as light waves did. What forced physicists to take de Broglie's idea seriously was that he actually predicted the *wavelength* an electron should have! He said this wavelength would be *h* divided by the electron's momentum:

$$\lambda = \frac{h}{mv}$$

This equation, of course, is the same as the one that gives the wavelength associated with a photon, except that the photon's momentum is *mc* instead of *mv*.

De Broglie's formula made it possible to test his prediction by experiment. Sure enough, three years after his idea was published, two scientists at the Bell Telephone Laboratories in New York found he was right. C. J. Davisson and L. H. Germer shot a beam of electrons at a nickel crystal; the rows of atoms in the crystal served as a diffraction grating, and the electrons scattered by this grating fell on a screen in an interference pattern very much like the one produced by photons. Only waves could form such a pattern. What was more, the electron wavelength measured by this experiment agreed exactly with de Broglie's prediction.

At about the same time, George P. Thomson in England sent beams of electrons through thin films of gold and he also found that they produced diffraction patterns (see Figure 29), in this

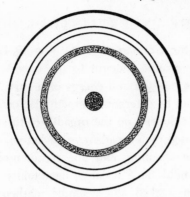

FIGURE 29. Diffraction of an electron beam by a thin gold foil. The spacing between the circles depends on the energy of the electrons and the spacing of the atoms in the gold crystal.

case resembling those of X-rays. (George P. was the son of J. J. Thomson, the discoverer of the electron; both father and son received Nobel prizes in physics.)

All the elementary particles have since been found to show the properties of waves. They can be thought of as wave packets, which is to say, probability packets: the intensity of the wave at any point represents the probability of finding the particle at that point.

The wavelengths of electrons are considerably shorter than those of photons; that is why only the very narrow spacing of atoms in a crystal can diffract them. It also explains why the electron microscope can resolve objects too small to be seen with an ordinary light microscope: the shorter electron wavelengths pick out viruses, for instance, which are so much smaller than the wavelengths of light that the light merely flows around them.

From the equations relating wavelengths to energy, we can calculate that an electron with the energy of 100 electron-volts has a wavelength of 1.22×10^{-8} of a centimeter. For a photon, this wavelength represents an energy of 10,000 electron-volts.

⁓⁓⁓ THE UNCERTAINTY PRINCIPLE

In 1927 the German physicist Werner Heisenberg gave some very concentrated thought to the uncertainty question—the fact that the position and energy of a particle (such as the photon) could not be determined exactly. He concluded that the uncertainty must depend on the breadth of the wave packet: a particle represented by a broad wave pocket would have a small uncertainty in momentum, and one represented by a narrow wave packet would have a large uncertainty in momentum. Heisenberg then worked out a simple mathematical equation relating the uncertainties in the position and momentum of a particle to each other:

$$\Delta x \cdot \Delta p \approx \frac{h}{2\pi}$$

In this equation Δx (delta x) is the uncertainty in the position of the particle, and is roughly the size of the wave packet. The uncertainty in momentum, Δp, is related to the spread in the wavelength necessary to make up the wave packet. The equation says, in a nutshell, that the uncertainty in momentum times the uncertainty in position is approximately equal to $h/2\pi$.

(Note that this equation is very similar to the one relating the size of the radio pulse to the bandwidth of a radio transmitter, which we discussed on page 176. As a matter of fact, one equation can be converted into the other. It may seem astonishing that we can take an equation that concerns the broadcasting of radio waves and convert it into an equation that applies to probability wave packets representing photons and other elementary particles. What this illustrates is that we are talking about the properties of wave packets in general—it doesn't matter what kind of waves they are.)

Heisenberg's equation states a fundamental law which has become known as the *Heisenberg Uncertainty Principle*. It is an underlying postulate of quantum physics, basic to all thinking about atoms, molecules, and elementary particles.

If we pass a beam of electrons through a narrow slit, the electrons will fall over a wider area on the other side of the slit, just as photons do (see Figure 30). We cannot tell just where any

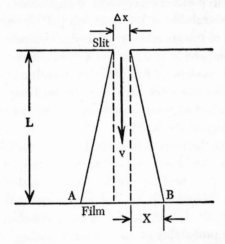

FIGURE 30. Diffraction of electrons passed through a narrow slit. The width of the slit (Δx) represents the uncertainty in the electron's position, and the width of the diffraction pattern (A-B) represents the uncertainty in velocity.

individual electron traverses the slit, so the width of the slit represents the uncertainty in the electron's position. Nor can we predict exactly where the electron will land on the film. This uncertainty in the velocity of the electron is measured by the width of the diffraction pattern.

We know from experiment that when the slit is made narrower, the diffraction pattern becomes wider. This means that when we try to make the uncertainty in position smaller, we end up by making the uncertainty in velocity greater. In other words, the more precisely we try to locate the electron, the less knowledge we have of its velocity.

The situation is usually described in terms of the effect that the act of observation has on the particle. When we deal with an elementary particle, we are dealing with an object so small that even the photons we use to detect it will change its position or velocity. Therefore no possible method of observation can determine both its position and velocity at any instant.

The unpredictability of the electron's path is one of the most basic aspects of the uncertainty principle. This point has aroused storms of controversy and has revolutionized not only physics but much of modern philosophy. Nineteenth-century scientists and philosophers took the view that, if you knew all the facts, you could predict all future events in the universe; that is, with exact knowledge of the positions and motions of all the atoms in the universe at the present time and with a sufficiently powerful computer, you could tell everything that was going to happen tomorrow. We can no longer make such a grandiose claim. The uncertainty principle tells us that we cannot make exact predictions about the future motions of even one electron. We can only give the probability of an electron traveling along a specified path, and we can only talk about the average motion of many particles.

This does not mean that the fundamental laws of conservation of energy and momentum are worthless. We can be certain that all particles must obey those laws, even though we cannot predict precisely where they are going or what will happen to them.

The uncertainty principle applies to all particles and bodies whatever their mass. But the equation tells us that as the mass increases, the uncertainty in velocity decreases. In the single-slit experiment, a beam of protons produces a much narrower diffraction pattern than a beam of electrons—about 1,800 times narrower, because the proton's mass is 1,800 times that of the electron. In other words, the uncertainty in the proton's motion is reduced 1,800-fold.

The uncertainty declines rapidly as we get to bodies big enough to be visible. Even a dust mote is heavy enough to mask its wave nature: its path through a slit is so straight that no diffraction effect can be measured.

This is reassuring. It means that when we talk about bodies large enough to see and touch, we can use the old-fashioned equations of mechanics and be sure they will give the right answers. Satellites will travel in predictable courses, and machines will work according to design. It is only when we deal with the activities of electrons, atoms, and molecules that the "quantum-mechanical" effects are important. This is true even in many situations in which particles act not as individuals but in unison. For example, quantum principles underlie the workings of transistors, the binding of atoms into molecules, the emission of light from matter in wavelengths that can be analyzed with a spectroscope, the superconductivity of metals cooled by means of liquid helium, the behavior of iron in a magnetic field, and many, many other everyday affairs.

It is interesting and amusing to speculate on situations in which the uncertainty principle may operate even on a gross scale. Let's imagine an experiment with two perfect spheres the size of a baseball. In a vacuum chamber free of vibration and all other disturbances except the effect of gravitation, we glue one sphere to the floor and drop the other on it. We drop it very carefully so that it hits precisely the apex of the stationary sphere and bounces straight up.

According to the ideas of classical physics, if the spheres are perfectly elastic the dropped ball will bounce straight up and down indefinitely. But the uncertainty principle says that there is a definite probability the ball will land just a tiny bit off center each time it falls. This tendency will be magnified at each bounce: the sidewise motion will become larger and larger, and after ten or twelve bounces there is a large probability that the ball will be far enough out to hit the floor instead of the stationed sphere.

The ball behaves as if according to chance, says the uncertainty principle; it is impossible to predict precisely the direction it will take on any bounce. Scientists and philosophers of the "deterministic" school (to which the late Albert Einstein belonged) would say this is nonsense: if we knew all the variables involved, we could tell exactly which way the ball would bounce. But most physicists working in the field of quantum theory believe it is really impossible to predict exactly where a particle will go, and the best we can do is predict probabilities.

If this is true, the human race is completely at the mercy of chance in a very fundamental sense. Think of a cosmic-ray particle (a proton) coming into the earth's atmosphere after many millions of years of wandering in space. The billion-electron-volt proton strikes an atom in the air with explosive force, producing a burst of electrons, photons, mesons, and fragments of the atomic nucleus which showers down on the ground. According to the uncertainty principle, no one could predict which atom would be hit or where the debris would fall. One of the high-speed mesons happens to dart through a man's body (of course, he does not feel it) and hits a gene in a chromosome within one of his reproductive cells. Again, the uncertainty principle avers, it is entirely a matter of chance which person and which gene is hit, and how the gene is altered. The man may later become the father of a child who carries the effects of the gene mutation, which may be unimportant (a change in eye color) or serious (hereditary hemophilia).

Thus a long chain of unpredictable events, triggered by a single cosmic-ray particle whose path could have been foreseen by nobody in the universe, produces a human change which will be transmitted widely through the population in future generations. Life is indeed full of uncertainties beyond man's control or understanding.

CHAPTER 11

~~~~~~~~~~~~~~~~~~~~~~~~~

Elementary Particles

~~~~~~~~

The very concept of an "elementary particle" has come a long way from its simple beginning. There was a time when the atom was considered the ultimate, indivisible elementary particle. Then atoms were found to be made of electrons, protons, and neutrons. Today, as we find the proton and neutron composed of various kinds of mesons, we are in a state of uncertainty as to what are the most "elementary" particles.

Similar changes have been taking place in our notion of "force." In the early part of this century, physicists gave up the attempt to picture fields of force by means of concrete models. This was a healthy change, for it swept the air clean of weird ideas of vortices, strains in the ether, and so on. Physics got along fine just by exploring the influence and effects of forces, without worrying much about exactly what a field of force really was. But the new philosophy left unanswered the old question about "action at a distance." This question remains very puzzling when, for instance, we try to explain how the force of gravity is transmitted over the 93 million miles between the sun and the earth.

Einstein offered a highly abstract answer. He said the mass of the sun caused the space around it to be "curved" so that the planets traveled along curved paths as "the shortest distance between two points." Although "the curvature of space" was a notion so abstract that it was very hard to visualize, it did make specific predictions about the orbits of planets, and these were found to be correct.

In the past few decades, physicists specializing in the theory of elementary particles have attempted another approach to the problem of the transmission of forces through space. They have simply abandoned the idea of "action at a distance" in thinking about interactions between particles; the force involved is transmitted, they say, by packets of energy, or "quanta," passing back and forth between the interacting bodies. The old-fashioned field of force has been replaced by a rush of particles of various types, interacting according to a few specific laws.

This concept is the basis of "quantum field theory"—a branch of physics which is perhaps the farthest out on the frontiers of learning at the present time. As a new and difficult subject, its ideas are not yet completely understood. Some of its predictions may be subject to change as more discoveries are made.

One of the reasons scientists have found it necessary to build this new and somewhat strange theory is that they have discovered elementary particles interacting in new ways which the old forces could not explain. Aside from the well-known attractions and repulsions, high-energy particles show a tendency on colliding with each other to create new particles, and sometimes to annihilate each other. Cosmic rays descending from space produce many such new particles when they hit the atoms in the air, and our accelerators can create the same particles by bombarding the atoms of targets within the machines. To understand how these new particles behave, and what functions they perform inside the nucleus, is one of the aims of the physics of elementary particles.

∿∿∿ PARTICLE PROPERTIES

The "classical" elementary particles with which we experiment are the electron, the proton, the neutron, and the photon. Each has certain specific properties, the most basic of which are the mass and the electric charge.

To measure these quantities, you must first of all get a supply of the particles you are studying. This is the reason scientists build particle accelerators—machines which produce beams of the various kinds of elementary particles, accelerating them to the desired energy.

One of the simplest kinds of particle accelerator is the cathode-ray tube; this provides a stream of low-energy electrons. To produce protons, you start with hydrogen gas, stripping the electrons off the hydrogen atoms, leaving behind the bare protons. This may be done by passing an electric current through a container of the gas. A small hole at one end of the container allows the protons to be drawn out by an electric field. They are then accelerated by one of several methods: the van de Graaff generator, the cyclotron, the synchrotron, etc. The amount of energy required depends on the experiment to be done. For an experiment to measure the mass of the proton, low-energy protons will do. But when we use these particles as projectiles to smash nuclei and create new particles, we need accelerators that can speed them up to many millions or billions of electron-volts.

Having equipped ourselves with a beam of the particles we want, we then measure or study them by subjecting them to interactions with other particles or with an electric or magnetic field. The effectiveness of our experiment depends heavily on the sensitivity of our devices for detecting the interaction. This has become a science in itself. We now have an elaborate array of detectors: Geiger counters, scintillation counters, solid-state detectors, cloud chambers, bubble chambers, spark chambers, photographic emulsions—all in many different sizes and shapes.

The earliest experiment in elementary-particle physics was the measurement of the mass and electric charge of the electron. When J. J. Thomson measured the deflection of cathode rays (electrons) in electric and magnetic fields, he found the ratio of the electron's charge to its mass. Later the American physicist Robert A. Millikan, with his famous "oil-drop" experiment, and other experimenters discovered ways to measure the electron's charge separately. It then became easy to calculate its mass. At ordinary velocities (amounting to less than a few thousand electron-volts) the electron's mass is the same as its rest-mass for all practical purposes.

We know that a hydrogen atom consists of one electron and one proton. The charge on the electron has arbitrarily been defined as negative, while the charge on the proton is called positive. We also know that the hydrogen atom as a whole (the combination of the electron and proton) has no electric charge; it is electrically neutral, as evidenced by the fact that hydrogen atoms do not attract or repel charged particles. This means that the amount of positive charge on the proton must exactly equal the amount of negative charge on the electron. Knowing the amount of charge on the proton, we can find its mass by measuring the deflection of a beam of protons in an electric or magnetic field. These measurements show that the proton mass is about 1,836 times that of the electron.

The photon has no electric charge at all. Consequently a beam of photons is not deflected from its path when it is passed through an electric field. As for the mass of the photon, we know that there is no such thing as its rest-mass, for photons exist only when moving at the speed of light. The moving photon, however, does have mass, which is just as real as the mass of any other particle. We have seen that the photon, by virtue of its momentum, can kick an electron into motion.

Most of the studies of elementary particles have been made by means of "scattering" experiments: a beam of particles is shot at a target to see how the particles bounce off the atoms of the target. The experiments have shown, first of all, that the laws of conservation of energy and momentum hold true for collisions between the smallest particles, moving with the highest velocities we can produce.

How do we know this is so? Well, for example, suppose we shoot a beam of low-energy electrons into a cloud chamber, which makes their tracks visible. Occasionally we see that an electron track suddenly branches into two tracks shooting off in different directions. The nature of the tracks makes clear that the electron must have hit another electron in an atom of the gas in the cloud chamber, knocking the target electron off in one direction while the projectile recoiled in another direction. We find that the angle of the fork in the track is always 90 degrees. This is exactly the result we would expect from an elastic collision. It shows that energy is conserved in a collision of electrons. If we apply a magnetic field to the cloud chamber, the amount of curvature it produces in the electron tracks confirms that the total energy and the total momentum of the two electrons are the same after the collision as before.

When the beam we shoot into the chamber is at a higher energy (more than several thousand electron-volts), then the angle of the forked track after a collision is less than 90 degrees. This is because of the relativistic increase in the mass of the incoming electron. Accurate measurement of the fork-angle verifies that not only are the conservation laws obeyed, but also the laws of relativity.

It was the conservation laws that led to the discovery of the neutron in 1932 by the British physicist James Chadwick and his collaborators. Certain radioactive materials (polonium and beryllium) had been found giving off a mysterious radiation which was able to penetrate great thicknesses of lead. Moreover, the same radiation, on hitting a piece of paraffin, knocked out protons carrying energies up to five million electron-volts! Where did all the energy come from? And how did this strange radiation pass through lead? No known radioactive emissions could produce these effects.

Chadwick came up with a simple solution. Everything could be explained if one supposed that the unknown radiation consisted of uncharged particles. A neutral particle could easily pass through matter, for it would not be repelled by the electric forces of the atomic nuclei. If this particle carried considerable energy and had about the same mass as the proton, it could knock out a high-energy proton when it collided with the nucleus of a hydrogen atom in the block of paraffin.

Chadwick's guess about the existence of the neutron was soon confirmed. Since it is electrically neutral, the neutron does not produce tracks in a cloud chamber or any other interaction that makes the particle itself directly detectable. But it readily enters into reactions with atomic nuclei which result in the emission of photons, protons, or alpha particles. These emissions have a characteristic pattern which identifies neutrons as the source of the reaction and tells the energy of the neutrons in each case, so that with special counters it is possible to "detect" the neutrons and measure their energy.

ᜰᜰᜰ THE STRUCTURE OF NUCLEONS

The nucleus of an atom is made up of neutrons and protons bound together in a more or less stable structure. Both of these particles are called *nucleons*. They differ principally in two respects: charge (the proton is positive and the neutron neutral) and mass (the neutron has a little more mass than the proton). The extra mass makes the neutron unstable: it tends to change into a proton, and in doing so emits an electron. This does not mean that the neutron simply consists of an electron stuck to a proton. The situation is much more complicated.

Like charged particles, the neutron has a little magnetic field connected with it, so that it behaves like a tiny bar magnet. This means that an electric current must circulate within the neutron. Its current must be different from that of the proton, because the neutron's and proton's magnetic fields differ in strength. In recent years a group led by Robert Hofstader at Stanford University has been investigating the structure of nucleons by scattering experiments with high-energy electrons. (For this work Hofstader received the 1961 Nobel prize in physics.) He found that each nucleon can be thought of as consisting of a "cloud of mesons." The only essential difference between the neutron and the proton is that in the proton the electric charges on the mesons add up, whereas in the neutron they cancel out. In fact, the neutron and proton may be thought of as being two aspects—or states—of a single particle. This concept is important in the theory of how nucleons are held together within the nucleus.

⁓⁓ CONSERVATION OF CHARGE

We have noted that the electron has just one unit of negative electric charge and the proton one unit of positive charge. Whenever we find a "particle" with more charge than this unit, we know that it must be a combination of particles. An example is the alpha particle (actually this is the nucleus of the helium atom, but it is also emitted as a particle from certain radioactive nuclei). The alpha particle contains two protons and two neutrons, and its total charge is two units.

Nature abhors unbalanced electric charges. It insists on matching up a negative charge with a positive charge whenever possible. Indeed, this can be stated as a universal law. Reactions between elementary particles which would result in unbalanced charges are forbidden. For example, a neutral particle cannot be transformed into two negative particles. If it breaks down into two charged particles, one must be positive and the other negative.

This principle is called the law of conservation of charge. Obviously its effect is to restrict the range of possible reactions among particles, just as all the other conservation laws put restrictions on the behavior of matter and energy. We now know of more than 30 different "elementary" particles. Were it not for the conservation laws, we would have to consider an enormous number of possible reactions among them. But thanks to these laws, the permitted reactions are definitely limited.

⁓⁓ SPIN

In its orbital travel around the atomic nucleus, an electron has a certain amount of energy and a certain amount of angular momentum. The amount may differ, depending on the orbit. But only certain particular amounts of energy and angular momentum are permitted to the electron: that is, it is restricted to certain *energy levels*. This restriction arises out of the wave-packet nature of the electron, and it is analogous to the restriction on the vibration of a violin string. The string may vibrate with a certain fundamental frequency, with twice this frequency, three times this frequency, and so on. But it cannot have a frequency in the intermediate ranges. The electron is in the same fix.

The electron in its atom has a stable energy level which corresponds to the fundamental. On absorbing a quantum of energy, it rises to a higher level. But it usually remains in that excited state no longer than a millionth of a second; the electron promptly drops back to its stable level, and in so doing gets rid of the excess of energy by emitting a photon of light of a certain wavelength, determined by the amount of energy it is shedding. In a very hot gas, many millions of electrons are continually being excited to various unstable energy levels, and their continual return to lower levels results in the emission of light of various wavelengths.

The discoverer of this principle was the late Niels Bohr, the great Danish physicist who will go down in history as the chief architect of atomic theory in the twentieth century. He was led to his picture of the structure of the atom by a mysterious observation that had been made in 1885 by the German physicist Johann Jakob Balmer. When hydrogen gas is heated, it emits light at a number of particular wavelengths. Balmer had found that nine of these wavelengths could be predicted by a simple numerical formula, even though he did not know the reason for the existence of this formula. To explain the "Balmer series," Bohr conceived the picture of the atom as a system of orbiting electrons around the nucleus which can occupy only certain energy levels and emit the Balmer lines in the spectrum as they drop from level to level. The electron's energy levels, in other words, are *quantized*.

The angular momentum of an electron in its atom also is

quantized. The electron may have 0, 1, 2, 3, or some other whole number of units of angular momentum—but not part of a unit.

The electron not only has an angular momentum around the nucleus, but, as we have seen, it also has a spin—an intrinsic angular momentum of its own. This fact, too, was established by study of the light emitted by heated substances. On close examination of their emission spectra, it was found that two lines sometimes were very close together. The intense yellow line in the spectrum of sodium, for example, is actually a double line. At first thought this may seem to contradict the quantum idea. But it turned out that the electron's spin explained the two lines. When its spin is in the same direction as its orbital motion, the electron's energy is slightly different from that when the spin is in the opposite direction. Therefore two electrons in the same orbit but with opposite spins will emit light of slightly different wavelengths when they drop to a lower level.

The fact that the electron spin can be oriented only in two positions (rather than three or more) leads to the conclusion that the amount of angular momentum connected with the spin is ½ unit, rather than one unit. The reasons for this belong to the more technical realms of quantum theory. We must always keep in mind that the behavior of the electron is described by a wave equation. The detailed structure of the electron is not yet known, but there is no doubt that it is more than just a solid body spinning on its axis.

The spin magnitude turns out to be a fundamental property of elementary particles. The proton and the neutron, like the electron, have ½ unit of spin. The photon, on the other hand, has a spin of one unit, and as a result it behaves differently from electrons, neutrons, and protons.

Their difference in behavior stems from a famous principle discovered by Wolfgang Pauli, the Viennese-born physicist who worked at Zurich, Switzerland, and later at the Institute for Advanced Study in Princeton. His principle states that no two particles in the atom can have the same amount of energy and angular momentum; it is therefore called the *Pauli exclusion principle.*

In the case of the electron, this means that the lowest orbit of the atom (with zero angular momentum) can hold either one electron or two electrons of opposite spins, which give them slightly different energies. If a third electron is added to the atom (forming lithium), it must go into a higher energy level. As a result, the various elements are made up of successive "shells" of electrons, so arranged that there are no two electrons of equal energy and momentum. The shell structure accounts for the periodic table of the elements.

The same thing is true of the atom's nucleus; there, too, the protons and neutrons are arranged in "shells" because they must obey the exclusion principle. The arrangement of the neutrons and protons determines whether the nucleus will be stable or radioactive, what kind of particle it will emit if it is radioactive, what its half-life (rate of radioactive breakdown) will be, and so on.

All particles that have ½ unit of spin obey the exclusion principle. They are called *fermions,* after Enrico Fermi, the Italian genius who did important work in investigating the consequences of Pauli's principle before creating the first atomic pile). All other particles, possessing spins of zero, one, or two units, are called *bosons,* for the Indian physicist S. N. Bose, who worked out some of their theoretical properties. The most important boson is the photon. Bosons are not at all restricted by the exclusion principle: we can pile as many photons as we like in any confined space—the only limitation is that the container must be strong enough to withstand the intensity, or pressure, of the radiation.

The Pauli exclusion principle is a fundamental law of nature. It controls the arrangement of the electrons in every atom and thereby determines the chemical properties of every element. It also has a great influence on the forces that bind atoms together in molecules and crystals.

⌇⌇⌇ THE NEUTRINO

Perhaps the greatest triumph of the law of conservation of energy was the prediction of the existence of the neutrino. Here was a particle so elusive that it defied all efforts to detect it, yet physicists were certain that it existed because the conservation of energy demanded it. And in the end the law proved itself in a most spectacular way.

It all began with a strange case of lost energy in a radio-active reaction. The reaction is known as beta-decay, which means the breakdown of a nucleus or particle by emission of a beta-particle—the name given to an electron that comes out of the *nucleus*. The transformation of a neutron into a proton by emission of an electron, which we discussed in the last chapter, is an example of beta-decay. Some atomic nuclei have too many neutrons for stability, and in such cases one of the neutrons locked in the nucleus is apt to change into a proton, with the result that the nucleus shoots out an energetic electron. One of the best-known nuclei of this kind is radioactive cobalt-60; it decays into nickel-60 by emitting a beta-particle (electron).

Now the strange situation that mystified the physicists was their finding that almost invariably the beta-particle coming out of cobalt-60 (or a similar nucleus) carried less energy than it should. The difference in mass between cobalt-60 and nickel-60 tells how much energy the beta-particle should have; it rarely possessed that amount. What happened to the missing energy?

Furthermore, some angular momentum disappeared also, for it turned out that the spins of the particles did not add up properly. Take the beta-decay of a neutron into a proton and an electron. The neutron's spin is ½ unit. Therefore the spins of its two products also should add up to ½ unit. But since the proton and the electron each has ½ unit of spin, their combined spins can only add up to 1 (if the spins are parallel) or 0 (if the spins are opposite in direction). Again, the question: What happens to the missing ½ unit of spin?

It was Wolfgang Pauli who suggested the answer. If the conservation laws were correct, he said, there must be another particle coming out of the nucleus along with the beta-particle. This hypothetical particle must carry the missing energy and spin.

The trouble was, the supposed particle did not show up in any of the physicists' measurements or detecting instruments. The fact that it could not be detected told something about what properties it must have, if it existed. It must be a particle with no measurable rest-mass, no electric charge, and almost no ability to interact with other particles. Judging from the failure to catch it with the thickest lead barriers and the most sensitive instruments, it appeared that the particle was so elusive that it could flit right through the whole earth without being deflected from its path in the slightest!

Nevertheless, all physicists became convinced of its existence, and Enrico Fermi gave it a name—neutrino ("little neutral one"). For 26 years after Pauli invented the particle in 1930, the physicists put the neutrino into their equations as something quite real, although no one had ever found one. And then at last, in 1956, the neutrino was trapped.

Next to a big nuclear reactor of the Atomic Energy Commission on the Savannah River in Georgia, an elaborate system of detection devices was set up. It was known that the flux of neutrinos from this radioactive pile must be about 30 times more intense than the flood of neutrinos pouring from the sun. Frederick Reines and Clyde L. Cowan of the Los Alamos Scientific Laboratory were in charge of the experiment. They had devised a scheme for detecting the neutrino by looking for the reverse of the beta-decay reaction that releases it from a neutron. That is to say, they hoped to catch the reaction in which a proton absorbs a neutrino and is transformed into a neutron, becoming neutral in charge by emitting a positron (a particle just like an electron, but with a positive electric charge).

Their idea worked. The scintillation counters they had set up caught one or two such reactions per hour, each signaling the capture of a neutrino. It was a great day for physics and the vindication of the conservation laws.

∿∿∿ ANTI-MATTER

When we bombard matter with particles of high energy (more than a million electron-volts), we enter a world of esoteric events. To start with, suppose we shoot a million-volt beam of photons at a thin piece of metal in a cloud chamber. Out of the metal comes a stream of particles whose tracks identify them as electrons. But if we turn on a magnetic field, the tracks divide into two groups, one curving to the right, the other to the left (see Figure 31). From the direction of the magnetic field, we

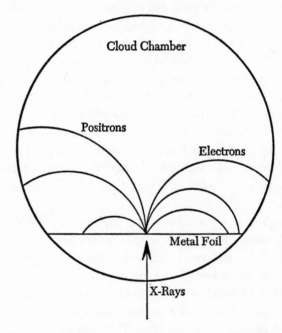

FIGURE 31. Production of oppositely charged particles by a high-energy beam of X-ray photons.

know that the particles going to the right are definitely electrons. Their opposite numbers, going to the left, must be just like electrons but with a positive electric charge. In other words, the particles come in pairs—one negative, one positive.

Now the total kinetic energy of each pair, as measured by the deflection of the two particles in the magnetic field, is less than the energy of the photon that produced them—in fact, just 1.02 million electron-volts less. That "lost" energy represents the conversion of the photon mass into the masses of the two particles. We had to supply this energy, by using photons of more than 1.02 million electron-volts (Mev), to create the two particles.

Here we have a new phenomenon, completely unpredicted by classical physics but understandable on the basis of Einstein's $E = mc^2$ formula. All the conservation laws are obeyed. The disappearance of one particle and the emergence of a pair of particles in its place is a little startling, but not altogether surprising in the light of the theories of quantum physics. In fact, this very phenomenon—the existence of a positive counterpart of the electron—was predicted by the British theoretical physicist P. A. M. Dirac years before the particle was actually discovered.

The positive "electron" is called, naturally, the *positron*. It was first detected among the products of cosmic rays in a cloud chamber by Carl D. Anderson of Caltech in 1932. The positron is now firmly established as a member of the elementary-particle family. Like a beta-particle, it is emitted from certain radioactive nuclei.

Although it is a perfectly stable particle, the positron cannot defend its single state for more than a very brief period. Left to itself, it would last indefinitely, but the moment it meets an electron (which is bound to happen before it has traveled very far), it is annihilated. Both the positron and the electron vanish in a flash of radiation, and in their place are left two photons, each with an energy of 0.51 Mev. The photons immediately flee from the spot, traveling in opposite directions. The "annihilation" of the electron and positron is the inverse of the pair-production process.

The verification of the existence of the positron was a great success for theoretical physics. Dirac had derived his prediction from a study of the wave equation describing the electron. According to this equation, he said, there should be electrons possessing a "negative" amount of energy. Negative energy certainly is a strange idea, but Dirac tried to explain it by the following model: Suppose that all space is filled with a sea of negative-energy electrons. They do not interact with ordinary matter, so we do not even know they are there. However, when an energetic photon comes along and gives its energy to one of these negative-energy electrons within an atom's electric field, the particle is raised to positive energy and shows all the properties of an electron. Its rise leaves behind a hole in the sea of negative-energy electrons (see Figure 32). The hole behaves like a posi-

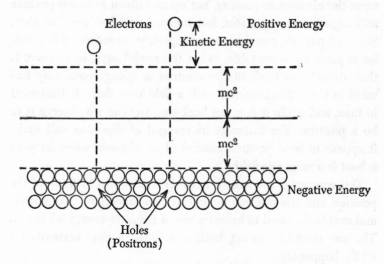

FIGURE 32. Dirac's model of the electrons moving up and down between the negative-energy and positive-energy states. Raising an electron to positive energy requires a photon with energy at least equal to 2 mc^2.

tively charged particle; this (as you have guessed) is the positron. The "meeting" of an electron and a positron, and their mutual "annihilation," occurs when an electron drops into this hole. Actually, according to Dirac's model, neither an electron nor a positron is created or destroyed; all that happens is that an electron moves up and down between negative and positive energy states—it absorbs energy when it goes up and emits energy when it goes down.

Dirac's model is consistent with all the observed behavior of electrons and positrons. But the notion of an infinite sea of undetectable negative-energy electrons seems somewhat artificial. Other models have been proposed by theoretical physicists. A current favorite is one suggested by Richard P. Feynman of Caltech.

Feynman's concept may seem just as odd as Dirac's. He pictures the electron as moving, not up and down between positive and negative energy states, but *forward and backward in time.* Since all particle reactions are completely reversible, this premise is perfectly acceptable. What the model says, in essence, is that, though we think of the electron as going continually forward in time, its encounter with a field may drive it backward in time, and while it is going backward in time we observe it to be a positron. For instance, its reversal of direction will make it appear to be a positron instead of an electron when its path is bent in a magnetic field.

This concept is convenient because it allows us to think of the positron and the electron simply as two aspects of one particle and avoids the need to invent a sea of negative-energy electrons. The one electron moving back and forth in time accounts for all the happenings.

The models, however, are merely attempts at explanation; we do not need them to describe what actually happens in the laboratory. We can still speak of the creation and annihilation of particles.

The Dirac interpretation of the wave equation predicted that for every particle there should exist an anti-particle. Just as there is an anti-electron (the positron), there must also be an anti-proton (a negatively charged proton).

Physicists knew that it would take a great deal of energy—at least six billion electron-volts (*Bev*)—to create the anti-proton. When a synchrotron of this power was built at the University of California Radiation Laboratory in the 1950s, they promptly began to bombard a copper target with six-Bev protons. Sure enough, out of the energetic collisions between the fast protons and the copper nuclei came definitely identifiable anti-protons.

On colliding with the target, each six-Bev proton produces two new particles and then goes flying off in a new direction. The new particles, representing conversion of 1.9 Bev of the fast proton's kinetic energy into mass, are a proton and an anti-proton. As soon as an anti-proton meets a proton, they annihilate each other, just as a positron and an electron do. The tremendous consequent release of energy (1.9 Bev) produces not only photons (in the form of gamma rays) but also several kinds of mesons.

What about the anti-neutron? High-energy particle collisions should create an anti-particle to the neutron, but how can we tell it from a neutron, in view of the fact that it has no electric charge? To distinguish them we must look into their inner structure. Although these particles have no charge, they do have electric currents circling within them. In the neutron and anti-neutron these currents go in opposite directions, so that their little magnetic fields are seen to have opposite polarity.

One particle that has no distinguishable opposite number is the photon. In this case we say that the photon is its own anti-particle.

Creating anti-particles every day in their laboratories, physicists naturally speculate about the possibility that somewhere, far from our own world, there may be a galaxy made up of anti-particles. In this anti-galaxy, atoms would consist of anti-protons and anti-neutrons with positrons circling around the nucleus. Everything would behave exactly as in our world. The inhabitants of the anti-world would not know that theirs was different from ours—nor would we. Only if the anti-galaxy came together with an ordinary galaxy would the difference be known: both galaxies would promptly annihilate each other and vanish in a great flash of photons! At the moment, however, this is pure speculation, for there is no evidence that such a catastrophe has ever occurred.

~~~~~ ## THE ELECTROMAGNETIC INTERACTION

The recent exploration of quantum physics has led to a beautifully simple explanation of the actions of electric charges and electromagnetic fields. Basically, all the reactions and interactions of electromagnetic forces rest upon just one action: the emission of photons by charged particles.

What causes an electron to emit a photon? We note first of all that a free, undisturbed, unexcited electron cannot emit a photon; this would not conserve momentum and energy. The electron may radiate a photon if it is deflected from its path by another charged particle: this reaction (called *Bremsstrahlung*) is what produces X-rays when an electron beam hits a target. Also, an electron in an atom may emit a photon of light on dropping from a higher to a lower orbit. In each case the action is abrupt and unpredictable for any single electron: the electron suddenly emits its photon and, by a recoil effect, the photon goes off in one direction while the electron goes off in another. We can predict the event only in terms of probability—the probability that an electron will emit a photon under given circumstances within a given time.

It turns out that the electric repulsion between two electrons depends simply on an exchange of photons between them. Thus the "electric field" results from a process of photons moving back and forth between the two electrons, continually being emitted and absorbed. These photons are called "virtual photons," because they are never observed directly. But our picture of a mutual emission and absorption of photons is able to explain all the reactions that take place between charged particles.

We write the equation for an electron's reversible emission and absorption of a photon this way:

$$e \leftrightarrow e + \gamma$$

The use of the Greek letter gamma as the symbol for a photon comes from "gamma-ray." The double-ended arrow denotes, as usual, the fact that the reaction is reversible.

The same formula covers the various reactions of the electron and its interaction with another electron or a positron: that is to say, emission or absorption of a photon, exchange of a virtual photon between two electrons, mutual annihilation of an electron and a positron with emission of one or more photons, and the production of an electron-positron pair by a high-energy photon (see Figure 33). To represent the annihilation (or production) of an electron-positron pair, for instance, we simply put a line over the e on the right side of the above equation to signify that it is a positron and bring it over to the left side:

$$e + \bar{e} \leftrightarrow \gamma$$

All this applies in just the same way to the proton or any other charged particle. We can substitute p (for proton) in place of e in the equations above. Essentially the formula defines what we mean by an "electric charge." A charged particle is one that "couples" to a photon in the way described above.

〰〰〰 MESONS

The force that holds the protons and neutrons together in an atomic nucleus is still not well-understood. We know certain things about it: that the force depends on an exchange of "virtual" particles among the nucleons, that it acts only over a very short range (less than 3×10^{-13} of a centimeter), and that its strength depends on the direction of the nucleons' spins—it is

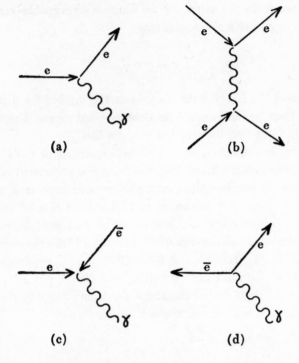

FIGURE 33. Interactions of an electron: (a) emission of
a photon, (b) the exchange of a virtual photon between two electrons, (c) the mutual annihilation of an electron and a positron, (d)
the creation of an electron-positron pair by an
energetic photon.

stronger when the spins are in the same direction than when they
are in opposite directions.

Something of a paradox arises here, however. The Pauli exclusion principle forbids two identical particles to join together.
This means that two protons (or two neutrons) with parallel
spins cannot stick together as a stable combination. However,
a neutron and a proton with parallel spins can form a stable
pair. This is actually the way they join up in all nuclei, from the
smallest nucleus (the one-proton-one-neutron deuteron, which is

quite stable) to the largest. As a result, we have a pairing and shell arrangement in the nuclei.

The strength of the nuclear binding force is much greater than the electric force between two charged particles. For example, in an alpha particle (the nucleus of a helium atom), there are two protons and two neutrons. The nuclear attraction between the protons and neutrons is a great deal stronger than the electric repulsion between the two protons.

It was the Japanese physicist Hideki Yukawa who first suggested (in 1935) that the strong nuclear force was maintained by the exchange of particles between the nucleons. He calculated that the cementing particle had to have a rest-mass 200 times that of the electron. No such particle was known. Then, in 1938, C. D. Anderson and S. H. Neddermeyer at Caltech announced that they had discovered, in the cosmic rays, a particle which seemed to possess about the mass that Yukawa had predicted. Because the mass was between that of the electron and the proton, the particle was named the "mesotron," later shortened to *meson*.

At first this seemed to be just the particle required to fit in with Yukawa's theory—the quantum of the nuclear-force field. The only trouble was that, whereas Yukawa's particle had to interact very strongly with atomic nuclei, the observed mesons interacted with them very weakly—the particles passed right through considerable thicknesses of matter.

For ten years the meson remained a puzzle. It was finally solved in 1948 by C. F. Powell and his co-workers at the University of Bristol in England. Closely studying the tracks of cosmic-ray particles recorded in photographic emulsions that had been sent to high altitudes (in balloons and on mountain tops), they found a new meson of greater mass than the one already known. The tracks showed that this heavy meson quickly decayed into the known lighter one (see Figure 34).

The answer seemed clear. The heavy meson (which Powell named the pi-meson, or pion) was Yukawa's particle. It had the right mass and other necessary properties to provide the nuclear

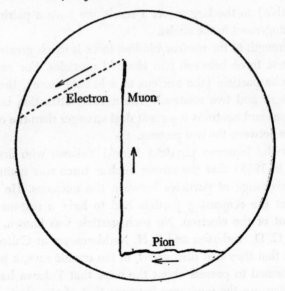

FIGURE 34. The decay of the heavy meson (pion) into the lighter one (muon), followed by the muon's decay into an electron.

binding force. The reason it had not been found earlier is that the pions produced by cosmic rays in the upper atmosphere break down into the light mesons (mu-mesons, or muons) before they reach the ground.

Why does the meson suddenly change direction when it changes from a pion to a muon, as in Figure 34? Physicists decided that, if momentum was to be conserved, another particle must be emitted (aside from the electron into which the meson eventually decayed). Naturally they thought of the neutrino, which had saved the conservation laws in the beta-decay situation. At first they gave the name "neutretto" to the particle that carried off the missing momentum in the pion case, but after a time they decided this must be the same as the neutrino.

Yet some physicists suspected that there might be more than one kind of neutrino. To check on this idea, experiments were set up in the two most energetic accelerators in the world—the

30 Bev machine at the Brookhaven National Laboratory and a similar one of the European Organization for Nuclear Research (CERN) in Geneva. In July 1962 the investigators announced that the neutrino connected with the creation of a muon was indeed different from the neutrino associated with the creation of an electron in beta-decay.

The mesons started a new chapter in particle research. Physicists were no longer satisfied with trying to catch a few of them in the debris produced by the cosmic rays falling in from space. They therefore built huge machines which can create mesons in great quantities and produce beams of them—indeed, even beams of anti-protons. As a result, they have turned up an unsuspected profusion of particles—well over 30 at the latest count. The particles discovered to date are listed in the table below.

Like the other particles, each meson has its anti-meson. In the pion group there are the positively charged (pi plus) and the negatively charged (pi minus) pions, plus the neutral pion (which is its own anti-particle). The muon behaves very much like an oversized electron and is negative in charge, while the anti-muon is positive. Just as there is no neutral electron, there is no neutral muon.

Several mesons heavier than the pion have been found, and for a time the overabundance of new particles was extremely disturbing. However, we are learning how to fit these new particles into a simplified scheme, so that order is coming out of chaos.

The lambda, sigma, and xi particles, together with the neutron and proton, are all called *baryons* (from the Greek word for "heavy"). When we include their anti-particles, they make up a sizable number of particles to keep in mind. But it is now beginning to appear that all of these apparently separate particles are different aspects of just *one* particle, the baryon. The neutron, the proton, and the heavy mesons may be looked at as various states of this baryon, with various amounts of energy, while the anti-baryons are baryons going backward in time.

According to this model, the electron, the two kinds of neutrino,

THE ELEMENTARY PARTICLES

PARTICLE	ELECTRIC CHARGE	MASS IN MEV	SPIN	AVERAGE LIFETIME IN SECONDS	ANTI-PARTICLE
Leptons					
ν (neutrino)	0	0	½	stable	$\bar{\nu}$ (anti-neutrino)
e⁻ (electron)	−e	0.511	½	stable	e⁺ (positron)
μ⁻ (mu minus)	−e	106	½	2.26×10^{-6}	μ⁺ (mu plus)
Bosons					
γ (photon)	0	0	1	stable	itself
Π⁰ (pi zero)	0	135	0	$< 10^{-15}$	itself
Π⁺ (pi plus)	+e	140	0	2.6×10^{-8}	Π⁻ (pi minus)
K⁺ (K plus)	+e	494	0	1.2×10^{-8}	K⁻ (K minus)
K⁰ (K zero)	0	498	0	1×10^{-10} and $6 \times 10^{-8*}$	$\overline{K}{}^0$ (anti-K zero)
Baryons					
p (proton)	+e	938	½	stable	$\bar{p}$ (anti-proton)
n (neutron)	0	940	½	1.0×10^{3}	$\bar{n}$ (anti-neutron)
Λ (lambda)	0	1115	½	2.5×10^{-10}	$\overline{\Lambda}$ (anti-lambda)
Σ⁺ (sigma plus)	+e	1190	½	0.8×10^{-10}	$\overline{\Sigma}{}^-$ (anti-sigma minus)
Σ⁰ (sigma zero)	0	1192	½	$\sim 10^{-20}$	$\overline{\Sigma}{}^0$ (anti-sigma zero)
Σ⁻ (sigma-minus)	−e	1196	½	1.6×10^{-10}	$\overline{\Sigma}{}^+$ (anti-sigma plus)
Ξ⁰ (xi-zero)	0	∼1311	½	$\sim 2 \times 10^{-10}$	$\overline{\Xi}{}^0$ (anti-xi zero)
Ξ⁻ (xi-minus)	−e	1319	½	2×10^{-10}	$\overline{\Xi}{}^+$ (anti-xi plus)

* The K⁰ and $\overline{K}{}^0$ have two average lifetimes depending on the type of reaction by which they decay.

and the muon are thought of as different states of one particle, the *lepton* (from the Greek word for "small"). The pion is a different sort of entity. It is a quantum of energy, and it is thought of as the carrier of the force between the baryons in the same way that we think of the photon as the carrier of the force between charged particles such as electrons.

We are thus left with only two basic particles: the lepton and the baryon, together with the few quanta (photons, pions, K-mesons) which dash back and forth between the particles to provide the forces we observe when the particles interact with each other. The study of elementary particles is the study of the ways in which the particles interact with one another. Just as we learn about the structure of atoms and molecules by studying chemical reactions, we expect to learn about the more fundamental structure of matter by studying the reactions between elementary particles.

〰 STRONG NUCLEAR INTERACTIONS

What do we mean by a "strong" nuclear interaction? In simple language, "strong" here is the measure of the eagerness of the particles to enter into the reaction. Given the opportunity, the particles do not wait around: they react very, very promptly—within billionths of a second or less. The strength of a nuclear interaction is usually measured in terms of the length of this interval, or, to put it another way, the shortness of lifetime of the particles involved.

One example of a strong interaction is the production of a pion by a collision between two high-energy protons:

$$p + p \rightarrow \pi^+ + p + n$$

This reaction yields a pi-plus pion, a proton, and a neutron. (In physicists' shorthand, the Greek pi stands for a pion, mu for a muon, and so on.)

Another example is the production of two strange particles by the collision of a pion and a proton, for instance:

$$\pi^- + p \rightarrow K^0 + \Lambda$$

We find that, for reasons unknown, baryons never break down of their own accord into lighter particles. For example, a proton cannot decay into a positron plus a photon, or into some combination of pions. In other words, the proton is completely stable, even though there is reason to believe that it consists of a combination of mesons. Although we do not know the fundamental reasons behind this behavior, we can note, as a general rule, that "nucleon charge" is always conserved. A proton (or any other baryon, regardless of its electric charge) is considered to have one unit of positive "nucleon charge." An anti-baryon has one negative unit. In any reaction involving the heavy particles, the total nucleon charge of all the particles (taking plus and minus signs into account) is the same before and after the reaction. In the first of the two equations above, the total nucleon charge on each side of the equation is two; in the second, it is one (for the only baryons involved are the proton, on the left side of the equation, and the lambda, on the right side).

The force that binds neutrons and protons together within the nucleus is the result of a strong interaction—the exchange of pions between the nuclear particles. This is very similar to the exchange of photons that produces the electric force between electrons or between protons. In the nucleus there are three basic interactions:

$$p \leftrightarrow n + \pi^+$$
$$p \leftrightarrow p + \pi^0$$
$$n \leftrightarrow n + \pi^0$$

The first of these can be reversed by moving the pi-plus pion to the other side of the equation and changing it to its antiparticle, the pi minus. This gives:

$$p + \pi^- \leftrightarrow n$$

This reaction means that a proton can change to a neutron either by emitting a pi plus or by absorbing a pi minus. Likewise, a neutron can change to a proton by emitting a pi minus or absorbing a pi plus. When a neutron and proton are very close to each other, the proton can emit a pi plus, which is immediately absorbed by the neutron. This results in an attractive force between the two nucleons. Since the neutron and proton have exchanged positions in the reaction, this is known as an "exchange force." The neutron and proton can also interact without exchanging identities, by shuttling a pi zero back and forth. In like manner, the attractive force between two protons or two neutrons is represented as an exchange of a pi zero between the particles involved.

The same interactions govern the scattering of neutrons and protons encountering each other outside the nucleus. Just as the path of a comet around the sun is the result of the gravitational attraction, so the path of a neutron traveling near a proton has a shape which depends on the form of the nuclear force. When we bombard a target of hydrogen with neutrons, and measure the number of neutrons scattered in different directions, we are finding out details concerning the interaction between neutrons and protons. (A comet swung by the sun into a hyperbolic orbit in interplanetary space might be considered a cosmic scattering experiment.)

Experiments such as these are the most important way of learning about the nature of nuclear forces. We learn from them that the strength of the force pulling two nucleons together depends, in a complex way, not only on the distance between them but also on their velocities and the directions of their spins. So far, experiments are our only guide to the nature of the forces, for we have no theory that can predict what the forces should be like. It must be confessed that the present theory of strong nuclear interactions is not capable of giving very good numerical answers to problems or predicting the exact result of many experiments. Nevertheless, it is useful for suggesting new experiments to do and what types of nuclear reactions are possible.

When we try to calculate the probability of a given reaction taking place, we run into trouble, because the equations cannot be solved even in an approximate way. If further advances are to be made, we need some imaginative new ideas.

⁓⁓⁓ WEAK NUCLEAR INTERACTIONS

A "weak" nuclear reaction is one that occurs much more reluctantly than a "strong" reaction. An example is the change of a neutron into a proton and an electron. The half-life of a free neutron (the average duration of its existence before it breaks down) is about 12 minutes, which is really an enormous length of time for an unstable particle to hold together. In contrast, an atomic nucleus made unstable by absorption of a fast neutron will emit a gamma-ray photon in a very short fraction of a second; this reaction takes place about 10^{18} times faster than the decay of the neutron (assuming the same amount of energy has to be emitted in both cases).

Weak nuclear interactions have been studied by physicists for many years. The classic case is beta-decay, which includes not only the free neutron's breakdown with emission of an electron but also, of course, all the decays of radioactive nuclei resulting from the change of a neutron into proton within the nucleus. As we have seen, in this reaction a neutrino is always emitted along with the electron. For technical reasons, it is actually an anti-neutrino that is emitted in this reaction (the symbol for which is nu with a line over it, $\bar{\nu}$). The equation goes:

$$n \leftrightarrow e^- + \bar{\nu} + p$$

If we change the electron to its anti-particle, the positron, and move it to the left side of the equation, we get:

$$n + e^+ \leftrightarrow \bar{\nu} + p$$

This means that a neutron can join with a positron to form a proton plus an anti-neutrino. The natural (that is, easy) direction for this reversible reaction is from left to right, because that releases energy, whereas the reverse requires an input of energy. To make the reaction go from right to left, we must supply a very energetic anti-neutrino. This, in fact, is the way neutrinos were detected in the experiment of Reines and Cowan. They put large tanks of water in the path of the intense stream of anti-neutrinos coming from a nuclear reactor. When an anti-neutrino was absorbed by a proton in the tank, it would produce a positron, which could then be detected. However, the interaction between anti-neutrinos and protons is so weak that only a very few such interactions took place.

If, in the same equation, we substitute a neutrino for the anti-neutrino and put it on the other side of the equation, as the rule allows us to do, we have:

$$n + e^+ + \nu \leftrightarrow p$$

The reaction from right to left takes place commonly in certain radioactive nuclei, which have so much extra energy that one of the protons changes into a neutron, emitting a positron and a neutrino.

Another weak reaction is the decay of a muon into an electron:

$$\mu \leftrightarrow e + \nu + \bar{\nu}$$

Weak interactions are believed to be responsible for the decay of the "strange particles" listed in the table on page 212. In general, it seems that in all reactions whereby a heavy particle breaks up spontaneously into lighter particles, some weak interaction plays a part.

～～ PARITY

To cap our brief excursion in the world of elementary particles—and, in fact, our whole exploration of the laws of physics—we come at last to a development which has been one of the most exciting events in modern physics: the repeal of one of the conservation laws which had been taken for granted for some years.

The principle involved was the concept known as "mirror symmetry." In physics, this concept assumes that if you looked at the universe in a mirror, everything would look and behave exactly the same—in other words, there would be no difference whatever between a right-handed and left-handed universe, and you could not tell one from the other. To take a common example, the mirror image of your left hand looks just like a right hand.

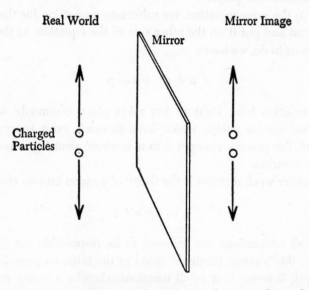

FIGURE 35. Repulsion of charged particles is unchanged in the mirror image.

Let us examine a couple of examples in physics. Two charged particles repelling each other appear identical whether you see them directly or look at their image in a mirror (see Figure 35). If we consider an electric current and its magnetic field, the situation is not quite the same, because this has direction: a current running clockwise looks counterclockwise in the mirror, and the magnetic field likewise is reversed (see Figure 36). An electron beam directed toward the mirror will be deflected to the right in the real world and to the left in the "looking-glass world." Nevertheless, there is no essential difference between the two images—they are completely symmetrical. If we change the

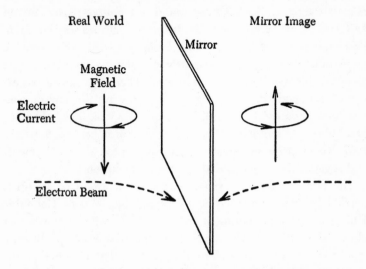

FIGURE 36. Mirror image of a magnetic field or deflection of an electron beam reverses the direction.

word "clockwise" to "counterclockwise" and "left" to "right," we make the image world the same as the real world. All our experiments show that electromagnetic interactions indeed have mirror symmetry; no reaction involving electromagnetic fields is altered one whit if we arbitrarily change our language and start using the word "right" in place of "left."

In the atomic world, this rule of left-right symmetry similarly prevailed—until recently. Atomic physicists elevated the rule to a law called the conservation of parity. Parity is a property of elementary particles and atomic systems, derived in a technical way from quantum mathematics. A particle, or group of particles, is said to possess either "even" or "odd" parity. In any reaction or interaction, parity must be conserved—the total parity of the particles involved must not change. This concept of parity implies that an elementary particle will look exactly the same if you twist it through half a revolution: the north pole of the spinning particle will look exactly like the south pole, and the right side will be exactly like the left side.

The strong nuclear interactions obey the rule perfectly: so far every strong reaction has been found to conserve parity. But in 1956 two young physicists at the Institute for Advanced Study in Princeton, Chen Ning Yang and Tsung Dao Lee, discovered a *weak* interaction which apparently did not conserve parity. It involved the beta-decay of two mesons. There was no way to explain their mode of decay except by throwing the law of conservation of parity overboard! Yang and Lee took that bold step: in a history-making paper (for which they promptly received the 1957 Nobel prize in physics), they presented their arguments and suggested experiments to test their conclusion.

The first to take up the challenge was a group of scientists headed by a woman physicist, Chien-Shiung Wu of Columbia University. Their experiment was designed to find out whether electrons emitted in the beta-decay of a radioactive substance would come out in a preferred direction—that is, whether the reaction would show a distinct "handedness." They used cobalt-60 as their radioactive material, cooled it to a very low temperature in liquid helium so that the spins of the cobalt nuclei could be controlled more easily, and applied a magnetic field to line up the spins along the field. Then they set up counters to detect the electrons emitted by the cobalt in the direction of the magnetic field, and in the opposite direction.

If electrons came out in about equal numbers in both directions, symmetry (*i.e.*, parity) would be conserved. If substantially more electrons went in one direction than the other, beta-decay would prove to be right-handed or left-handed (as the case might be). In a mirror, this difference could be detected. Symmetry and the conservation of parity would be overthrown.

Dr. Wu's experiment vindicated Yang and Lee. Many more electrons were counted at one counter than at the other. Other experimenters in various laboratories got the same results. It was established beyond doubt that weak nuclear interactions violated the "rule" of left-right symmetry, and that in this realm of physical events the "law" of conservation of parity did not hold.

What is responsible for the lack of symmetry in the emission of beta-particles? Theoretical physicists explain it this way: When the electron is emitted, an anti-neutrino simultaneously comes out of the nucleus in the opposite direction. Unlike other particles, the neutrino and the anti-neutrino always spin in a fixed direction—the neutrino counterclockwise (looking along its direction of motion) and the anti-neutrino clockwise. This fact, for the first time, provides a standard for defining right and left.

Suppose you are communicating with a scientist on another planet and he wants to know what you mean by "right-hand." You can tell him to set up the cobalt-60 experiment. He finds the direction in which most of the electrons are emitted, and this tells him that the direction of the magnetic field is opposite to that. Once he knows that direction, you and he can both agree in saying that the direction of deflection of an electron beam by the magnetic field is *to the right* (or to the left, if you choose to use that word instead).

The breakdown of parity conservation attracted much attention because it seemed to be a clear-cut violation of a cherished conservation law. However, when the evidence was carefully examined, it turned out that conservation of parity had never really been tested in a reaction involving a weak nuclear interaction. The symmetry laws had worked so well for all other interactions that everybody simply assumed they were good under all circumstances. The new finding proved again what everybody had already known: whenever you extend a law into an area where it has never been tested, you run the risk of finding that it no longer holds.

Are the other conservation laws threatened now? Hardly. Conservation of energy and momentum have withstood too many tests in all conceivable circumstances to be seriously questioned now. Until an observation or experiment comes along that shows a real violation of these laws, we can continue to rely on them.

Indeed, we can restore the law of mirror symmetry to usefulness if we replace each particle with its anti-particle every time we exchange the words right and left in describing a situation. For example, suppose that somewhere there is a world made up of anti-particles, with positrons in place of our electrons, anti-protons in place of protons, and so on. In that "looking-glass world" the cobalt-60 experiment will turn out exactly like ours. The positrons will go in the same direction as our electrons (see Figure 37), and anti-man's left hand will be the same as our right hand.

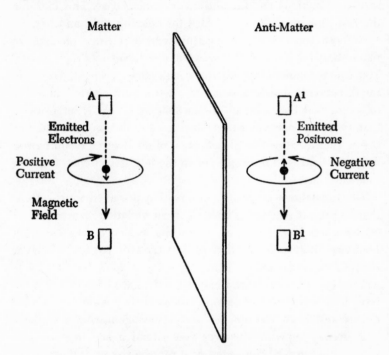

FIGURE 37. The symmetry of matter and anti-matter. The latter is a mirror image of the former.

Left or right, the laws of physics in any case must be the same in that anti-universe as in ours.

CHAPTER 12

~~~~~~~~~~~~~~~~~~~~~~~~

Where Do We Stand Now?

~~~~~~~~

Our rapid survey of modern physics has made clear that the behavior of the physical universe—as far as man has been able to observe it—is ruled by a few conservation laws and four types of interaction among elementary particles. Fundamentally, physicists believe, everything that happens in the universe is determined by interactions between the particles. As Professor Feynman has said, if we knew and understood all the particles and their "couplings," we would have "physics in a nutshell."

We can summarize the basic laws governing particle interactions as follows:

Conservation of Momentum: In a system of particles the total momentum is always constant.

Conservation of Angular Momentum: In a system of particles the total angular momentum is always constant.

Conservation of Energy: In a system of particles the total energy is always constant.

Time Reversal: The laws describing the interactions of elementary particles do not depend on the direction of time.

Mirror and Charge Symmetry: The laws describing the interactions of elementary particles are unchanged if *left* and *right* are interchanged and particles are replaced by anti-particles.

Conservation of Electric Charge: In a system of particles the total number of electric charges is always constant. (In adding up charges, we give positive charges a value of +1 and negative charges a value of −1).

Conservation of Nucleon Charge: In a system of particles the total number of nucleon charges is always constant. (In adding up nucleon charges, we give protons, neutrons, and other baryons a value of +1; anti-protons, anti-neutrons, and other anti-baryons have a value of −1.)

To explain certain details of the reactions among mesons, physicists also invoke a few special, abstruse conservation laws, such as conservation of "strangeness."

Then there are Newton's laws of motion (or their equivalent), which allow us to predict how objects will behave in response to the basic forces. And most fundamental of all are the two postulates of relativity: (1) the laws of nature are the same for every observer, regardless of his position or motion; and (2) the speed of light is the same for all observers.

In attempting to understand these laws we have found ourselves beset with mysteries and uncertainties. We may console ourselves with the fact that if we find these matters hard to understand, the greatest scientists in the world also find themselves at the limit of their comprehension in dealing with them. The theories we have described of the nature and origin of physical forces are by no means complete or final. All we can say is that, as of now, this is the best picture we have. It makes a useful model, a framework of thought, to guide physicists in looking for answers to the many outstanding problems.

For example, we are still very much in the dark as to how the gravitational force is transmitted. But the quantum theory suggests a possible explanation. We have seen that electromagnetic forces may be described as the exchange of photons between charged particles, and the nuclear binding force as the exchange of mesons between nucleons. In the same way, the gravitational force might be considered to be conveyed by *gravitons*—the "quanta" of the gravitational field. We can predict what some of the poperties of the "graviton" might be. Presumably it has no mass, no electric charge, and a spin of 2 (in comparison with the photon, which has a spin of 1). The gravitational force is so weak, however, that we cannot conceive of any way of detecting the interaction of "gravitons" with matter—even if they exist.

The weakness of the gravitational interaction is itself a prime mystery. If, for comparison, we take the strength of the gravitational force as one, then on that scale the strength of the weak nuclear force is 10^{25} (ten trillion trillion times stronger!), the electromagnetic force 10^{36}, and the strong nuclear force 10^{38}.

There is nothing in the theory of matter that gives any sort of reason for this huge spread in strengths and for these particular figures. Some scientists believe that such a theory will be worked out some day. But if it is, no doubt still deeper and more difficult questions will emerge. There is no sign of impending unemployment, or lack of problems to solve, in the realm of physics.

～～～ DO WE KNOW ALL THE LAWS?

Do the four basic types of interaction we have discussed represent all the forces existing in the universe?

The fact that other forces have not been discovered does not prove that no others exist. We are inclined to think that all the kinds of force strong enough to produce noticeable effects in the universe should have been found by now. But perhaps we have not been looking in the right places. Perhaps, at one extreme, there are strange forces connected with particles of tremendously high energies; and, at the other extreme, forces too weak for us to detect with the means at our disposal.

We can ask the same question about the laws of nature: Are there any laws not yet discovered? No doubt there are, but these are likely to be rather special, not as sweeping as the grand conservation laws. A more serious question is whether the conservation laws are completely and forever correct as we have stated them. After all, these laws are only as good as the accuracy of our measurements. At best, our observations are always subject to a small margin of error. Therefore we cannot be absolutely sure that the total energy of a system after a reaction is always precisely the same as before the reaction. In that sense, our statement of the laws is more exact than it has a right to be. But long, searching, cumulative experience entitles us to say that there is an extremely high probability the laws are basically true.

On these laws as a foundation, science has advanced steadily and rapidly toward a more meaningful understanding of the universe, and also toward useful applications of the forces of nature.

~~~~~~~~~~~~~~~~~~~~~~

Derivation of Conservation of Kinetic Energy from Conservation of Momentum

~~~~~~~~~

In the study of collisions between two bodies, the center of mass of the two bodies is commonly taken as the starting point for all measurements. Let us say we have two spheres, moving toward each other with the velocities v_1 and v_2 relative to a fixed point on the ground. After the collision, they bounce away from each other with velocities v_3 and v_4 relative to the fixed point (see Figure 38). The center of mass of the two bodies is a point somewhere between them, and it is moving with a constant velocity relative to the ground point. If we locate this center of mass and find its velocity (V_c), we can then find the velocities of the spheres relative to the center of mass (which we will call V_1 and V_2 when they are moving toward each other, and V_3 and V_4 when they are moving apart).

A system in which all velocities are measured relative to the center of mass is called a center-of-mass (CM) system. With reference to the center of mass, the total momentum of the bodies must be zero at all times. Therefore we can say that:

$$m_1V_1 = m_2V_2 \quad \text{and} \quad m_1V_3 = m_2V_4$$

Examining Figure 38, we see that the velocity of each body in the CM system can be related to its velocity relative to the ground:

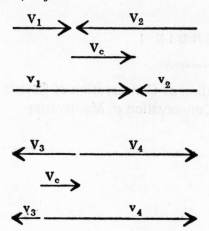

FIGURE 38. Addition of velocity vectors. The velocity of each body relative to the ground is equal to its velocity with respect to the center of mass plus the velocity vector of the center of mass with respect to the ground (V_c).

$$V_1 = v_1 - V_c \qquad\qquad V_3 = v_3 + V_c$$
$$V_2 = v_2 + V_c \qquad\qquad V_4 = v_4 - V_c$$

From this we find that, for instance:

$$V_c = v_1 - V_1$$

Now we note from the earlier equation that:

$$V_1 = \frac{m_2}{m_1} V_2$$

Since $V_2 = v_2 + V_c$, this equation can be written:

$$V_1 = \frac{m_2}{m_1} (v_2 + V_c)$$

Now we substitute this value of V_1 in the equation $V_o = v_1 - V_1$, which becomes:

$$V_o = v_1 - \frac{m_2}{m_1} (v_2 + V_o)$$

By simplifying and rearranging, we get:

$$(m_1 + m_2) V_o = m_1 v_1 - m_2 v_2$$

The left side of this equation is the momentum the two bodies would have if they were both moving with the velocity V_o. The right side is the actual momentum of these two bodies with respect to the ground. Since the two momenta are equal, this proves our assertion that the center of mass of a group of bodies moves just as if all the bodies were assembled at the center of mass.

Now we come to the reason for introducing the center-of-mass idea in the first place. In the CM system, the center of mass is a fixed point. It is the point where the collision takes place. If you were at that point, you would see the colliding bodies approaching you and then receding from you, but you would feel that you were standing still. If you put a concrete wall at that point, m_1 and m_2 would rebound from the wall exactly as if they were bouncing from each other.

But we said that when a perfectly elastic body bounces from a rigid wall, its velocity remains unchanged. Therefore, as a result of assuming the spheres to be *elastic*, we can say that the velocities of the bodies before and after colliding are the same, or:

$$V_1 = V_3 \text{ and } V_2 = V_4$$

By squaring both sides of each equation and multiplying by the corresponding masses, we have:

$$m_1 V_1{}^2 = m_1 V_3{}^2 \text{ and } m_2 V_2{}^2 = m_2 V_4{}^2$$

Adding these two equations together gives:

$$m_1 V_1{}^2 + m_2 V_2{}^2 = m_1 V_3{}^2 + m_2 V_4{}^2$$

This equation tells us that the kinetic energy of the two bodies in the CM system is the same after the collision as before.

We now want to find the kinetic energy relative to the ground point. We substitute in the foregoing equation the velocities in terms of ground speed (*i.e.*, $V_1 = v_2 - V_c$, etc.), and we get:

$$m_1 (v_1 - V_c)^2 + m_2 (v_2 + V_c)^2$$
$$= m_1 (v_3 + V_c)^2 + m_2 (v_4 - V_c)^2$$

After some algebra we find that:

$$m_1 v_1{}^2 + m_2 v_2{}^2 - 2V_c (m_1 v_1 - m_2 v_2)$$
$$= m_1 v_3{}^2 + m_2 v_4{}^2 - 2V_c (m_2 v_4 - m_1 v_3)$$

From the law of conservation of momentum we know that $m_1 v_1 - m_2 v_2 = m_2 v_4 - m_1 v_3$, so we can remove these equalities from the equation above; thus it reduces to:

$$m_1 v_1{}^2 + m_2 v_2{}^2 = m_1 v_3{}^2 + m_2 v_4{}^2$$

This is the final result. We have shown that the law of conservation of momentum predicts the conservation of kinetic energy in the case of collisions between two perfectly elastic bodies. This follows from the fact that, if we multiply both sides of this equation by ½ (½mv^2 being the formula for kinetic energy), then the left side is the total kinetic energy before the collision (as measured from the ground), and the right side is the kinetic energy after the collision.

APPENDIX 2

The Transformations of Relativity

We start with two coordinate systems S and S_1, which are together in space at the instant a flash bulb is set off at the origin (O) of these systems (see Figure 39). These coordinate systems have a velocity v relative to each other. The observer in S sees S_1 moving in the x direction with velocity v, and the observer in S_1 sees S moving with the same velocity in the opposite direction along x.

Both observers must see the flash of light travel away from the origin with the same velocity, c. The distance the light travels in the S system, during a time t, is ct. This must be true in any direction. If the light spreads out equally in all directions, at the end of time t it has extended to fill a sphere whose radius is r. Thus we can write down (using the Pythagorean theorem):

$$r^2 = x^2 + y^2 + z^2 = c^2t^2 \tag{1}$$

Exactly the same formula is true in the S_1 system, because the flash was set off when the origin of S_1 coincided with the origin of S. So, while the two systems are separating from each other, the observer in S_1 also sees the light fill a spherical shell in his own system, and we say:

$$r_1^2 = x_1^2 + y_1^2 + z_1^2 = c^2t_1^2 \tag{2}$$

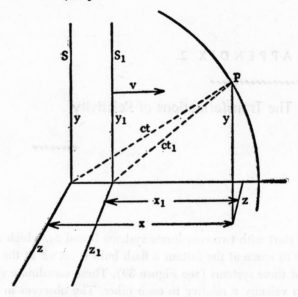

FIGURE 39. Coordinate systems used in finding the Lorentz transformations.

Notice that the speed of light is the only thing that is the same in both systems. The two equations describe a point (p) lying on the shell. Even though they describe the same point in space, the observer in S sees the point at the position (x, y, z, t) in his system, and the observer in S_1 sees the point at the position (x_1, y_1, z_1, t_1). Our aim is to write a set of equations which will tell us what the position (x, y, z, t) is if we know (x_1, y_1, z_1, t_1), and vice versa.

Subtracting Equation 2 form Equation 1, and transposing some terms, we find that:

$$x^2 + y^2 + z^2 - c^2t^2 = x_1^2 + y_1^2 + z_1^2 - c^2t_1^2 \qquad (3)$$

We now look for a transformation similar to the Galilean transformation, but one which will allow c to be the same in both systems. The y and z coordinates of the position are not affected by motion in the x direction, so we can say that $y = y_1$ and $z = z_1$. For the x coordinate we try a transformation of the form:

$$x = a(x_1 + vt_1) \tag{4a}$$

$$\text{and} \quad x_1 = a(x - vt) \tag{4b}$$

The a must be determined by our fundamental postulates. The same quantity is used in going from x to x_1 as in going from x_1 to x, for it does not depend on the direction of motion. Also, we expect a to depend on the velocity v in such a way that it becomes equal to one when v becomes small compared to the speed of light. When this happens, Equations 4a and 4b become the same as the ordinary Galilean transformation, which we know is good for small velocities.

From Equation 4a we solve for t_1 and find:

$$t_1 = \frac{1}{v}\left(\frac{x}{a} - x_1\right) \tag{5}$$

Put into this the value of x_1 found in Equation 4b:

$$\begin{aligned} t_1 &= \frac{1}{v}\left(\frac{x}{a} - ax + avt\right) \\ &= at - \frac{x}{v}\frac{(a^2 - 1)}{a} \end{aligned} \tag{6}$$

In the same manner, we find that:

$$t = at_1 + \frac{x_1}{v}\frac{(a^2 - 1)}{a} \tag{7}$$

If we put Equations 4b and 6 into the right side of Equation 3, we have:

$$\begin{aligned} x^2 + y^2 + z^2 - c^2t^2 &= a^2(x - vt)^2 + y^2 + z^2 \\ &\quad - c^2\left[at - \frac{x}{v}\frac{(a^2 - 1)}{a}\right]^2 \end{aligned} \tag{8}$$

Rearranging terms, and canceling the y and z terms, which are the same on both sides of the equation, we have:

$$x^2 - c^2t^2 = \left[a^2 - \frac{(a^2 - 1)}{a^2} \frac{c^2}{v^2} \right] x^2$$
$$+ 2 \left[(a^2 - 1) \frac{c^2}{v^2} - a^2 \right] vxt$$
$$- (c^2 - v^2) a^2 t^2 \qquad (9)$$

If this equation is to be true for any values of x and t, each term on the left must equal each term on the right. There is no term with the combination xt on the left, so the xt term on the right must equal zero. This means that:

$$(a^2 - 1) \frac{c^2}{v^2} - a^2 = 0 \qquad (10)$$

Solving this for a^2, we find:

$$a^2 = \frac{1}{1 - \dfrac{v^2}{c^2}} \qquad (11)$$

and

$$a = \frac{1}{\sqrt{1 - \dfrac{v^2}{c^2}}} \qquad (12)$$

In addition,

$$\frac{a^2 - 1}{a} = \frac{v^2/c^2}{\sqrt{1 - v^2/c^2}} \qquad (13)$$

Substituting this into Equations 4 and 5, we obtain our final result, the Lorentz transformation equations:

$$x = \frac{x_1 + vt_1}{\sqrt{1 - v^2/c^2}} \quad \text{(14a)} \qquad\qquad x_1 = \frac{x - vt}{\sqrt{1 - v^2/c^2}} \quad \text{(14b)}$$

$$y = y_1 \qquad\qquad \text{(15a)} \qquad\qquad y_1 = y \qquad\qquad \text{(15b)}$$

$$z = z_1 \qquad\qquad \text{(16a)} \qquad\qquad z_1 = z \qquad\qquad \text{(16b)}$$

$$t = \frac{t_1 + x_1 v/c^2}{\sqrt{1 - v^2/c^2}} \quad \text{(17a)} \qquad\qquad t_1 = \frac{t - xv/c^2}{\sqrt{1 - v^2/c^2}} \quad \text{(17b)}$$

〰〰 THE LORENTZ-FITZGERALD CONTRACTION

A yardstick pointed in the x direction is moving in that direction with velocity v. We think of it as being at rest in the S_1 system, with one end at $x_1 = 0$ and the other end at $x_1 = L_1$. Its length in the S_1 system is L_1. At the time $t = 0$, we take an instantaneous picture of this rod with a camera located in the S system. We look at this picture and ask: What are the locations of the two ends of the rod in the S system?

Without going to the trouble of actually taking a picture, we can answer this question by using Equation 14b. We use this, rather than 14a, because we have specified that $t = 0$. We do not specify what t_1 is, and it may not be zero. The end of the yardstick that is at $x_1 = 0$ in S_1 is found to be at $x = 0$ in S. The other end in S is seen to be at:

$$x = L_1 \sqrt{1 - v^2/c^2}$$

This tells us the length of the rod in S, so we can say that the length of the moving rod is seen by the camera to be:

$$L = L_1 \sqrt{1 - v^2/c^2}$$

That is less than L_1, its length at rest.

~~~~ ADDITION OF VELOCITIES

An object in the S_1 system starts at the point $x_1 = 0$ at the time $t_1 = 0$. It moves with a constant velocity u_1 (relative to S_1), and in the time t_1 it travels a distance x_1. By definition, $u_1 = x_1/t_1$. How fast does this object travel according to the observer at rest in system S?

He sees a velocity given by the formula:

$$u = \frac{x}{t} = \frac{x_1 + vt_1}{t_1 + x_1 v/c^2}$$

$$= \frac{x_1/t_1 + v}{1 + \frac{x_1\,v}{t_1\,c^2}}$$

$$= \frac{u_1 + v}{1 + u_1\,v/c^2}$$

This is the formula for addition of velocities. If u_1 and v each is equal to c, then this formula says that $u = c$. If u_1 and v are less than c, then u must always be less than c. This is another way of showing that a body cannot travel faster than light.

~~~~ THE MASS INCREASE

We consider two colliding spheres as seen in system S and S_1, and we assume as a basic postulate that conservation of momentum is satisfied in both systems. We will show that for this to be true, we cannot take the masses of the spheres to be constant, but we must define a variable mass, given by the formula:

$$m = \frac{m_0}{\sqrt{1 - u^2/c^2}}$$

m_o being the rest-mass, and u the velocity of the body relative to the observer. (The velocity of a body is usually denoted by v, but in this Appendix we reserve v for the relative velocity of the two systems.) For our two colliding spheres we shall designate the rest-masses as m_a and m_b. Since the momentum of a body is mu, the momentum of the first sphere, for example, is given by:

$$mu_1 = \frac{m_a u_1}{\sqrt{1 - u_1^2/c^2}}$$

As seen by the observer in S_1, the total momentum of the two spheres before the collision is equal to the total after the collision—that is:

$$\frac{m_a u_1}{\sqrt{1 - u_1^2/c^2}} + \frac{m_b u_2}{\sqrt{1 - u_2^2/c^2}} = \frac{m_a u_3}{\sqrt{1 - u_3^2/c^2}} + \frac{m_b u_4}{\sqrt{1 - u_4^2/c^2}} \quad (1)$$

We now wish to see if the same kind of equation can be satisfied in S. Assuming the equation above is true, is the following equation also true?

$$\frac{m_a u_a}{\sqrt{1 - u_a^2/c^2}} + \frac{m_b u_b}{\sqrt{1 - u_b^2/c^2}} = \frac{m_a u_c}{\sqrt{1 - u_c^2/c^2}} + \frac{m_b u_d}{\sqrt{1 - u_d^2/c^2}} \quad (2)$$

From the formula for addition of velocities (see page 236), we can show that:

$$u_a = \frac{u_1 + v}{1 + \dfrac{u_1 v}{c^2}} \qquad u_b = \frac{u_2 + v}{1 + \dfrac{u_2 v}{c^2}}$$

$$u_c = \frac{u_3 + v}{1 + \dfrac{u_3 v}{c^2}} \qquad u_d = \frac{u_4 + v}{1 + \dfrac{u_4 v}{c^2}} \quad (3)$$

By use of a certain amount of algebra, we find that:

$$1 - \frac{u_a^2}{c^2} = \frac{(c^2 - v^2)(c^2 - u_1^2)}{(c^2 + u_1 v)^2} \quad (4)$$

Similar expressions are found for u_b, u_c, and u_d. Substituting Equations 3 and 4 into Equation 2, we find that:

$$\frac{m_a\,(u_1 + v)}{\sqrt{c^2 - u_1{}^2}} + \frac{m_b\,(u_2 + v)}{\sqrt{c^2 - u_2{}^2}} = \frac{m_a\,(u_3 + v)}{\sqrt{c^2 - u_3{}^2}} + \frac{m_b\,(u_4 + v)}{\sqrt{c^2 - u_4{}^2}} \quad (5)$$

This can be simplified by the following procedure. Dividing both sides of Equation 1 by c, we obtain:

$$\frac{m_a u_1}{\sqrt{c^2 - u_1{}^2}} + \frac{m_b u_2}{\sqrt{c^2 - u_2{}^2}} = \frac{m_a u_3}{\sqrt{c^2 - u_3{}^2}} + \frac{m_b u_4}{\sqrt{c^2 - u_4{}^2}} \quad (6)$$

Subtracting Equation 6 from Equation 5, we are left with:

$$\frac{m_a v}{\sqrt{c^2 - u_1{}^2}} + \frac{m_b v}{\sqrt{c^2 - u_2{}^2}} = \frac{m_a v}{\sqrt{c^2 - u_3{}^2}} + \frac{m_b v}{\sqrt{c^2 - u_4{}^2}} \quad (7)$$

When this is multiplied by c/v, we have, finally:

$$\frac{m_a}{\sqrt{1 - u_1{}^2/c^2}} + \frac{m_b}{\sqrt{1 - u_2{}^2/c^2}} = \frac{m_a}{\sqrt{1 - u_3{}^2/c^2}} + \frac{m_b}{\sqrt{1 - u_4{}^2/c^2}} \quad (8)$$

We now see that the left side of this equation is the total mass of the two spheres as seen in S_1 before the collision, whereas the right side is the total mass after the collision. If we multiply both sides of the equation by c^2, then the two sides of the equation represent the energy in S_1 before and after the collision. We may now review the logic which the mathematics represents. Equations 1 and 2 represent conservation of momentum in systems S_1 and S, respectively. Equation 8 represents conservation of energy in S_1 and was obtained from Equations 1 and 2. Since we assume that conservation of energy holds true, this shows that momentum is consistently conserved in both systems if the mass of each body is allowed to vary according to the relativistic formula and if we transform velocities between the two systems by Equation 3.

APPENDIX 3

The Mössbauer Effect

Cobalt-57 is a radioactive isotope which has become a very valuable research tool. Its nucleus decays into iron-57, which immediately (in about one ten-millionth of a second) emits a gamma-ray photon with an energy of about 14,000 electron-volts. The emitted photon has a very good probability of being absorbed by any stable iron-57 atom it encounters, because it has exactly the right amount of energy to be captured by that nucleus. This is called "resonance absorption." It is much like the pickup of a radio wave by a radio receiver sharply tuned to the wave's frequency.

The iron-57 atom is one of the most sharply tuned receivers in nature. The reason has to do with the conservation of momentum. Most atoms, on emitting a gamma-ray, recoil a bit. This recoil, of course, uses up part of the energy the atom has available for the creation of the photon. As a result, the photon has less energy than it would have if there were no recoil, and consequently its frequency is a bit lower. Therefore it is not at the right frequency for resonance absorption by an atom like the one that emitted it. The unusual thing about iron-57 is that its atoms do not recoil when they emit their gamma-ray photons. These photons have a rather low energy, and besides, the crystal lattice of the metal holds the iron atoms rigidly in place.

Because of the lack of recoil, virtually all the energy released by the nucleus goes into the creation of the gamma ray, so that it has exactly the right energy to be in resonance with an iron-57 atom. That is why iron-57 is such a sharp receiver of the gamma-ray emissions from the decay of cobalt-57.

The discovery that certain radioactive isotopes emit their gamma-rays without losing energy to recoil of the atom was made in 1958 by a young German physicist, R. L. Mössbauer. For this discovery (called the "Mössbauer effect") he shared the 1961 Nobel prize in physics. The effect has been used for many important experiments which depend upon very precise measurements of small changes in the frequency of electromagnetic radiation. One of these experiments was R. V. Pound's confirmation of the effect of gravity on radiation, as predicted by the theory of relativity.

REFERENCES

PHILOSOPHY AND HISTORY OF SCIENCE

Bertrand Russell, *Human Knowledge*—Simon & Schuster, New York (1948).

Hans Reichenbach, *The Rise of Scientific Philosophy*—University of California Press (1959).

Herbert Butterfield, *The Origins of Modern Science*—Collier Books (1962).

RELATIVITY

L. D. Landau and G. B. Rumer, *What Is Relativity?*—Basic Books (1960).

Hans Reichenbach, *The Philosophy of Space and Time*—Dover Publications (1957).

D. W. Sciama, *The Unity of the Universe*—Doubleday & Company (1961).

ELEMENTARY PARTICLES

Otto R. Frisch, *Atomic Physics Today*—Basic Books (1961).

Chen Ning Yang, *Elementary Particles*—Princeton University Press (1962).

ARTICLES IN *Scientific American*:

"Neutrino Astronomy," by Philip Morrison (August, 1962).

"Gamma-Ray Astronomy," by W. L. Kraushaar and G. W. Clark (May, 1962).

"Hypernuclei," by V. L. Telegdi (January, 1962).

"How Cells Communicate," by Bernhard Katy (September, 1961).

"The Eötvös Experiment," by R. H. Dicke (December, 1961).

"Gravity," by George Gamow (March, 1961).

"The Muon," by Sheldon Penman (July, 1961).

"The Mössbauer Effect," by Sergio De Benedetti (April, 1960).

"Things that Go Faster than Light," by M. A. Rothman (July, 1960).

"The Force between Molecules," by Boris V. Derjaguin (July, 1960).

"The Nuclear Force," by Robert E. Marshak (March, 1960).

"High-Energy Cosmic Rays," by Bruno Rossi (November, 1959).

"The Exclusion Principle," by George Gamow (July, 1959).

"The Weak Interactions," by S. B. Treiman (March, 1959).

"The Atomic Nucleus," by R. E. Peierls (January, 1959).

"Anti-Matter," by Geoffrey Burbidge and Fred Hoyle (April, 1958).

"The Principles of Uncertainty," by George Gamow (January, 1958).

"Elementary Particles," by Murray Gell-Mann and E. P. Rosenbaum (July, 1957).

"The Overthrow of Parity," by Philip Morrison (April, 1957).

"Inertia," by Dennis Sciama (February, 1957).

"Pions," by Robert E. Marshak (January, 1957).

INDEX

absolute motion, 123

"absolute space," 64

absorption, resonance, 239

acceleration, absolute, 123; defined, 38; inertia and, 144–145

accelerator, particle, 137, 191, 210–211

"action at a distance," 78, 189

air resistance, 10

Aldrich, J. M., 1

Alembert, Jean d', 48

alpha particle, 195

alternating current, 111

Anderson, Carl D., 202, 209

angular momentum, components of, 92–93; conservation of, 52–67, 223; defined, 53–54; of electron, 195–196; gyroscope and, 62–64; potential energy and, 83–84, 90–91; *see also* momentum, angular

angular velocity, 53, 59–60

anti-baryon, 214

anti-electron, 204

anti-galaxy, 205

anti-gravity, 99

anti-matter, 97–98, 201–206; mirror symmetry and, 221–222

anti-meson, 211

anti-neutrino, 216–217, 221

anti-neutron, 205

anti-proton, 204–205, 211

Aristotle, 68–69

atom, 11; structure of, 17–18, 103

atomic bomb, 131

Atomic Energy Commission, 200

atomic particles, 95–96, 134–135, 189–222; *see also* elementary particles

atomic physics, mass in, 24

atom-smashing machines, 11, 137, 191, 210–211

attraction, versus repulsion, 100–102; gravity as, 97

balance, between two masses, 27

Balmer, Johann Jakob, 196

bandwidth, in broadcasting, 175–177; uncertainty principle and, 184

baryon, 211, 214

baseball, path of, 15

Bell Telephone Laboratories, 182

bell curve, 152

Berkeley, George, 122–124

Bernoulli, Johann and Daniel, 48

beryllium, 193

beta-decay, 199, 210, 216, 220

beta-particle, 199

binding energy, of nucleus, 103, 142, 207, 209, 214

black-body radiation, 168

Bohr, Niels, 196

Bose, S. N., 198

bosons, 198

Brahe, Tycho, 73, 76

brain, in learning process, 14

Bremsstrahlung, 206

Broglie, Louis de, 182

Brookhaven National Laboratory, 211

bullet, trajectory of, 60

calculus, 78

canonical equations, Hamilton's, 86

Carnot, Sadi, 50

carrier frequency, 175

cathode-ray tube, 102, 191

causation, time and, 18–20

causes, search for, 10

Cavendish, Henry, 97

center-of-mass system, 227

centripetal force, 106

Chadwick, James, 193

chance, laws of, 147, 162–163; *see also* probability

change, energy relations in, 43–44

charge, conservation of, 195; irreversible, 162; meaning of, 207; symmetry of, 223

chemical reaction, electricity from, 49

Chen Ning Yang, 220

Chien-Shiung Wu, 220

classical physics, versus modern, 24, 42, 64, 115, 127, 165–166, 187, 190–191

Clausius, Rudolf, 161

clocks, relativity of, 128, 131–133

cloud chamber, 95, 192, 201

cobalt-57, 239

cobalt-60, 199; "handedness" and, 221–222

cohesive forces, 103–106, 142, 207, 209, 214

coin-tossing, probability and, 148

comet, as "scattering," 215

compression wave, 120

Compton, Arthur Holly, 174

Compton effect, 174

confidence range, 155–157

conservation laws, 21, 26–27; complexity of concepts in, 47–51; duality of, 48; "repeal" of, 218; summary of, 223–224; symmetry and, 91–92

conservation of charge, 195

conservation of energy, 36–51, 223; relativity and, 135–136

conservation of heat, 159–161

conservation of kinetic energy, 227–230

conservation of momentum, 21–35, 135–136, 223, 227–230

coordinate systems, 125–126, 231–232

Coriolis force, 107–108

cosmic rays, 133, 190, 202, 209; mesons from, 210–211; probability and, 188

cosmology, 51

Cowan, Clyde L., 200

curved space, 140, 189–190

cycles and epicycles, 68

cyclotron, 191

da Vinci, Leonardo, *see* Vinci, Leonardo da

Davisson, C. J., 182

Democritus, 69

Descartes, René, 47, 78

determinism, 187–188

deuterium, 142

deuteron, 208

deviation, standard, 155

Dicke, R. H., 145

diffraction, of electrons, 182–183

Dirac, Paul A. M., 202–203

distance, force and, 39

distribution curve, 151–154

Doppler effect, 133, 140

dynamics, 84

earth, gravitational field of, 11; as gyroscope, 66; as non-symmetrical sphere, 91; rotation of, 58–60; tilt of axis, 66–67

Einstein, Albert, 43–44, 116, 188; curved-space concept, 140, 189–190; mass-energy equation, 137, 173, 202; photoelec-

tric effect, 168–170; Principle of Equivalence, 138; relativity theory, 65, 96, 115–116, 124–129; summary of theories, 129–130

elastic forces, 103–106

electrical energy, 42

electrical potential, 82

electric charge, accelerated, 111–112; conservation of, 223–224; inverse-square law and, 82; photons and, 207; unbalanced, 195

electric current, from chemical reaction, 49

electric field, charge of, 109; "creation" of, 98–99; inverse-square law and, 99–100; versus magnetic, 100–101

electricity, generation of, 49; laws of, 19–20; nature and work of, 8–9

electromagnetic field, 99–103; and accelerated charge, 111–112; disturbances in, 165; Hamilton's equations for, 88–89; interaction in, 206–207; relativity and, 141; similarities to gravitational field, 143; strength of, 102–103

electromagnetic radiation, photons in, 170

electromagnetic waves, 117–121

electron, 9, 14; angular momentum of, 197; attraction and repulsion among, 103; as beta-particle, 199; cloud-chamber tracks, 193; emission of, 216; exchange of photons between,

electron (*cont'd*)
206; as lepton, 211–213; and magnetic field, 11; mass of, 191–192; movement in time, 204; negative-energy, 202; photons and, 44; positron and, 202; quantized energy levels in, 196–197; shell structure of, 198; wavelength of, 182; uncertainty principle and, 184–186

electron diffraction, 182–183, 185

electron microscope, 183

electron–positron pair, 207

electron spin, 101, 103, 195–196, 208–209

elementary particles, 10–14, 89, 95–96, 189–222; charge of, 192; field and, 98–99; mass changes in, 134–135; rest-mass of, 174, 209, 237; scattering of, 192; spin in, 196–197; symmetry of, 93; as wave packets, 183; waves and, 18

energy, binding, 80, 142, 207, 209, 214; conservation of, 36–51, 135–136, 223; "creation" of, 48; defined, 36; electrical, 42; heat, 47; interchangeability of, 80; kinetic, 36, 39–42 (*see also* kinetic energy); mass and, 38; potential, 43–44, 48, 88–91; symmetry and, 93–94; total, of system, 42, 82–87; units of, 45–46; various concepts of, 47–51; wavelength and, 183–184

energy levels, of electrons, 196

energy–matter relationships, 44

entropy, defined, 160–161; laws of, 147–157

equivalence, principle of, 138; *see also* mass-energy equivalence

error, probability of, 158

ether, concept of, 8, 115, 129

European Organization for Nuclear Research, 211

exchange force, in nucleus, 215

exclusion principle, Pauli's, 197

existence, basic fact of, 13

facts, accepted, 13–20

falling bodies, law of, 70–73

Faraday, Michael, 100

Fermat, Pierre de, 148

Fermi, Enrico, 198, 200

fermions, 198

Feynman, Richard P., 204

field, acceleration of, 111–112; change of, 108–113; linear and non-linear, 141, 143

field theory, 9, 95–121

Fitzgerald contraction, 127, 133, 235

Fitzgerald, George, 115, 127

forces, cohesive and elastic, 103–106, 142, 207, 209, 214; defined, 38, 46; distance and, 39; versus energy, 80; fields of, 9–12, 95–121; gravity as, 7, 96–99; inverse-square law and, 76, 79, 99–100, 109; momentum and, 37; versus potential energy, 80–81; types of, 95; units of, 46

frame of reference, absolute, 123, 127

frequency, Compton effect and, 174; in photoelectric effect, 168; of wave, 117

frequency distribution, 151–154

friction, 82–83, 105

future, time and, 102–103

Galilean transformation, 126, 128, 130

Galilei, Galileo, 6–7, 69–73, 123, 126, 144

gamma-ray photon, 216, 239

gamma rays, 34, 205, 207

gas, diffusion of molecules in, 150–151; pinch effect in, 102; pressure of, 105; theromdynamics of, 159–161

Gaussian distribution, 152–154

Geiger counter, 175, 191

gene mutation, cosmic rays and, 188

Germer, L. H., 182

glaciers, 60

glue, 105

Goddard, Robert H., 2–3, 31

gravitation, force of, 96–99; inertia and, 143–144; law of, 77; quantum theory and, 224–225; relativity and, 137–143; universal, 15–16, 76; variation in, 17

gravitational constant, 76, 145

gravitational field, 7–12; nonlinear, 141–143; photons in, 138–139; potential energy and, 81; similarities with electromagnetic, 143; strength of, 91;

symmetry of, 91; weakness of, 96–97, 225

gravitational red-shift, 139–140

"gravitol," 9–10

"gravitons," as quanta, 224–225

gravity, 5–6, 16; acceleration of, 71, 75, 144; as attraction, 97; center of mass and, 28; as constant, 20; effect of on radiation, 240; and gyroscopic movement, 61–63; inverse-square law of, 76, 79; weight and, 22

gravity shield, 98

Greek letters, use of, 53–54

Greek philosophers, 68–69

group velocity, 121

gyroscope, 63–65

half-life, 198

Hamilton, Sir William Rowan, 84

Hamiltonian expression, 85–86

harmonic motion, 111

heat, conservation of, 159–161; and conservation of energy, 48–49; mechanical energy and, 47–50

Heisenberg, Werner, 184–188

helium atom, 195

Helmholtz, Hermann von, 50

Hertz, Heinrich, 165–166

Hofstader, Robert, 194

Hoyle, Fred, 51

Huygens, Christian, 79

hydrodynamics, energy in, 38

hydrogen atom, 17, 192

hydrogen gas, Balmer lines in, 196; protons from, 191

hydrogen light, 17

impulse, momentum and, 37

inertia, 23, 106–108; cause of, 143–146; moment of, 57; principle of, 72; in projectile path, 74–75

inertial guidance, 63

interference, of electrons, 182; of light, 177

inverse-square law, 99–100; in electrical field, 109; of gravitational field, 76, 79

ionized gas, 102

ion propulsion, 33–34

iron-57, 239

Joule, James Prescott, 49–50

Kepler, Johann, 73, 76, 79

kilogram, standard, 24

kinetic energy, 36, 39–42; in change of state, 105; conservation of from conservation of momentum, 227–230; Hamilton's principle and, 85–88; mass and, 136–137; paradox of, 45; and *vis viva*, 79

K-mesons, 212–213

knowledge, philosophy of, 14

Lagrange, Joseph-Louis, 80–84

law of nature, defined, 5–12

laws: conservation of charge, 195; conservation of energy, 18, 36–51, 199; conservation of momentum, 2, 21–35; of entropy, 147–157; of falling bodies, 70–73; of gravity, 5–7, 77; inverse-square, 76, 79, 99–100, 109; Kepler's, for planetary motion,

73–74; knowledge of, 225–226; of motion, 28, 38, 68–94, 224; Pauli exclusion principle, 197–198; probability, 147–157, 162–163; of quantum physics, 165–188; of random motion, 16–17, 29; of relativity, 122–146; summary of, 223–225; of thermodynamics, 159–161; undiscovered, 225–226

learning, assumptions underlying, 14

Leibniz, Gottfried Wilhelm von, 47, 79

Lenard, Philipp, 168

lepton, 213

Liebig, Justus von, 50

light, as constant value, 126–129; as electromagnetic radiation, 116; interference effect, 177; photons and, 171; pressure of, 34; refraction of, 121; speed of, 114, 116, 126, 129, 174; travel of, 113–114; wave-particle, nature of, 166, 182; *see also* photon

light-beam propulsion, 34

light quanta, 169

linear field, 141

liquid, molecule distribution in, 150–151

logic, reason and, 14, 76

Lorentz, Hendrik, 115, 127

Lorentz-Fitzgerald contraction, 127, 133, 235

Lorentz transformation, 128–131, 235

Los Alamos Scientific Laboratory, 200

Mach, Ernst, 124, 127, 144

magnet, permanent, 101

magnetic field, 9; charged particles in, 89; charge of, 109; in cloud chamber, 201; around conductor, 102; "creation" of, 99; electrons and, 11, 101, 192; inverse-square law and, 109; and ion propulsion, 34; of neutron, 194

magnetism, electricity and, 165

mass, center of, 27; in classical physics, 24; energy and, 38; gravitational field and, 99; gravitational versus inertial, 144; kinetic energy and, 40–41, 136–137; measurement of, 24–25; momentum and, 135–136; relative motion and, 128; total, 44; and uncertainty principle, 186–187; velocity and, 186; versus weight, 22

mass-energy, conservation of, 44

mass-energy equivalent, 43–44, 136–137, 173, 202

mass increase, equations for, 236–237; relativity and, 134–137

matter, annihilation of, 202, 207

matter–energy relationship, 23, 44

Maxwell, James C., 100, 165–166

Mayer, Robert, 50

mechanical energy, heat and, 49

mechanics, development of, 78–90

meson, 11, 90, 188–189, 207–213; as baryon, 211; beta-decay of, 220; from cosmic rays, 210–211; discovery of, 209; nucleon and, 194–195; pi and mu, 90, 209–212, 217; relativistic time effects and, 133

mesotron, 209

meteorites, 34

Michelson, A. A., 114

Michelson-Morley experiment, 114–115, 126–127

Millikan, Robert A., 191–192

mirror symmetry, concept of, 93–94, 218–223

modulation, in wave train, 120

Mössbauer, R. L., 240

Mössbauer effect, 140, 239–240

molecules, diffusion of, 150–151; random motion of, 29

momentum, angular, 52–67 (*see also* angular momentum, components of); change of, 37; conservation of, 21–35, 223, 227–230; defined, 25; energy and, 36; Hamiltonian and, 88; of isolated system, 26; ordinary versus angular, 54–55; of photon, 174, 192; potential energy and, 83; rate of change of, 74; relativistic, 135–136

moon, acceleration and velocity of, 75; gravity and, 16

Morley, E. W., 114

Morse code, 175

motion, absolute, 123; laws of, 28, 38, 68–94, 224; reversible, 159; speed and, 122; three-dimensional, 88; uniform, 74

moving bodies, angular momentum of, 54

mu-meson (muon), 90, 210–212, 217

nature, "facts" of, 13–20; law of, 5–12; "why" of, 7–11
Naturphilosophie, 50
Neddermeyer, S. H., 209
negative and positive charges, 9, 15, 98, 100, 192
negative energy, 202–203
neutretto, 210
neutrino, 11, 199–200, 210; emission of, 216; two kinds of, 210–212
neutron, 11; attraction to proton, 208–209; as baryon, 211; detection of, 194; magnetic field of, 89, 194; versus proton, 194–195; scattering of, 215
neutron spin, 93
Newton, Sir Isaac, 6–7, 16, 23, 28, 38, 47, 64, 122–123, 144; laws of motion, 28, 38, 73–78, 224
New York Times, The, Goddard editorial, 2
Nobel prize, 170, 194, 220, 240
non-linear field, 141–143
normal distribution curve, 152
nova, 143
nuclear power, defined, 46–47
nuclear reactions, strong and weak, 213–217
nucleon, 194–195; charge of, 214, 224
nucleus, 11–12; binding force in, 142, 207, 209, 214; pairing and shell arrangement in, 208–209; structure of, 194

Oberth, Hermann, 2
orbital velocity, 75
organization, change of to disorganization (entropy), 160–161
oscillation, 112

parity, concept of, 217–222
particle accelerator, 137, 191, 210–211
particles, elementary, *see* elementary particles
Pascal, Blaise, 148
past, causation and, 18–20; versus future, 162–163
Pauli, Wolfgang, 197–200
Pauli exclusion principle, 197–198, 208
Peltier, Jean, 49
percentage uncertainty, 156
periodic table, 198
perpetual-motion machines, 1, 48–49, 97, 161
phase velocity, 118–121
Phoebus, 68
Phosphoros, 68
photoelectric cells, 18
photoelectric effect, 167, 175
photon, 11–14, 44, 96, 170–181; as boson, 198; charge of, 192; in cloud chamber, 201–202; comparative energies of, 171–172; electrons and, 44; emission of, 206, 208, 216; energy-spread of, 171–172, 180; equation for, 207; gamma-ray, 239–240; in gravitational fields, 138; interference and, 177–178; momentum of, 192; prob-

photon (*cont'd*)
    ability behavior of, 179; properties of, 173–175; as quanta, 170–171, 213; size of, 175–181; "uncertainty" of, 181; wavelength of, 183–184; X-ray, 174
physics, classical, *see* classical physics
pi meson (pion), 90, 209–215
pinch effect, in ionized gas, 102
Planck, Max, 168–169
Planck's constant, 169
Planck's formula, 173
planetary motion, Kepler's laws of, 73–74
planets, gravitation and, 16, 74, 189–190; sun and, 10
plasma rockets, 33
Plato, 68
Poincaré, Henri, 115, 127
polls, reliability of, 157
polonium, 193
positive and negative charges, 9, 15, 98, 100, 192
positrons, 11, 202, 216–217
potential energy, 41–42; as binding energy, 141–142; concept of, 80–81; conservation of, 91; of elementary particles, 90; Hamilton's principle and, 85–89; heat and, 48; momentum and, 91; transformation of to kinetic, 43–44
Pound, R. V., 140, 240
Powell, C. F., 209
power, defined, 46–47
precession, 62
prediction, physical laws and, 147

probability, laws of, 147–157; photon behavior and, 179
probability wave packet, 179–180, 184
proportionality constant, 145
propulsion methods, 29–35
proton, 11–12, 34, 188, 194; as baryon, 211; in magnetic field, 89; versus neutron, 194–195, 209
psychic force, 96
public-opinion polls, 157

quanta, nature of, 169–173, 190
quantum mechanics, 17–18, 165–188; gravitation and, 224–225

radar, speed of, 121
radiation, effect of on gravity, 240; production of, 112–113
radiation field, 112
radio, photons of, 172; uncertainty principle and, 184
radioactivity, 157, 166, 193; and conservation of energy, 42
radio broadcasting, 175–177, 184
radio waves, 112, 166
radium, 42
random motion, 16–17, 29
random walk, 150–151
reaction, versus action, 74; propulsion by, 2–3, 31
reason, logic and, 14, 76
Redheffer, Charles, 1
regularity, in universe, 15
Reichenbach, Hans, 158
Reines, Frederick, 200

Reines-Cowan, experiment, 217

relativity, 65, 96, 115–116, 127–130; laws of, 122–146; mass increase and, 134–137; results of theory, 131–143; transformations of, 231–234

repulsion, electrical, 100–102

resonance absorption, 239

rest-mass, 136–137, 174; and mass increase, 237; in nucleus, 209

reversible motions, 159

rifling, of gun barrel, 60

rocket, conservation of momentum in, 32

rocket propulsion, 2–3, 29–35

roller-coaster, potential energy of, 82

rotation, of earth, 58–60; kinetic energy of, 57–58; relativistic, 133–134

Rowland, H. A., 101

Royal Society of London, 79

Savannah River plant, AEC, 200

scattering effects, 192, 215

Schelling, Wilhelm Joseph von, 50

Scientific American, 1

scientific determinism, 187–188

scientific predictions, 157–158

scintillation counter, 175, 191, 200–201

scissor blades, velocity of, 119–120

Seebeck, Thomas Johann, 49

seesaw, 21

semi-conductors, 89

senses, learning through, 14

sideband frequencies, 175

signal velocity, 121

skewed curve, 153

sound waves, 114

space, coordinates in, 125; curved, 140, 189–190

space propulsion methods, 29–35

spaceship, frame of reference of, 128; gravitational forces in, 107; inertia of, 146; launch of, 30; Lorentz-Fitzgerald contraction in, 133–134; relativistic momentum of, 135–136

spark gap, 166–167

speed, relative, 122, 124–125

spin, electron, 101–103, 195–196; neutron, 93; parallel, 208–209

spinning bullet, path of, 60–61

Sputnik, 3

standard deviation, 155

stars, red-shift of, 139–140

state, change of, 105

steady-state hypothesis, 51

steering, in space, 29–30

Stevin, Simon, 70

"strangeness," conservation of, 224

sun, gravitation of, 10, 16, 74, 189–190

supernatural laws, 8

surface adsorption, 105

symmetry, conservation and, 91–92; and laws of motion, 90–94; mirror, 93–94, 218–223

synchrotron, 191

Terrell, James, 134

theory, assumptions of, 13

thermodynamics, laws of, 159–161

Thompson, Benjamin, Count Rumford, 49

Thomson, George P., 182

Thomson, J. J., 168, 183, 191

thrust, rocket, 31–32

time, awareness of, 162–163; causation and, 18–20; "dilation" of, 131–133; as dimension, 93; direction of, 162–164; regularity principle and, 19; relativity of, 128; reversal of, 223

time delay, in change of field, 110–111

tops, spinning, 63–66

torque, defined, 56–57; and earth's axis, 66

trajectories, factors affecting, 15; inertia and, 74–75

transformation equations, 125–126; in relativity theory, 231–234

transistors, 18

Tsung Dao Lee, 220

ultraviolet light, and Compton effect, 175; electric current and, 167–168

uncertainty principle, 181–188

uncertainty, probability and, 155–157

uniformity, in universe, 16–18

units, physical, 45–47

universe, density of, 145; regularity and uniformity in, 16–18

uranium, fission of, 18; mass-energy relations in, 43

V-2 rockets, 3

vacuum, "impossibility" of, 69

van de Graaff generator, 191

vectors, addition of, 228, 236

velocity, angular, 53, 57–60; change of, 72; kinetic energy and, 40–41; mass and, 186; phase, in waveguide, 118; of rocket, 32–33; rotation and, 52; signal or group, 121; and uncertainty principle, 186

velocity vectors, addition of, 228, 236

Venus, 68

vibrating electric charge, 111

Vinci, Leonardo da, 69–70

"virtual" particles, 206–207

vis viva, 79–80

Volta, Alessandro, 49

wave, modulation of, 120; propagation and travel of, 113–116; velocity of, 117

waveguide, speed of waves in, 116

wavelength, of electron, 182; of photon, 173

wave packet, 190; photon as, 173–176; probability and, 179; uncertainty principle and, 184

wave-particle problem, 18, 166–167

weight, versus mass, 22

wetting, solid surfaces, 105

whirlpool theory, 8

Wilson, C. T. R., 95

wind direction, 108

work, defined, 46, 50

work–energy equivalence, 50
Worlds in Collision, 66

X-rays, 18, 113, 166, 171; diffraction of, 182–183; photons of, 172–173; production of, 206; scattered, 174

Yukawa, Hideki, 209

Ziolkowsky, Constantin, 31